SpringerBriefs in Service Science

Series Editor

Robin Qiu, Division of Engineering & Information Science, Pennsylvania State University, Malvern, PA, USA

Editorial Board Members

Saif Benjaafar, Industrial and Systems Engineering, University of Minnesota, Minneapolis, MN, USA

Brenda Dietrich, Cornell University, New York, USA

Zhongsheng Hua, Zhejiang University, Hefei, Anhui, China

Zhibin Jiang, Management Science, Shanghai Jiao Tong University, Shanghai, China

Kwang-Jae Kim, Pohang University of Science and Technology, London, UK

Lefei Li, Department of Industrial Engineering, Tsinghua University, Haidian, Beijing, China

Kelly Lyons, Faculty of Information, University of Toronto, Toronto, ON, Canada

Paul Maglio, School of Engineering, University of California, Merced, Merced, CA, USA

Jürg Meierhofer, Zurich University of Applied Sciences, Winterthur, Bern, Switzerland

Paul Messinger, Alberta School of Business, University of Alberta, Edmonton, Canada

Stefan Nickel, Karlsruhe Institute of Technology, Karlsruhe, Baden-Württemberg, Germany

James C. Spohrer, IBM University Programs World-Wide, IBM Almaden Research Center, San Jose, CA, USA

Jochen Wirtz, NUS Business School, National University of Singapore, Singapore, Singapore

SpringerBriefs present concise summaries of cutting-edge research and practical applications across a wide spectrum of fields. Featuring compact volumes of 50 to 125 pages, the series covers a range of content from professional to academic.

Typical publications can be:

A timely report of state-of-the art methods

A bridge between new research results, as published in journal articles

A snapshot of a hot or emerging topic

An in-depth case study

A presentation of core concepts that students must understand in order to make independent contributions

SpringerBriefs are characterized by fast, global electronic dissemination, standard publishing contracts, standardized manuscript preparation and formatting guidelines, and expedited production schedules.

The rapidly growing fields of Big Data, AI and Machine Learning, together with emerging analytic theories and technologies, have allowed us to gain comprehensive insights into both social and transactional interactions in service value co-creation processes. The series SpringerBriefs in Service Science is devoted to publications that offer new perspectives on service research by showcasing service transformations across various sectors of the digital economy. The research findings presented will help service organizations address their service challenges in tomorrow's service-oriented economy.

Shiliang Cui • Zhongbin Wang • Luyi Yang

Innovative Priority Mechanisms in Service Operations

Theory and Applications

Shiliang Cui
Georgetown University
Washington, WA, USA

Zhongbin Wang
Tianjin University
Tianjin, China

Luyi Yang
University of California, Berkeley
Berkeley, CA, USA

This work was supported by University of California, Berkeley Foundation

ISSN 2731-3743   ISSN 2731-3751 (electronic)
SpringerBriefs in Service Science
ISBN 978-3-031-30840-6   ISBN 978-3-031-30841-3 (eBook)
https://doi.org/10.1007/978-3-031-30841-3

This title is freely available in an open access edition with generous support from the Library of the University of California, Berkeley.

© The Editor(s) (if applicable) and The Author(s) 2023. This book is an open access publication.
Open Access This book is licensed under the terms of the Creative Commons Attribution 4.0 International License (http://creativecommons.org/licenses/by/4.0/), which permits use, sharing, adaptation, distribution and reproduction in any medium or format, as long as you give appropriate credit to the original author(s) and the source, provide a link to the Creative Commons license and indicate if changes were made.
The images or other third party material in this book are included in the book's Creative Commons license, unless indicated otherwise in a credit line to the material. If material is not included in the book's Creative Commons license and your intended use is not permitted by statutory regulation or exceeds the permitted use, you will need to obtain permission directly from the copyright holder.
The use of general descriptive names, registered names, trademarks, service marks, etc. in this publication does not imply, even in the absence of a specific statement, that such names are exempt from the relevant protective laws and regulations and therefore free for general use.
The publisher, the authors, and the editors are safe to assume that the advice and information in this book are believed to be true and accurate at the date of publication. Neither the publisher nor the authors or the editors give a warranty, expressed or implied, with respect to the material contained herein or for any errors or omissions that may have been made. The publisher remains neutral with regard to jurisdictional claims in published maps and institutional affiliations.

This Springer imprint is published by the registered company Springer Nature Switzerland AG
The registered company address is: Gewerbestrasse 11, 6330 Cham, Switzerland

Preface

The service sector encompasses a diverse range of tangible and intangible services, including car repair, garbage collection, healthcare, and information services, among others (see below for more examples). As such, the service sector plays a crucial role in both personal life and the economic growth of society. However, a common and often frustrating experience for customers seeking service is waiting in line. Whether it's at a gas station, an ATM machine, a popular restaurant, or when contacting customer-service representatives, waiting can be a source of dissatisfaction. Therefore, effectively managing individuals' wait time for service is of utmost importance for both service managers and researchers studying service operations.

The most socially acceptable rule of waiting in line is the first-come, first-served principle. However, priority mechanisms that grant latecomers earlier access to services are also prevalent. These mechanisms are employed to maximize profits for service providers (e.g., priority boarding for airlines or skip-the-line passes for theme parks), accommodate people in need (e.g., wheelchair access at the Louvre Museum, which saves an average of 2 hours of waiting time, or Hong Kong's public housing program, which prioritizes single elderly applicants), or even save lives (e.g., triage systems in emergency departments).

While traditional priority schemes have been extensively studied in the literature (a brief review can be found in Chap. 1), a new and innovative set of priority mechanisms has emerged with advancements in mobile technology and the gig economy. Unfortunately, these innovative priority mechanisms in service operations have not received the same level of research attention. Specifically, how do these mechanisms impact the behavior of self-interested customers? What are the implications for service providers' profits, throughput, consumer surplus, and social welfare? These are the questions we seek to address throughout this book. In the following sections, we provide a brief overview of the contents of each chapter.

Chapter 1 serves as an introduction to the book. It offers a brief history of research on priority queues with self-interested customers and serves to motivate the content presented in the subsequent chapters which showcase the latest research on innovative priority mechanisms in service settings.

Chapter 2 presents the research on trading service positions. This practice involves customers mutually agreeing upon the order in the waiting line through the exchange of positions with appropriate monetary compensation.

Chapter 3 examines the research on line-sitting services. This practice involves customers hiring others (known as line-sitters) to wait in line on their behalf.

Chapter 4 delves into the research on queue-scalping. This practice involves individuals (or scalpers) proactively joining a waiting line with the intention of selling their spot later.

Chapter 5 explores the research on referral priority programs. This emerging business practice grants existing customers on the waitlist priority access to service if they successfully refer new customers to join the waitlist.

Chapter 6 investigates the research on distance-based priority policies. This practice involves giving higher service priority to customers who must travel longer distances to access the service, thereby providing them with a new incentive to seek service.

Chapter 7 focuses on the research on in-queue priority purchase policies. This practice enables customers to pay for upgrades in service priority at any time during their wait in the queue, even if they initially choose not to do so upon arrival.

Each chapter in this book is based on state-of-the-art research from the authors and others. We thank INFORMS, Elsevier, and Springer for their permission to use published material in the book. We express our gratitude to the editor of this book series and the production team at Springer for providing us with the opportunity to share this knowledge with a broader audience. We also extend our thanks to the University of California, Berkeley for their support in making this book open access.

The collaboration among the book's authors began in the fall of 2017, when we all resided in the Washington, DC-Baltimore region. Our collective goal was to understand the most innovative service operations practices of the time. This book represents a culmination of six years of collaborative research, involving numerous paper revisions, countless remote and face-to-face meetings, and, most importantly, the cultivation of trust and friendship. The world has undergone significant changes in recent years due to the COVID-19 pandemic, presenting both challenges and new research opportunities. Therefore, this book marks not the end but the beginning of a fascinating research journey.

Washington, WA, USA	Shiliang Cui
Tianjin, China	Zhongbin Wang
Berkeley, CA, USA	Luyi Yang

Contents

1 A Brief Review of Research on Priority Queues with Self-Interested Customers 1
  1 Introduction 1
  2 Unobservable Queues 2
    2.1 Priority Pricing 2
    2.2 Priority Auctions 4
  3 Observable Queues 5
  4 Emerging Research Directions 6
  References 6

2 Auctions for Trading Queueing Positions 9
  1 Introduction 9
  2 Model Setup 11
  3 Baseline Auction 12
    3.1 Trading Rules 12
    3.2 Auction Equilibrium 13
  4 Social Welfare and Service Provider's Revenue 16
    4.1 Social Optimization 17
    4.2 Service Provider's Revenue Maximization 18
  5 Trading Through an Intermediary 20
    5.1 Baseline Auction with a Trade Participation Fee 20
    5.2 Augmented Auction: Trading Rules and a Motivating Example 21
    5.3 Auction Equilibrium 22
    5.4 Optimal Auction Parameters and Structure 24
    5.5 The Value of Trading vs. FIFO 27
  6 Conclusion Remarks 29
  References 30

3 Line-Sitting Services 33
  1 Introduction 33
  2 Model Preliminaries and FIFO Benchmark 34

		2.1 FIFO Benchmark	35
	3	Line-Sitting	35
		3.1 Comparison Between Line-Sitting and FIFO	39
	4	Accommodating Line-Sitting or Selling Priority?	42
		4.1 Priority Purchasing	42
		4.2 Comparison Between Priority and FIFO	44
		4.3 Comparison Between Line-Sitting and Priority	44
	5	Three-Way Comparison	47
	6	Endogenizing Service Fee B	48
	7	Finitely Many Line-Sitters	49
	8	Pre-commitment Payment	50
		8.1 Revenue of the Line-Sitting Firm	51
		8.2 Welfare Implications	52
	9	Concluding Remarks	53
		References	54
4	**Queue Scalping**		55
	1	Introduction	55
	2	Model Description	56
	3	Analysis of the Single-Scalper Model	59
		3.1 What Queues Are Susceptible to Scalping?	60
	4	Analysis of the Multi-Scalper Model	61
		4.1 What Queues Are Susceptible to Scalping?	63
	5	Impact of Queue-Scalping	65
		5.1 System Throughput	65
		5.2 Consumer Surplus	66
		5.3 Social Welfare	67
	6	The Long-Run Capacity Response	68
	7	Comparison with Line-Sitting	70
	8	Effect of Queue Information	71
	9	Concluding Remarks	73
		References	74
5	**Referral Priority Programs**		75
	1	Introduction	75
	2	Model	76
		2.1 Queueing Preliminaries	78
	3	Equilibrium	80
		3.1 Equilibrium Referral Strategies	80
		3.2 Existence of Equilibria and Structural Results	81
	4	Effectiveness of the Referral Priority Program	82
		4.1 Analytic Results	83
		4.1.1 System Throughput	84
		4.1.2 Customer Welfare	85
		4.2 Summary	87
	5	Extensions	89

	6	Optimal Pricing, Referral Reward Program, and Comparison	89
		6.1 Pricing in the Referral Reward Program	90
		6.2 Numerical Comparison	91
	7	Optimal Scheduling in Referral Priority Programs	93
		7.1 Numerical Illustrations	95
		7.2 Capacity Implications	97
	8	Concluding Remarks	97
	References		97

6 Distance-Based Service Priority — 99

1. Introduction — 99
2. Model Preliminaries and FIFO Benchmark — 100
   - 2.1 FIFO Service Discipline — 102
3. Distance-Based Service Priority Policy — 103
4. Comparison between Priority and FIFO Policies — 106
5. Two-Dimensional Service Area — 112
6. Optimal Service Fee B — 113
7. Comparison to Price Discrimination Strategy — 115
   - 7.1 Comparing PDS to the FIFO Benchmark — 115
   - 7.2 Comparing PDS to the Priority Policy — 116
8. Concluding Remarks — 116

References — 117

7 In-Queue Priority Purchase — 119

1. Introduction — 119
2. Model Description — 120
3. Simultaneous Upgrade Rule — 121
   - 3.1 Equilibrium Definition — 122
   - 3.2 Analysis — 125
     - 3.2.1 Step 1: Equilibrium Structure — 127
     - 3.2.2 Step 2: Nonexistence of Pure-Strategy Equilibria — 129
   - 3.3 A Small Buffer System — 129
4. Sequential Upgrade Rule — 130
   - 4.1 Equilibrium Definition — 130
   - 4.2 Sufficiently Light or Heavy Traffic — 132
   - 4.3 Small Buffer Systems — 134
     - 4.3.1 $K = 2$ — 134
     - 4.3.2 $K = 3$ — 136
5. Concluding Remarks — 138

References — 138

Chapter 1
A Brief Review of Research on Priority Queues with Self-Interested Customers

1 Introduction

Priority queues are prevalent in service operations. For example, theme parks and ski resorts often allow customers to purchase premium tickets to join express lines. Everything Everywhere (EE), a leading telecommunications company in the UK, once offered "Priority Answer" that enabled customers to pay £0.50 to jump the queue for a service call. E-commerce platforms and shipping companies charge higher prices for faster deliveries. The US Citizenship and Immigration Services (USCIS) expedites case processing for an extra fee. The celebrated $c\mu$ rule establishes that giving priorities to customers with higher waiting costs and shorter processing times minimizes the total holding costs. Therefore, when done right, priority scheduling can increase revenue and social welfare. However, customers are delay- and price-sensitive. Offering priorities will impact customers' self-interested joining behavior, and when customers self-select into priorities, service providers must ensure that customers choose the "right" priority by charging them the "right" priority prices or, more generally, by designing the "right" priority mechanisms. This chapter reviews the theoretical literature on priority queues of self-interested customers, with a focus on pay-for-priority schemes.

Earlier research in this space typically assumes that priorities can be assigned to different classes of customers based on some publicly known attributes, but customers in each class can freely decide whether to join the queue based on the price and expected wait time of the class. Hence, the focus is on the pricing of a multi-class priority queue and control of arrival rates (see, e.g., Chapter 4 of Stidham 2009). The assumption of assigning priorities according to known customer attributes fits various practical applications even to this date. For example, in COVID-19 testing, priorities can be based on symptoms (Yang et al. 2022); in government services, priorities can be given to those who travel from afar (such distance-based priorities are studied in Wang et al. 2022a and will be reviewed in Chap. 6).

In many other applications, however, such customer attributes are unavailable, and priorities must be self-selected. This calls for a pay-for-priority scheme in which customers who pay a higher price receive a higher priority. We review the literature on pay-for-priority schemes in this chapter. In particular, Sect. 2 reviews papers that assume an unobservable queue. The vast majority of the literature adopts this assumption, partly because of its tractability. It is also assumed that customers differ in their delay sensitivity, on the basis of which, they choose their priority level. This literature can be further divided into two streams in terms of implementation: one on priority pricing and, the other, priority auctions. The commonly investigated performance measures are revenue and social welfare. Section 3 reviews papers that assume an observable queue. Unlike its unobservable-queue counterpart, this observable-queue literature typically assumes that customers have the same delay sensitivity (for tractability) and decide whether to purchase priority based on the ever-evolving real-time queue length. Section 4 concludes the chapter by highlighting new research trends in this area of rational priority queueing.

2 Unobservable Queues

2.1 Priority Pricing

This literature studies the following mechanism: the service provider posts a menu of prices and expected wait times; a higher price is associated with a shortened expected wait time (and therefore a higher priority class). Each arriving customer decides whether to join the queue and, if so, which price to pay (and therefore which priority class to join).

The seminal paper of Mendelson and Whang (1990) studies the incentive-compatible socially optimal priority pricing scheme. Their paper employs a model of a discrete set of customer classes. Within each class, customers have the same delay sensitivity and the same expected service requirement, but still differ in service valuation (drawn from a continuous distribution). Mendelson and Whang (1990) show that if all customers have the same expected service requirement, the socially optimal price charged to each class should be equal to the externalities a customer imposes on others, and it is also incentive-compatible in the sense that customers prefer the price and wait time of their own class to those of other classes. The socially optimal pricing scheme implements the $c\mu$ rule, with customers with higher delay sensitivity being charged a higher price and receiving a higher priority.

In a similar model, Afèche (2013) studies the priority pricing problem from a revenue-maximizing service provider's perspective. Instead of prespecifying a particular scheduling policy such as strict priority, Afèche (2013) applies the achievable region method due to Coffman and Mitrani (1980) and casts the revenue-maximization problem into a mechanism design framework. The paper shows that the service provider should sometimes artificially inflate the waiting time of low-priority customers in the optimal mechanism to stimulate demand for high priority. This strategy is referred to as "strategic delay."

Further, Afèche and Pavlin (2016) study a model in which customer-type rankings are lead-time dependent and find that the optimal mechanism not only may involve strategic delay but also pricing out the middle and pooling some customers into a single FIFO (first-in-first-out) class despite their differences in delay sensitivity.

Gavirneni and Kulkarni (2016) study how a continuum of customers self-select into priority when two priority classes are available. Nazerzadeh and Randhawa (2018) further show that in this setting, a coarse service grade of granting only two priority classes is asymptotically optimal for a revenue-maximizing service provider. Their model assumes that customers' unit waiting cost depends on their service valuation. Gurvich et al. (2019) compare how revenue maximization differs from social-welfare maximization. They find that in the asymptotic regime, the two objective functions will not lead to any significant difference in coverage (i.e., the total throughput is similar across the two) or coarseness (i.e., in both cases, having two priority classes suffices), but classification (the proportion of customers who purchase priority) is markedly different. They also find that selling priority can reduce consumer surplus and make all customers worse off despite its ability to improve social welfare (as the service provider appropriates the welfare gain).

Wang and Fang (2022) consider the effect of customer awareness on priority queues, and they find that social welfare and customer surplus are both non-monotone in the level of customer awareness. In particular, full or no customer awareness can be suboptimal from a social-welfare standpoint. Wang and Wang (2021) study the priority-purchasing behavior in retrial queues, and they show that the service provider's revenue is bimodal in the priority price. Wang et al. (2022b) propose a pay-to-activate-service (PTAS) scheme in a vacation queue where customers can pay to instantaneously end the server's vacation. By comparing it with the pay-for-priority scheme, they show that selling priority generates more revenue than PTAS when the system workload is high. Afeche et al. (2019) consider a pricing-and-prioritization problem when customers have heterogeneous demand rates. They show that prioritizing customers with higher demand rates may be revenue-maximizing even when customers are homogeneous in delay sensitivity.

While all the papers above study the case of a single service provider, a few papers study competition among service providers who practice priority pricing (Lederer and Li 1997; Allon and Federgruen 2009; Sainathan 2020). For a monopoly service provider, selling priority always improves revenue, and therefore, in principle, priority pricing will always be implemented (barring practical constraints). However, Sainathan (2020) shows that in a duopoly setting, priority pricing may not always arise in equilibrium even though it is a more desirable outcome for both service providers.

2.2 Priority Auctions

This literature studies the following mechanism: the service provider runs an auction in which each arriving customer submits a bid she would like to pay to join the queue, and a customer with a higher bid is served ahead of all customers with a lower bid. The early literature sometimes refers to priority auctions as queue bribery as they enable customers to bribe the service provider in exchange for an expedited service. While priority auctions sound rather different from priority pricing, they are equivalent from a mechanism design perspective as both can be translated into a direct revelation mechanism that induces customers to truthfully report types. However, models of priority auctions often assume a continuum of customer types and therefore a continuum of priorities yet those of priority pricing usually (and justifiably) consider a finite number of priority classes (even when customer types are continuous).

Kleinrock (1967) lays the foundation for the literature on priority auctions by deriving the expected waiting time expressions under continuous priorities. However, in his work, payment functions are exogenously given. Lui (1985) and Glazer and Hassin (1986) extend Kleinrock's model by deriving customers' endogenous bid functions in equilibrium. They show that the $c\mu$ rule can be achieved in this priority auction. In particular, Lui (1985) shows that allowing bribery (i.e., priority auctions) can induce faster service as it motivates the service provider to increase capacity. Hassin (1995) shows that the bidding mechanism in the priority auction is self-regulating in that it achieves both the socially optimal service order and arrival rate. This is because customers' bids factor in externalities, similar to the socially optimal priority prices chosen by Mendelson and Whang (1990). Hassin (1995) also shows that while running a priority auction can induce faster service, a revenue-maximizing service provider does not invest as much capacity as a social planner would. Afèche and Mendelson (2004) study priority auctions under a generalized delay cost structure that augments the standard additive model with a multiplicative component. They find that priority auctions perform better under multiplicative compared to additive delay costs. In the auction of Kittsteiner and Moldovanu (2005), customers possess private information on job processing time. They show how the convexity/concavity of the function expressing the costs of delay determines the queue discipline (i.e., shortest-processing-time-first (SPT), longest-processing-time-first (LPT)) arising in a bidding equilibrium.

Unlike the literature above that studies a single service provider, Gao et al. (2019) study two competing firms, one running a priority auction and the other charging a fixed price (this setup contrasts that in Sainathan 2020, who allows each firm to choose which scheme to adopt). Gao et al. (2019) show that in equilibrium, customers with either high or low waiting costs seek service from the priority-auction firm, whereas those with intermediate waiting costs choose the fixed-price firm. They also find that the priority-auction firm can be inherently favored in such a competition.

3 Observable Queues

This literature typically assumes that customers have the same waiting cost. Upon arrival, customers observe the queue length and decide whether to purchase priority (and more generally, which priority class to purchase); they may also decide whether to join the queue or balk.

Adiri and Yechiali (1974) study such a model and identify a threshold equilibrium whereby customers will purchase priority if and only if the total number of customers in the system is above a certain threshold. Hassin and Haviv (1997) extend Adiri and Yechiali (1974) to a model that incorporates mixed strategies. The authors show that multiple equilibria may exist. This is driven by the "follow the crowd" (FTC) behavior, i.e., a customer is more likely to purchase priority if more other customers purchase priority. Purchasing priority has dual purposes: it not only helps a buyer overtake non-buyers but also prevents a customer from being overtaken by future buyers. It is the latter incentive that induces the FTC behavior.

Alperstein (1988) identifies the optimal number of priority classes and the set of prices for a revenue-maximizing service provider. It shows that under full optimality, an arriving customer chooses the lowest priority price that is higher than any prices chosen by existing customers, and balks if the queue length reaches a threshold. As a result, while the model starts out with the FIFO discipline, full optimality results in a pure LIFO (last-in-first-out) discipline, which achieves the maximum social welfare (as shown by Hassin 1985). This result echoes with Hassin (1995) and demonstrates that pay-for-priority can regulate the queue by letting customers internalize their externalities.

Wang et al. (2019) compare the revenue of a pay-for-priority queue with balking, between the observable and unobservable settings. The authors find that the service provider is better off in the observable setting when the system load is either low or high, but benefits from withholding queue information when the system load is intermediate. Note that when the service provider in an unobservable queue can also charge an admission fee in addition to the priority price, then with homogeneous customers, priority pricing yields the same maximum revenue as FIFO pricing and achieves social optimality. In this case, the service provider entirely captures social welfare, leaving customers with zero surplus. On the other hand, in an observable queue, priority pricing attains social optimality when the number of priority classes is optimized, in which case, the service provider again extracts all surplus (Alperstein 1988). Since the maximum social welfare is higher when the queue is observable (as shown by Hassin 1986), it implies that the globally optimal strategy for the service provider is to disclose the queue length and practice optimal priority pricing.

The literature has studied alternative mechanisms. Erlichman and Hassin (2015) analyze a strategic-overtaking scheme in which customers observe the queue length and have the option of overtaking some of the customers already present in the queue by paying a fixed amount per overtaken customer. They show that implementing strategic overtaking can be more profitable for the service provider than selling priority. While all the papers above require customers to make a priority choice upon arrival, Wang et al. (2021) let customers pay and upgrade to priority at any time during their stay in the queue, even if they choose not to do so initially. We will review (Wang et al. 2021) in more details in Chap. 7.

4 Emerging Research Directions

We see two emerging trends in the research on rational priority queueing. The first trend is an increasing integration of queueing models with (sophisticated) economic tools, such as mechanism design/auction theory (Afèche 2013; Afèche and Pavlin 2016; Yang et al. 2017), cheap talk/information design (Yu et al. 2018), and dynamic games (Wang et al. 2021). These methodologies lend themselves to the setting of priority queues, which are often characterized by customers having private information about their priority preferences (i.e., waiting cost) and the service provider having private information about the dynamically evolving queue length.

Second, new applications, often driven by technological advances and societal concerns, also open up abundant new opportunities in this area of research. For example, Baron et al. (2022) show that prioritizing offline orders in omnichannel services eliminates channel interference and improves social welfare. Hu et al. (2022) explore privacy regulation when the service provider can use customers' disclosed information to offer different priorities. The phenomena of decentralized priority provisioning, whereby priority is not sold by the service provider, but emerges as a result of peer-to-peer or third-party transactions, are seen in trading auctions (Yang et al. 2017), line sitting (Cui et al. 2020), and queue scalping (Yang et al. 2021). These papers will be reviewed in more details in Chaps. 2–4 of this book. Finally, referral priority programs, where priority is obtained not from purchase, but by exerting referral effort, are increasingly used by technology startups (Yang and Debo 2019; Yang 2021) and will be reviewed in Chap. 5.

References

Adiri I, Yechiali U (1974) Optimal priority-purchasing and pricing decisions in nonmonopoly and monopoly queues. Oper Res 22(5):1051–1066

Afèche P (2013) Incentive-compatible revenue management in queueing systems: optimal strategic delay. Manuf Serv Oper Manag 15(3):423–443

Afèche P, Mendelson H (2004) Pricing and priority auctions in queueing systems with a generalized delay cost structure. Manag Sci 50(7):869–882

Afèche P, Pavlin M (2016) Optimal price-lead time menus for queues with customer choice: priorities, pooling and strategic delay. Manag Sci 62(8):2412–2436

Afeche P, Baron O, Milner J, Roet-Green R (2019) Pricing and prioritizing time-sensitive customers with heterogeneous demand rates. Oper Res 67(4):1184–1208

Allon G, Federgruen A (2009) Competition in service industries with segmented markets. Manag Sci 55(4):619–634

References

Alperstein H (1988) Note—Optimal pricing policy for the service facility offering a set of priority prices. Manag Sci 34(5):666–671

Baron O, Chen X, Li Y (2022) Omnichannel services: the false premise and operational remedies. Manag Sci 69(2):865–884

Coffman EJ, Mitrani I (1980) A characterization of waiting time performance realizable by single-server queues. Oper Res 28(3):810–821

Cui S, Wang Z, Yang L (2020) The economics of line-sitting. Manag Sci 66(1):227–242

Erlichman J, Hassin R (2015) Strategic overtaking in a monopolistic $M/M/1$ queue. IEEE Trans Autom Control 60(8):2189–2194

Gao J, Iyer K, Topaloglu H (2019) When fixed price meets priority auctions: competing firms with different pricing and service rules. Stochastic Syst 9(1):47–80

Gavirneni S, Kulkarni VG (2016) Self-selecting priority queues with Burr distributed waiting costs. Prod Oper Manag 25(6):979–992

Glazer A, Hassin R (1986) Stable priority purchasing in queues. Oper Res Lett 4(6):285–288

Gurvich I, Lariviere M, Ozkan C (2019) Coverage, coarseness and classification: determinants of social efficiency in priority queues. Manag Sci 65(3):1061–1075

Hassin R (1985) On the optimality of first come last served queues. Econometrica 53(1):201–202

Hassin R (1986) Consumer information in markets with random product quality: the case of queues and balking. Econometrica 54(5):1185–1195

Hassin R (1995) Decentralized regulation of a queue. Manag Sci 41(1):163–173

Hassin R, Haviv M (1997) Equilibrium threshold strategies: the case of queues with priorities. Oper Res 45(6):966–973

Hu M, Momot R, Wang J (2022) Privacy management in service systems. Manuf Serv Oper Manag 24(5):2761–2779

Kittsteiner T, Moldovanu B (2005) Priority auctions and queue disciplines that depend on processing time. Manag Sci 51(2):236–248

Kleinrock L (1967) Optimum bribing for queue position. Oper Res 15(2):304–318

Lederer PJ, Li L (1997) Pricing, production, scheduling, and delivery-time competition. Oper Res 45(3):407–420

Lui FT (1985) An equilibrium queueing model of bribery. J Polit Econ 93(4):760–781

Mendelson H, Whang S (1990) Optimal incentive-compatible priority pricing for the $M/M/1$ queue. Oper Res 38(5):870–883

Nazerzadeh H, Randhawa RS (2018) Near-optimality of coarse service grades for customer differentiation in queueing systems. Prod Oper Manag 27(3):578–595

Sainathan A (2020) Technical note—pricing and prioritization in a duopoly with self-selecting, heterogeneous, time-sensitive customers under low utilization. Oper Res 68(5):1364–1374

Stidham S Jr (2009) Optimal design of queueing systems. CRC Press, New York

Wang J, Cui S, Wang Z (2019) Equilibrium strategies in $M/M/1$ priority queues with balking. Prod Oper Manag 28(1):43–62

Wang Z, Fang L (2022) The effect of customer awareness on priority queues. Nav Res Logist (NRL) 69(5):801–815

Wang Z, Cui S, Fang L (2022a) Distance-based service priority: an innovative mechanism to increase system throughput and social welfare. Manuf Serv Oper Manag 25(1):353–369

Wang Z, Liu Y, Fang L (2022b) Pay to activate service in vacation queues. Prod Oper Manag 31(6):2609–2627

Wang Z, Wang J (2021) Strategic priority-purchasing and joining rules in a retrial queue. IMA J Manag Math 32(2):161–194

Wang Z, Yang L, Cui S, Wang J (2021) In-queue priority purchase: a dynamic game approach. Queueing Systems 97:343–381

Yang L (2021) Invite your friend and you'll move up in line: Optimal design of referral priority programs. Manuf Serv Oper Manag 23(5):1139–1156

Yang L, Cui S, Wang Z (2022) Design of covid-19 testing queues. Prod Oper Manag 31(5):2204–2221

Yang L, Debo L (2019) Referral priority program: leveraging social ties via operational incentives. Manag Sci 65(5):2231–2248

Yang L, Debo L, Gupta V (2017) Trading time in a congested environment. Manag Sci 63(7):2377–2395

Yang L, Wang Z, Cui S (2021) A model of queue scalping. Manag Sci 67(11):6803–6821

Yu Q, Allon G, Bassamboo A, Iravani S (2018) Managing customer expectations and priorities in service systems. Manag Sci 64(8):3942–3970

Open Access This chapter is licensed under the terms of the Creative Commons Attribution 4.0 International License (http://creativecommons.org/licenses/by/4.0/), which permits use, sharing, adaptation, distribution and reproduction in any medium or format, as long as you give appropriate credit to the original author(s) and the source, provide a link to the Creative Commons license and indicate if changes were made.

The images or other third party material in this chapter are included in the chapter's Creative Commons license, unless indicated otherwise in a credit line to the material. If material is not included in the chapter's Creative Commons license and your intended use is not permitted by statutory regulation or exceeds the permitted use, you will need to obtain permission directly from the copyright holder.

Chapter 2
Auctions for Trading Queueing Positions

1 Introduction

A queue constitutes a "miniature social system" in which the underlying fabric that ties individuals to society also guides the relationships between those in a queue (Mann 1969). In particular, the behavioral protocol of queueing collectively endorses the notion of "property rights" (Gray 2009), a fundamental part of the social fabric. An individual's *position* in a queue is considered by its occupant as her *property* that she temporarily *owns*. Tampering with one's position in a queue amounts to taking away someone's property and may be met with strong objection: Any attempt to cut in line may be disapproved since this infringes on the "bumped" customers' perceived property rights over their waiting positions. This is one of the reasons why the first-in, first-out (FIFO) queue discipline is predominant in many services systems. The FIFO rule ensures "a direct correspondence between inputs (time spent waiting) and outcomes (preferential service)" and thus manifests a basic principle of distributive justice (Mann 1969). However, the FIFO rule disregards queue occupants' heterogeneous time-sensitivities. The system would be more efficient if more time-sensitive customers jump ahead and get served faster. To that end, service providers often sell priorities to customers. For instance, EE, one of the largest telecommunications companies in the UK, once launched a new service feature called "Priority Answer" that allowed customers to pay £0.50 to jump the queue for a service call. This new feature soon created a huge uproar and irked many customers who complained they were not being treated fairly.

What goes awry with Priority Answer is that the proceeds go to the service provider, yet a longer wait is inflicted on the non-paying customers. The misalignment would be resolved if the monetary transfer were among customers themselves: impatient customers may be willing to pay to acquire the position of less impatient customers who are potentially willing to give away their spots for monetary gains. This calls for a two-sided marketplace where customers consensually *trade* their waiting spots. Such a marketplace enables waiting customers to voluntarily swap positions at mutually agreed prices. Since such swaps do not influence the positions of any other customers on the wait list, no customers are forcibly pushed back without being compensated. Thus, customers can have the best of both worlds: their proprietary entitlements to waiting positions are preserved as in the FIFO system while their diverging priority preferences are accommodated, improving system efficiency.

We study in Yang et al. (2017) how trading in a queue can be organized by simple auctions in an environment where customers are privately informed about their waiting costs. We design the optimal mechanisms from three different perspectives: social welfare, the service provider's revenue, and the revenue of the trading platform (which we refer to as the intermediary) that mediates trading. While the first two perspectives are common in the queueing literature, they implicitly rely on the assumption that the trading platform is and can be managed by the service provider, which may not necessarily be true in practice. Instead, the service provider may be inclined to delegate the trading platform to an intermediary for technological reasons and reputational concerns. First and foremost, the infrastructure that facilitates trade hinges on technology (e.g., mobile apps) that typically falls beyond the expertise of the service provider. Therefore, if a specialized intermediary is responsible for developing, deploying and maintaining the platform on behalf of the service provider, the service provider will not be distracted from its core competencies. In the restaurant industry, for example, dining reservation platforms (intermediaries) are typically not fully integrated with restaurants (service providers): examples include OpenTable which charges restaurants for each reservation, and a similar dining app, Reserve, which alternatively charges customers for each booking. Second, if the service provider were to operate and conceivably profit from a resale market of waiting positions (either directly by collecting fees for trading or indirectly via surcharges in service fees), there might be a backlash from customers given the sensitive nature of queue-jumping (as in the case of Priority Answer). To the extent that this results in a loss of goodwill, the service provider would rather be detached from the trading platform and leave it to a third-party intermediary to arbitrate swaps of waiting positions. This begs the question of what is the optimal mechanism to collect fees from trading customers for an intermediary, who has the potential of raising sizable revenues once the technology is scaled up.

The problem of trading waiting positions in a queue has been studied by several papers in the extant literature. Rosenblum (1992) assumes that customers' waiting costs are public information in their trading model and that future values of transactions are ignored. Our model relaxes these two strong assumptions: customers are privately informed of their own waiting costs and take into account the expected values of future transactions when they trade. Gershkov and Schweinzer (2010) formulate a mechanism design problem of rescheduling a fixed number of players in a clearing system where there is no arrival process and trading is completed before service starts. Since all customers are present at time zero, it is not clear how the initial property rights are formed, so they study different initial allocations and show that an efficient mechanism can be implemented if the initial schedule is random ordering but not if it is deterministic like FIFO. El Haji and

Onderstal (2019) experimentally examine how human subjects trade in a queueing environment similar to Gershkov and Schweinzer (2010). They provide evidence that organizing such a time-trading market can achieve a nontrivial amount of efficiency gains. Our model incorporates the operational dynamics of a queueing system where the order of arrivals naturally gives rise to the initial allocation. It allows us to study how trading impacts customers' endogenous queue-joining behaviors. While Gershkov and Schweinzer (2010) and El Haji and Onderstal (2019) mostly focus on the efficiency of the time-trading mechanisms, our work also incorporates the perspectives of the revenue maximizing service provider and intermediary.

2 Model Setup

Consider a congested service facility, modeled as an $M/M/1$ queueing system, that faces a population of delay-sensitive customers. Customers arrive at the system according to an exogenous Poisson process with rate Λ (market size). Each customer requests one unit of service. The service times are i.i.d. samples from an exponential distribution with mean $1/\mu$. Let $\rho \doteq \Lambda/\mu$. Customers have a common valuation V for service. For a customer with delay cost rate c, who experiences waiting time w, defined as the entire duration in the system, and money m after receipt of service, her utility is $V - c \cdot w + m$. For simplicity, we normalize initial money wealth for all customers at zero, but assume that they are not budget-constrained, so $m > 0$ means a customer is a net receiver; $m < 0$, a net payer. Customers differ in their delay cost rate c. Each customer's delay cost per unit time is an i.i.d. draw from a continuous distribution with a strictly increasing cumulative distribution function F and a finite, strictly positive and continuously differentiable probability density function f over the support $c \in \Xi \triangleq [\underline{c}, \overline{c}]$ and $0 \leq \underline{c} < \overline{c} < \infty$. Customers are risk-neutral and expected utility maximizers. To exclude the case where no customers have a positive net value even if served immediately, we assume $V > \underline{c}/\mu$.

Upon arrival, customers decide whether to join the service facility to obtain service, or balk. In case they do not join, they obtain the reservation utility, which we normalize to zero. The inter-arrival time distribution, the service time distribution, the delay cost distribution f and the service value V are common knowledge. The type of each individual customer (delay cost rates c) is her private information. Customers do not observe the system state upon arrival but can estimate the expected waiting time and the expected monetary transfer.

3 Baseline Auction

In this section, we study an auction-based trading mechanism that is budget-balanced among customers: all monetary transfers are internal within customers. This auction is the building block for subsequent results about the social planner, service provider and intermediary in Sects. 4 and 5.

3.1 Trading Rules

Auction Format In the baseline auction, upon arrival, a customer decides whether to join the queue or not. If the customer does not join, she earns a reservation utility of 0. If the customer joins, she submits a sealed bid b that can either be "No," or a price for one unit of time. We allow customers to bid "No" to reflect that trading is voluntary and that customers can always preserve their FIFO property right. The bid b represents the least amount she wants to receive for expecting to wait one additional unit of time and also the greatest amount she is willing to pay for one unit of the expected waiting time reduced. The queue is reorganized in such a way that the arriving customer swaps positions consecutively with those who place bids strictly lower than hers. In each transaction, the customer who jumps ahead (the buyer) compensates the one who moves back (the seller) by the seller's bid price times the expected waiting time exchanged. The existing customers who submitted bids strictly higher or those who submitted "No" are not affected in their waiting position. Nor are customers who bid the same amount as the buyer. Any customers with equal bids are served FIFO amongst themselves. Note that this auction follows a "pay-as-you-overtake" paradigm, since customers' realized payment as buyers depends on the actual number of customers they overtake. For simplicity, trading is instantaneous (transactions do not take any time) and preemptive-resume (customers at the server can suspend their service and sell their spot; service is resumed when this customer reaches the server again). Customers submit a bid before observing the queue length and commit to the bid throughout their stay in the system.[1]

Illustration 1 Consider an arriving customer who joins and participates in trading by submitting a price b'. Assume that there are four other existing customers in the system. Among them, the first, the second and the fourth customer participate in trading with bids b_1, b_2 and b_4 (with $b_1 \geq b' > b_2 > b_4$), respectively. The third bids "No" and thus does not participate in trading. Thus, before the new arrival, the system can be represented by (b_1, b_2, F, b_4), where F stands for a FIFO customer who bids "No". Adding the arriving customer (customer 5) who bids b' to the tail of

---

[1] After submitting their bid, customers could see the queue length, but this would be technically irrelevant to the bidding game since the trading process goes on autopilot once bids are collected from customers.

the queue, we have (b_1, b_2, F, b_4, b'), which is not (yet) ordered. Then, the auction swaps customer 5 and customer 4, yielding (b_1, b_2, F, b', b_4). Customer 5 makes a payment of b_4/μ to customer 4. Next, the auction swaps customer 5 and customer 2, yielding (b_1, b', F, b_2, b_4). Notice that the expected wait time of the FIFO customer does not change. Customer 5 makes a payment of $2b_2/\mu$ to customer 2 (because the latter moves back by two positions). Customer 5 does not swap positions with customer 1 since customer 1 bids weakly higher and they are served FIFO. Thus, the trading process is completed. The total payment customer 5 makes to the other customers is thus $(b_4 + 2b_2)/\mu$. Similarly, customer 5 expects a compensation of b' per unit of time if she ever moves back and swaps positions with other, later arriving customers who make a higher bid than b'.

3.2 Auction Equilibrium

Strategy We focus on pure strategies specified by two functions; the joining function $J : \Xi \mapsto \{\text{join, balk}\}$ specifies which customer types join or balk, and the bid function $b : \{c | J(c) = \text{join}\} \mapsto \mathbb{R}_+ \cup \{\text{No}\}$ specifies the bid of each customer type (either a price for one unit of time or "No"). Thus the effective arrival rate to the system is $\lambda \triangleq \Lambda \int_{\underline{c}}^{\overline{c}} \mathbf{1}\{J(c) = \text{join}\} dF(c)$, where $\mathbf{1}\{X\}$ is the indicator function of condition X.

Waiting Time and Utility Given the bid function $b(\cdot)$ and the joining function $J(\cdot)$, let $W : \mathbb{R}_+ \mapsto \mathbb{R}_+$ denote the mapping from a customer's bid to her expected waiting time. Since trading does not affect any joining customer who bids "No," it is immediate that these customers' expected waiting time is equal to the mean waiting time of an $M/M/1$ system: $W(\text{No}|b, J) = \frac{1}{\mu - \lambda}$. Note that this waiting time depends on the endogenously determined λ, the aggregate arrival rate of the system, and is not impacted by any individual, infinitesimal customer's action. Since customers submit their bid up front and make a commitment during their wait, they take into account all future transactions in the expected utility (note that this is one of the key distinctions from Rosenblum 1992). We assume that customers do not discount future payments. Let $P_p : \mathbb{R}_+ \mapsto \mathbb{R}_+$ be the function that maps a customer's bid to the total expected amount of money she *pays* as a buyer upon arrival; and $P_r : \mathbb{R}_+ \mapsto \mathbb{R}_+$ maps a customer's bid to the total expected amount of money she *receives* as a seller during her stay in the system.

Thus, given $b(\cdot)$ and $J(\cdot)$, the expected utility of a joining customer of type c who bids β is

$$U(c, \beta | b, J) = \begin{cases} V - cW(\beta|b, J) - P_p(\beta|b, J) + P_r(\beta|b, J), & \beta \in \mathbb{R}_+ \\ V - \frac{c}{\mu - \lambda}, & \beta = \text{No.} \end{cases}$$

(2.1)

Customer Equilibrium A symmetric pure-strategy Nash equilibrium is defined by the following conditions:

$$b(c) \in \arg\max_{\beta \in \mathbb{R}_+ \cup \{\text{No}\}} U(c, \beta | b, J), \quad \forall c \in \{c | c \in \Xi, J(c) = \text{join}\} \quad (2.2a)$$

$$U(c, b(c) | b, J) \geq 0, \quad \forall c \in \{c | c \in \Xi, J(c) = \text{join}\} \quad (2.2b)$$

$$U(c, \beta | b, J) \leq 0, \quad \forall c \in \{c | c \in \Xi, J(c) = \text{balk}\},$$

$$\forall \beta \in \mathbb{R}_+ \cup \{\text{No}\}. \quad (2.2c)$$

Condition (2.2a) states that for all the joining customers, the best response of the equilibrium bid function should be itself. Condition (2.2b) ensures that all joining customers get nonnegative expected utility and (2.2c) specifies that the balking customers in equilibrium have no incentive to join the system since their expected utility would not turn positive regardless of what she bids.

An equilibrium is said to achieve *efficiency* or be an *efficient schedule* if $b(c)$ is strictly increasing in c whenever $J(c) =$ join. If this holds, customers are effectively prioritized by the $c\mu$ rule.

It is immediate that there is a trivial equilibrium: all joining customers submit "No". Thus, nobody participates in trading and customers are served FIFO. This equilibrium holds in all auction settings in this paper. We analyze other equilibria that realize gains from trade. We indicate the equilibrium in the baseline auction by means of a superscript B.

Theorem 1 (Full Trading, Separating Equilibrium) *Under the baseline auction, there exists an equilibrium in which*

(i) $J^B(c) =$ *join for* $c \in [\underline{c}, \tilde{c}]$ *(and balk otherwise) with* $\tilde{c} \leq \overline{c}$, *i.e.,* $\lambda^B = \Lambda F(\tilde{c})$;
(ii) *the equilibrium bid function is strictly increasing and given by*

$$b^B(c; \tilde{c}) = c + \frac{\int_c^{\tilde{c}} (F(\tilde{c}) - F(s))^2 W^e(s; \tilde{c}) ds}{(F(\tilde{c}) - F(c))^2 W^e(c; \tilde{c})}, \quad c \in [\underline{c}, \tilde{c}]$$

where $W^e(c; \tilde{c}) = \frac{1}{\mu[1-\rho(F(\tilde{c})-F(c))]^2}$ *is the time customer c expects to wait given $\tilde{c}$;*
(iii) *the equilibrium expected utility of the joining customers, $U(c, b^B(c; \tilde{c}))$, is convex decreasing in c. Either $\tilde{c}$ uniquely solves $U(\tilde{c}, b^B(\tilde{c}; \tilde{c})) = 0$ or $\tilde{c} = \overline{c}$ if there is no solution.*

We illustrate Theorem 1 in Fig. 2.1. Unless otherwise stated, we use the parameters in Table 2.1 for numerical illustrations throughout the paper.

Theorem 1 suggests that customers follow a threshold policy in their joining decisions, and they balk if their waiting cost is high, i.e., c is greater than the cutoff value $\tilde{c}$. We henceforth use $\overline{W}(\tilde{c}) \triangleq \frac{1}{\mu - \Lambda F(\tilde{c})}$ to denote the expected FIFO waiting time. In this equilibrium, however, all the joining customers participate in trading.

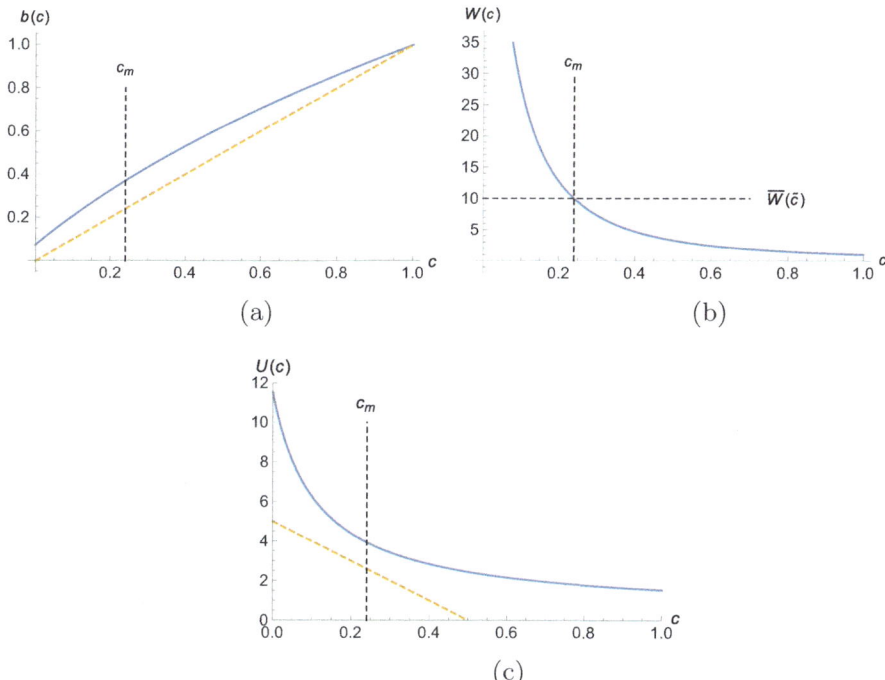

Fig. 2.1 The baseline auction. *Note.* The solid curves are the bidding function in (**a**), the expected waiting time in (**b**), and the expected utility under the auction. The dashed lines are a 45-degree line in (**a**), and the expected utility if customers are served FIFO under arrival rate λ^B in (**c**). In this example, $\tilde{c} = \bar{c} = 1$. (**a**) Biding function. (**b**) Waiting time. (**c**) Utility

Table 2.1 Model primitives for numerical illustrations

V	Λ	μ	F
5	0.9	1	$U[0, 1]$

Most importantly, the equilibrium bid function is strictly increasing and the expected waiting time is strictly decreasing in c, implying that the budget-balanced baseline auction implements an efficient schedule: any two customers with different waiting costs trade waiting spots with one another so that customers are prioritized in decreasing order of their waiting cost. The resulting expected wait time is illustrated in Fig. 2.1b.

Achieving allocative efficiency via a budget-balanced trading mechanism under private information is a nontrivial result under individual rationality in trading (cf. Myerson and Satterthwaite 1983). As illustrated in Fig. 2.1c, under this equilibrium, trading makes all the joining customers better off, i.e., their expected utility exceeds the utility they would get if they bid "No" and wait FIFO. The intuition is the following. Prior to trading, all customers expect FIFO waiting time, so the initial waiting time allocation is the same. This is analogous to having equal shares before partnership dissolution (cf. Cramton et al. 1987). When trading starts, customers may buy from existing customers, and may also sell to future arriving customers. The countervailing incentives as both buyers and sellers offset each other, making an efficient schedule possible.

We also highlight that one favorable feature of the budget-balanced auction is that it has very simple rules that do not require knowledge of customer valuations like V and F. An efficient schedule is automatically achieved by customers themselves. While the auction, in principle, allows for an arriving customer to overtake another customer who chooses not to participate in trading (without influencing her expected waiting time, e.g., customer 5 overtakes the FIFO customer in Illustration 1), this case never happens in equilibrium as all joining customers trade, i.e., any customer who is overtaken gets compensated at an agreed-upon price in equilibrium.

As illustrated in Fig. 2.1a, all the joining customers overbid, i.e., $b^B(c) > c$, except that customer $\tilde{c}$ bids truthfully, i.e., $\lim_{c \to \tilde{c}} b^B(c) = \tilde{c}$ ($\tilde{c} = \overline{c}$ in this example). This is a consequence of the auction rule that the seller's bid dictates the trading price in each transaction. Thus, customers have an incentive to inflate their bid as a seller to gain more revenue. As illustrated in Fig. 2.1c, customers' expected utility is downward sloping in their waiting costs, implying that the more impatient a customer is, the less she gains from joining the system; whereas the convexity of the curve implies that customers with extreme waiting costs (either very high or very low) have the most gains from trading relative to being served FIFO whereas customers with medium waiting cost reap the least relative gains. Customers with very low waiting cost favor trading since they are most willing to sell spots for money, i.e., $P_p(b^B(\underline{c})) = 0$ and $P_r(b^B(\underline{c})) > 0$; while those with high waiting cost benefit from trading since they are most willing to pay to skip the line, i.e., $P_r(b^B(\tilde{c})) = 0$ and $P_p(b^B(\tilde{c})) > 0$. Both incentives are weak for customers in the middle. In particular, there is one type of customers, c_m, who expects exactly the same waiting time as if she were served FIFO, i.e., $W^e(c_m; \tilde{c}) = \overline{W}(\tilde{c})$. Because of the convexity of the utility curve, c_m is also the type of customers whose gain in trading relative to FIFO is the smallest. Still, she strictly prefers trading to FIFO since $P_r(b^B(c_m)) > P_p(b^B(c_m))$, i.e., the amount she expects to receive exceeds the amount she expects to pay. In a nutshell, two types of customers warrant special attention: the one with the least patience who would be the most sensitive to joining; and the one with moderate patience who would be the most sensitive to trading.

4 Social Welfare and Service Provider's Revenue

In this section, we study how social welfare and the service provider (SP)'s revenue can be maximized using the trading mechanism proposed in Sect. 3.

4 Social Welfare and Service Provider's Revenue

4.1 Social Optimization

Definition 1 The maximum social welfare SW is determined by:

$$SW = \max_{\tilde{c} \in \Xi : \Lambda F(\tilde{c}) < \mu} \Lambda F(\tilde{c}) V - \Lambda \int_{\underline{c}}^{\tilde{c}} c W^e(c; \tilde{c}) dF(c). \qquad (2.3)$$

The socially optimal arrival rate $\lambda^{SW} = \Lambda F(\tilde{c}^{SW})$, where $\tilde{c}^{SW}$ is the maximizer of (2.3).

Definition 1 formalizes the concept of the social optimum in a centralized system where the social planner can dictate the arrival rate and scheduling policy. First, it is socially optimal to serve customers with the smallest waiting costs for any arrival rate and scheduling policy; thus, the social optimum requires a threshold joining policy, which coincides with the equilibrium structure of the baseline auction. Second, for any arrival rate, it is socially optimal to prioritize customers by the $c\mu$ rule, which is achieved by the equilibrium structure of our trading mechanism. It is natural to ask whether the baseline auction as a decentralized mechanism implements the social optimum. Proposition 1 indicates the answer is negative in general.

Proposition 1 $\lambda^B \geq \lambda^{SW}$ with equality if and only if $\lambda^B = \lambda^{SW} = \Lambda$. The social planner can achieve SW by running the baseline auction with an admission fee $p^{SW} = \int_{\underline{c}}^{\tilde{c}^{SW}} c \left[1 - \frac{F(c)}{F(\tilde{c}^{SW})} \right] \left[-\frac{\partial W^e(c; \tilde{c}^{SW})}{\partial c} \right] dc.$

Although the baseline auction achieves the "right" service order (efficiency), it does not attain the socially optimal arrival rate in general: in particular, customers with high waiting cost who should otherwise balk in social optimum join the system under the trading mechanism. This runs counter to the well-known result for the typical priority auction as in Kleinrock (1967) which is shown to be self-regulating in both the arrival rate and service order (Hassin 1995). The problem with the trading mechanism is that unlike in the priority auction, customers do not fully internalize the negative externalities inflicted on others. They do pay for the cost imposed on the existing customers if they jump over them; in fact, they are over-penalized in our auction since the trading price overstates the seller's waiting cost. However, they are not held accountable for the cost imposed on future arrivals; worse still, they can even earn rents on their waiting spots for future customers to buy. The inability to achieve the maximum social welfare is similarly found in the bilateral trading model in Myerson and Satterthwaite (1983), but takes a different form. There, maximizing social welfare is synonymous with achieving ex-post efficiency due to a fixed number of traders (one buyer and one seller). Their system is afflicted by the lack of ex-post efficiency, hence a loss in social welfare. Our queueing system attains efficiency for a given arrival rate, but customers' joining decisions are endogenous, precisely because of which, the system suffers from over-joining, again engendering a loss in social welfare. Fundamentally, this loss in social welfare is symptomatic of

Table 2.2 Comparisons of different mechanisms

	Baseline	Socially optimal	SP revenue maximizing	FIFO pricing
Social welfare	2.942	3.106	2.921	2.121
SP's revenue	0	2.121	2.381	2.011
Admission fee	0	2.592	3.439	3.505
Arrival rate	0.9	0.818	0.692	0.574
Percentage loss in SW	5.29%	0.00%	5.95%	31.72%

the presence of property rights: customers take the FIFO waiting time as their initial property and thus do not internalize the externalities inflicted on those who arrive later.

Like Naor (1969), an intuitive remedy to over-joining is to charge an admission fee p^{SW}. This fee can be interpreted as what the service provider charges for accessing the service facility, and thus it applies to all joining customers regardless of their trading decision. It is important to recognize that the admission fee only alters customers' joining incentives, but not their trading incentives since it decreases their utility if they trade just as much as it does the utility obtained from waiting FIFO. To the extent that all money flows are viewed as internal transfers, Proposition 1 shows that an appropriate admission fee can restore the social optimum. Charging a single admission fee and running the baseline auction for trading, this mechanism is *outcome equivalent* to the aforementioned priority auction that regulates both the arrival rate and service order (Hassin 1995), but customers' perception can be quite different. In our mechanism, the service provider charges a flat fee for admission and customers sort out the right service order by themselves through trading. Moreover, joining customers can also opt out of the auction and maintain their FIFO position, but it just so happens that they all voluntarily trade in equilibrium. The second and third column in Table 2.2 illustrate that charging the admission fee can reduce the arrival rate and eliminate the 5.39% social welfare loss in the baseline auction.

4.2 Service Provider's Revenue Maximization

Given the admission fee p and the baseline auction, the service provider's long-run average revenue is $p\lambda(p)$, where $\lambda(p)$ is the arrival rate under p. We show this structure raises the optimal revenue for the service provider under some technical assumptions we will introduce presently. Thus, finding the revenue-maximizing optimal mechanism reduces to pinning down the optimal admission fee.

Before we proceed, we define *virtual type functions* and assume they are monotone.

4 Social Welfare and Service Provider's Revenue

Definition 2 Denote by $f_r(\cdot)$ and $f_p(\cdot, \tilde{c})$ the receivers' and payers' virtual type functions, respectively:

$$f_r(c) \triangleq c + \frac{F(c)}{f(c)}, \qquad f_p(c; \tilde{c}) \triangleq c - \frac{F(\tilde{c}) - F(c)}{f(c)}.$$

ASSUMPTION 1 $\frac{df_r(c)}{dc} > 0$ and $\frac{df_p(c;\tilde{c})}{dc} > 0$ for all $c \in [\underline{c}, \tilde{c}]$ and $\tilde{c} \in [\underline{c}, \overline{c}]$.

Assuming monotone virtual type functions is common in the mechanism design literature. Monotone virtual types are satisfied by many common probability distributions, such as the uniform, normal, logistic and power function distributions, and the gamma and Weibull distributions with shape parameters greater than or equal to 1; any log-concave distribution has this property (Bagnoli and Bergstrom 2005).

The service provider is not bound by the form of mechanism we introduce (a flat admission fee plus the baseline auction). For example, it could revise the auction rule so as not to induce strict priority. Proposition 2 indicates, nevertheless, that it is optimal under Assumption 1 for the service provider to appeal to the same mechanism structure as the social planner does. The only difference is that the service provider should set a higher admission fee.

Proposition 2 *The service provider maximizes revenue by setting a price $p^M > p^{SW}$ and running the baseline auction.*

Given the mechanism structure, if the service provider's only lever were the admission fee, then it should be intuitive that the service provider would set a higher fee than is socially optimal. Naor (1969) has a similar result in a different queueing context. As a monopolist, the service provider would command a higher price than the efficient level to maximize its own revenue. Proposition 2 reveals that even if the service provider has more levers, it should stick to mechanisms that implement strict priority. The monotone virtual types in Assumption 1 guarantee that the service provider has the same incentive as the social planner in prioritizing customers. Otherwise, the service provider would prefer pooling, i.e., serving a class of customers by the FIFO rule despite differences in their waiting costs (cf. Katta and Sethuraman 2005).

Note that as one of the many implementations of the service-provider's optimal direct mechanism, the proposed trading mechanism in Proposition 2 is outcome equivalent to a priority auction with an optimally determined reserve price (cf. Lui 1985). Yet unlike the priority auction, there is no price discrimination by the service provider: all the payments generated in the baseline auction are transfers among customers; still, the same optimal revenue is achieved. We highlight that our proposed trading mechanism, albeit not the unique implementation of the optimal mechanism, is rather simple and that the flat admission fee is only for accessing the service facility, not for gaining priority, so it does not have the unfair connotation like the Priority Answer feature offered by EE.

Table 2.2 illustrates the service provider's optimal trading mechanism in column four, and the optimal pricing of a FIFO queue in column five. The FIFO price, p^F, is defined by

$$(p^F, \tilde{c}^F) = \arg\max_{(p,\tilde{c})} \; p \Lambda F(\tilde{c}), \quad \text{s.t.} \; V - p - \tilde{c}W(\tilde{c}) = 0. \tag{2.4}$$

Denote the FIFO revenue by $\Pi^F = p^F \Lambda F(\tilde{c}^F)$. While it is immediate that the trading mechanism outperforms FIFO pricing in its revenue performance (2.381 vs. 2.011), it is not clear how the admission fees in the two scenarios, p^M and p^F, compare. Since the exclusive source of revenue in both scenarios is the admission fee, one might expect the service provider who shifts from FIFO to trading to increase this price to extract more revenue. This intuition is correct if the full market is already captured by FIFO pricing, i.e., $\tilde{c}^F = \bar{c}$, but in general, the direction of the service provider's price adjustment is ambiguous. Table 2.2 shows a possibility that the service provider decreases the price (from 3.505 to 3.439) and achieves a higher revenue through a higher throughput. A lower price might be more palatable to customers and make them more receptive of the trading platform.

5 Trading Through an Intermediary

In this section, we study a setting in which the service provider delegates trading to a revenue-maximizing intermediary. The key distinction between the service provider and the intermediary is that the intermediary can only charge customers for using the trading platform (e.g., a trade participation fee), but not for access to the service facility (e.g., an admission fee). Since a high trade participation fee will make trading less attractive and eventually deter some customers from trading altogether, the intermediary's fee-structure will potentially affect customers' trading incentives.

5.1 Baseline Auction with a Trade Participation Fee

We start by considering a benchmark trading mechanism where an arriving customer must pay the intermediary an upfront trade participation fee H; then, the baseline auction is run as before. We refer to this as an "H auction." The intermediary's revenue is $H\lambda^T(H)$, where $\lambda^T(H)$ is the arrival rate of the customers who trade given H. By definition, trading customers are a subset of joining customers, i.e., $\lambda^T(H) \leq \lambda$ for any H.

Recall that in the baseline auction (where $H = 0$), all joining customers are strictly better off by participating in trading. Thus, the equilibrium structure identified in Proposition 1 remains valid if H is slightly positive. It is easy to see

5 Trading Through an Intermediary

that if the trade participation fee H is too high, then trading will no longer be favored over FIFO. Hence, there exists a threshold value $\overline{H}$ such that the equilibrium structure identified in Theorem 1 is preserved and all joining customers voluntarily trade ($\lambda^T(H) = \lambda$) if and only if $H \leq \overline{H}$.

Definition 3 $\overline{H}$ is such that $\lambda^T(H) = \lambda$ if and only if $H \leq \overline{H}$.

For convenience, we refer to the auction where $H = \overline{H}$ as the "$\overline{H}$ auction." In our running numerical example, at $H = \overline{H} = 1.342$, $U(c)$ in Fig. 2.1c would be tangent to the FIFO line, and the intermediary's revenue is 1.208. If $H > \overline{H}$, some customers with medium waiting costs (since they benefit the least from trading) will find trading too costly and thus refuse to trade by submitting "No," and this would lead to $\lambda^T(H) < \lambda$. The revenue-maximizing intermediary's is in a conundrum. On one hand, if it would like to get all joining customers to trade, its fee is bounded above by $\overline{H}$. One the other hand, if the intermediary wants to charge more aggressively (above $\overline{H}$), it must bear the cost of being unable to collect the fee from some joining customers: a direct loss of revenues via a decreased trading volume, plus, an indirect loss via a lower arrival rate as the non-trading (FIFO) customers downgrade the expected utility of those who trade.

To resolve this conundrum, we enrich the baseline auction with two trade-restriction prices that enable the intermediary to charge above $\overline{H}$ while still inducing voluntary trading of all joining customers. We shall show this is the optimal trading mechanism for the intermediary.

5.2 Augmented Auction: Trading Rules and a Motivating Example

Auction Format The augmented auction contains two trade restriction parameters $\underline{R}$ and $\overline{R}$ ($\underline{R} \leq \overline{R}$) in addition to the trade participation fee H. The trading rule is the same as before except that *if both customers' bids are within the interval $[\underline{R}, \overline{R}]$, they are barred from trading with one another and are served FIFO.* However, if only one of the two customers' bids are within $[\underline{R}, \overline{R}]$, trade still occurs between the two. This auction is referred to as an "$(H, \underline{R}, \overline{R})$ auction."

Illustration 2 Consider the illustrative scenario in Sect. 3 and assume that $b_4 < \underline{R} < b_2 < b' \leq b_1 < \overline{R}$. As before, the system prior to trading is represented by (b_1, b_2, F, b_4, b'). Only customer 4 and 5 swap positions, and the system after trading is represented by (b_1, b_2, F, b', b_4). Note that despite the fact that $b_2 < b'$, customers 2 and 5 do *not* swap positions since both of their bids fall in $[\underline{R}, \overline{R}]$.

Table 2.3 shows that when $H = 1.510$, $\underline{R} = 0.257$ and $\overline{R} = 0.425$, the intermediary's revenue would be 1.352 in the $(H, \underline{R}, \overline{R})$ auction, 11.9% higher than the revenue that would be achieved in the $\overline{H}$ auction. Note that the trade participation fee H in the augmented auction is higher than $\overline{H}$, yet all joining customers sign up for trading, which can be verified by recognizing the revenue (1.352) is equal to H (1.510) times λ (0.896).

Table 2.3 The intermediary's optimal $(H, \underline{R}, \overline{R})$ auction and the $\overline{H}$ auction

	Revenue	H	$\underline{R}$	$\overline{R}$	λ
Optimal augmented auction	1.352	1.510	0.257	0.425	0.896
$\overline{H}$ auction	1.208	1.342	–	–	0.9

5.3 Auction Equilibrium

To generate insights into how the augmented auction with trade restriction benefits the intermediary, we derive the equilibrium for the case when trading is free ($H = 0$, budget-balanced among customers), and compare that with the budget-balanced baseline auction. We indicate the equilibrium in the augmented auction by means of a superscript A. With a slight abuse of notation, we use $U(c, \beta)$ to denote the expected utility of customer c who bids β in the equilibrium of the augmented auction (including the trade participation fee).

Theorem 2 (Full Trading, Partial Pooling Equilibrium) *Under the augmented auction with given $\underline{R}$ and $\overline{R}$, when $H = 0$, there exists an equilibrium in which:*

(i) $J^A(c) = $ *join for $c \in [\underline{c}, \tilde{c})$ (and balk otherwise);*
(ii) *the equilibrium bid function is weakly increasing and given by*

$$b^A(c; c_r, c_p, \tilde{c}) = \begin{cases} c + \frac{\int_c^{c_r} (F(\tilde{c}) - F(s))^2 W^e(s; \tilde{c}) ds + K(\underline{R}, c_r, c_p, \tilde{c})}{(F(\tilde{c}) - F(c))^2 W^e(c; \tilde{c})}, & c \in [\underline{c}, c_r) \\ \overline{R}, & c \in [c_r, c_p] \\ b^B(c; \tilde{c}), & c \in (c_p, \tilde{c}] \end{cases}$$

(2.5)

where constant $K(\underline{R}, c_r, c_p, \tilde{c}) = (\underline{R} - c_r)(F(\tilde{c}) - F(c_r))^2 W^e(c_r; \tilde{c})$ and $c_r, c_p, \tilde{c} \in \Xi$ with $\underline{c} \leq c_r \leq c_p \leq \tilde{c}$ are a solution to the following equations:

$$[U(c_r, \underline{R}) - U(c_r, \overline{R})][c_r - \underline{c}][c_r - \tilde{c}] = 0 \quad (2.6a)$$

$$[U(c_p, b^A(c_p^+; c_r, c_p, \tilde{c})) - U(c_p, \overline{R})][c_p - \underline{c}][c_p - \tilde{c}] = 0 \quad (2.6b)$$

$$U(\tilde{c}, b^A(\tilde{c}; c_r, c_p, \tilde{c}))[\tilde{c} - \overline{c}] = 0; \quad (2.6c)$$

(iii) *the expected waiting time for customer $c \in [\underline{c}, \tilde{c}]$ is*

$$W^A(c; c_r, c_p, \tilde{c}) = \begin{cases} W^e(c; \tilde{c}), & \forall c \in [\underline{c}, c_r) \cup (c_p, \tilde{c}] \\ \frac{1}{\mu(1 - \rho F(\tilde{c}) + \rho F(c_r))(1 - \rho F(\tilde{c}) + \rho F(c_p))}, & \forall c \in [c_r, c_p]. \end{cases}$$

(2.7)

5 Trading Through an Intermediary

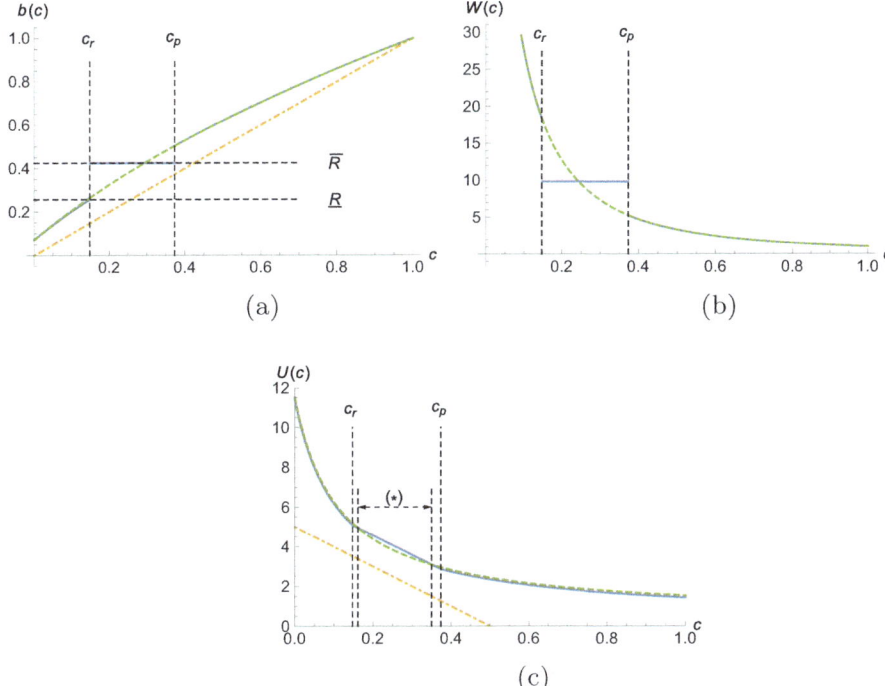

Fig. 2.2 The augmented auction. *Note.* $H = 0$, $\underline{R} = 0.257$, $\overline{R} = 0.425$. $\tilde{c} = 1$, $c_r = 0.148$, $c_p = 0.373$. The blue solid curves correspond to the equilibrium properties of the augmented auction; the green dashed curve, the baseline auction as in Fig. 2.1. The orange dot-dashed line is the 45-degree line in (**a**); the expected utility if customers are served FIFO under the same equilibrium arrival rate in (**c**). (∗) indicates the subset of customer types in the pooling segment that receive a higher expected utility than in the baseline auction. (**a**) Bidding function. (**b**) Waiting time. (**c**) Utility

Comparing Theorem 2 with Theorem 1 shows the effects of the trade restriction parameters, $\underline{R}$ and $\overline{R}$. While the bid function $b^A(\cdot)$ in (2.5) is still strictly increasing in $[\underline{c}, c_r] \cup (c_p, \tilde{c}]$, it is flat in $[c_r, c_p]$: these customers all bid $\overline{R}$ and thus do not trade with one another (see Fig. 2.2a). As a result, the waiting time schedule is no longer efficient since these customers all expect the same waiting time despite their different waiting costs (see Fig. 2.2b). Consequently, there is pooling of customers in $[c_r, c_p]$, who are served as a single FIFO class. As shown in the expression of $W^A(\cdot)$ in (2.7), for any given arrival rate, the expected waiting time for customers in $[\underline{c}, c_r) \cup (c_p, \tilde{c}]$ is still the efficient waiting time, i.e., trading allows these customers to be strictly prioritized over any other joining customer with lower waiting cost.

Similar to the baseline auction, adding $\underline{R}$ and $\overline{R}$ to the budget balanced auction does not discourage any joining customers from voluntarily participating in trading. As shown in Fig. 2.2c, all joining customers are better off by participating in trading than submitting "No." One noticeable difference of customers' expected utility in the augmented auction is that it decreases linearly in c for $c \in [c_r, c_p]$. This is by the linearity assumption of waiting costs. Customers in the pooling segment $[c_r, c_p]$ differ in their waiting costs but choose to bid the same amount and thus expect to wait the same amount of time and pay/receive the same amount of money.

5.4 Optimal Auction Parameters and Structure

When $H = 0$ in the augmented auction (the intermediary has no revenue), all customers strictly prefer trading. A slightly positive H will not alter this preference and the equilibrium bidding behavior in the augmented auction insofar as all joining customers trade. We show that this is indeed the optimal structure the intermediary wants to implement. Furthermore, the $(H, \underline{R}, \overline{R})$ auction is an optimal mechanism for the intermediary given the optimal auction parameters.

Theorem 3 (Optimality of the Augmented Auction) *The $(H^*, \underline{R}^*, \overline{R}^*)$ is an optimal mechanism for the intermediary with:*

$$H^* = \frac{\Pi(c_r^*, c_p^*, \tilde{c}^*)}{\Lambda F(\tilde{c}^*)} \tag{2.8a}$$

$$\overline{R}^* = \frac{c_p^* \overline{W}(\tilde{c}^*) + [\rho b^R(c_p^*; c_r^*, c_p^*, \tilde{c}^*)(F(\tilde{c}^*) - F(c_p^*)) - c_p^*]W^e(c_p^*; \tilde{c}^*)}{\rho(F(\tilde{c}^*) - F(c_r^*))\overline{W}(\tilde{c}^*)} \tag{2.8b}$$

$$\underline{R}^* = \frac{c_r^* W^e(c_r^*; \tilde{c}^*) - c_r^* \overline{W}(\tilde{c}^*) + \rho \overline{W}(\tilde{c}^*)[F(\tilde{c}^*) - F(c_p^*)]\overline{R}^*}{\rho W^e(c_r^*; \tilde{c}^*)[F(\tilde{c}^*) - F(c_r^*)]} \tag{2.8c}$$

where $\Pi(c_r, c_p, \tilde{c}) = -\Lambda \int_{\underline{c}}^{c_r} \left(W^e(c; \tilde{c}) - \overline{W}(\tilde{c})\right) f_r(c) dF(c) + \Lambda \int_{c_p}^{\tilde{c}} \left(\overline{W}(\tilde{c}) - W^e(c; \tilde{c})\right) f_p(c; \tilde{c}) dF(c)$ *and* $c_r^*, c_p^*, \tilde{c}^*$ *solve the following optimization problem:*

$$\max_{c_r, c_p, \tilde{c} \in \Xi: c_r \leq c_p \leq \tilde{c}} \Pi(c_r, c_p, \tilde{c}) \tag{2.9a}$$

s.t. $$\frac{1}{\mu(1 - \rho F(\tilde{c}) + \rho F(c_r))(1 - \rho F(\tilde{c}) + \rho F(c_p))} = \overline{W}(\tilde{c}) \tag{2.9b}$$

$$V - \int_{c_p}^{\tilde{c}} W^e(c; \tilde{c}) dc - c_p \overline{W}(\tilde{c}) \geq 0. \tag{2.9c}$$

The resulting equilibrium structure is the same as identified in Theorem 2. In particular,

$$U\left(c, b^A\left(c; c_r^*, c_p^*, \tilde{c}^*\right)\right) = V - c\overline{W}(\tilde{c}^*), \quad \forall c \in \left[c_r^*, c_p^*\right]. \tag{2.10}$$

Theorem 3 determines the optimal parameters $(H^*, \underline{R}^*, \overline{R}^*)$ by reverse engineering. Instead of characterizing the equilibrium outcome by solving (2.6a)–(2.6c) for $c_r, c_p, \tilde{c}$ under any given auction parameters $(H, \underline{R}, \overline{R})$, we first determine what the optimal outcome should be by obtaining $c_r^*, c_p^*, \tilde{c}^*$ from the optimization problem (2.9a)–(2.9c) and then determine the optimal auction parameters $(H^*, \underline{R}^*, \overline{R}^*)$ that can implement the optimal outcome using (2.8a)–(2.8c), where (2.8b) and (2.8c) are obtained from shuffling terms of (2.6a) and (2.6b).

Combining (2.9b) and $W^A(\cdot)$ in (2.7) implies that in the optimal auction, the expected waiting time for customers in $[c_r^*, c_p^*]$ is equal to the FIFO waiting time $\overline{W}(\tilde{c})$ (see Fig. 2.3b). Furthermore, (2.10) suggests that these customers' expected utility is equal to what they would get if they just bid "No" and wait FIFO (see Fig. 2.3c). This does not imply they do not trade at all: they still swap positions with customers *outside the pool* by selling their spot to higher bidders and buying positions from lower bidders, but on average trading does not realize any gains. The fact that they trade is crucial to achieving an efficient expected waiting time for

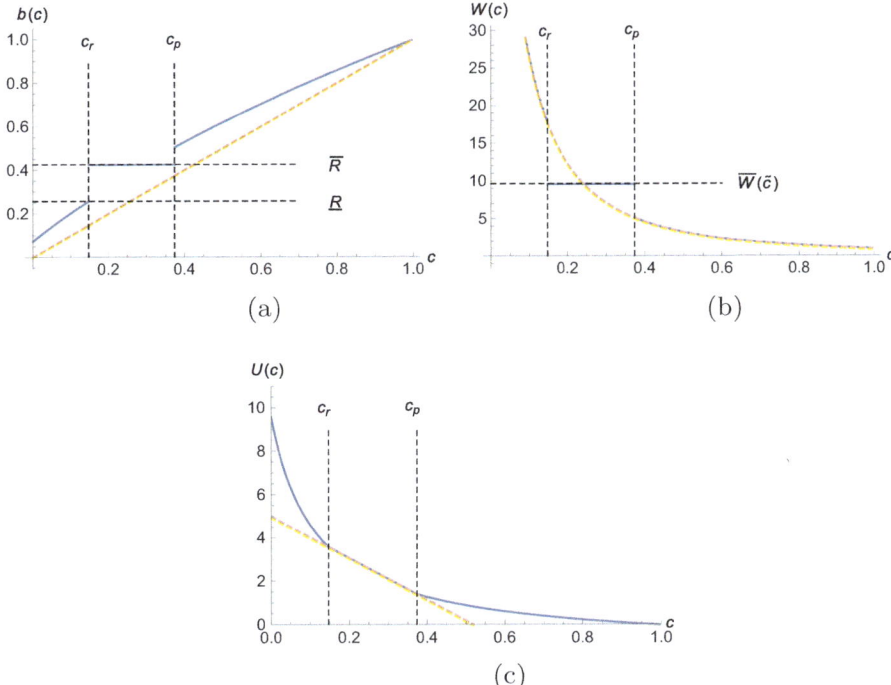

Fig. 2.3 The optimal $(H, \underline{R}, \overline{R})$ auction. *Note.* $H = 1.510$, $\underline{R} = 0.257$, $\overline{R} = 0.425$. $\tilde{c} = 0.995$, $c_r = 0.147$, $c_p = 0.373$. The solid curve corresponds to the equilibrium properties of the auction; the dashed curve is the 45-degree line in (**a**); the efficient waiting time function in (**b**); the expected utility if customers are served FIFO under the same equilibrium arrival rate in (**c**). (**a**) Bidding function. (**b**) Waiting time. (**c**) Utility

customers outside the pool $[\underline{c}, c_r^*) \cup (c_p^*, \tilde{c}^*]$. The augmented auction is designed to only prohibit trading within the pool.

In brief, the optimal auction has the following two features:

(1) All joining customers participate in trading.
(2) The schedule is efficient in $[\underline{c}, c_r^*) \cup (c_p^*, \tilde{c}^*]$ but customers in $[c_r^*, c_p^*]$ expect FIFO waiting time.

Theorem 4 (Optimality of Trade Restriction) *The optimal auction should always have $\underline{R}^* < \overline{R}^*$, and thus $c_r^* < c_p^*$.*

Theorem 4 shows that the intermediary would like to restrict trading to a certain extent to fully exploit its control over the trading channel. As a result, it sets $\overline{R}^*$ strictly above $\underline{R}^*$ so that pooling occurs in the intermediary's optimal auction and the schedule is not efficient. This extends the classical result in Myerson and Satterthwaite (1983) about the intermediary's trade restriction incentives in bilateral trading to a queueing context where customers can be both buyers and sellers. After all, the intermediary is a monopolist who wants to restrict output under the efficient level to command a higher price. Note that if the service provider operates the trading platform as in Sect. 4.2, it can simply exercise its monopoly power by charging a higher admission fee (which reduces arrivals). By contrast, the intermediary's trade participation fee cannot be forced upon customers even after they join the system, so setting a higher fee as an intermediary should be done in a more nuanced way that reduces the amount of trading among customers and creates a pooling segment. As we argue in Sect. 5.3, trade restriction generates value to customers in the middle who are most sensitive to trading by letting them avoid undesirable trades. This value added, in turn, passes on to the intermediary by enabling it to charge a higher trade participation fee (we shall formally establish this in Corollary 1).

Let $\lambda^* = \Lambda F(\tilde{c}^*)$ be the optimal effective arrival rate under the $(H^*, \underline{R}^*, \overline{R}^*)$ auction. Let λ^{FIFO} be the effective arrival rate if all joining customers are served FIFO. In the FIFO system, a customer of type c receives an expected utility of $V - c\overline{W}(\tilde{c}^{\text{FIFO}})$, where $\tilde{c}^{\text{FIFO}}$ satisfies $\lambda^{\text{FIFO}} = \Lambda F(\tilde{c}^{\text{FIFO}})$. Let $\lambda^{\overline{H}}$ be the effective arrival rate if the intermediary charges $\overline{H}$ in the H auction. Likewise, $\tilde{c}^{\overline{H}}$ is defined such that $\lambda^{\overline{H}} = \Lambda F(\tilde{c}^{\overline{H}})$. Proposition 3 orders the three arrival rates.

Proposition 3 $\lambda^{FIFO} \leq \lambda^* \leq \lambda^{\overline{H}}$. *In particular, if not all customers join in the optimal auction, i.e., $\lambda^* < \Lambda$, then $\lambda^{FIFO} < \lambda^* < \lambda^{\overline{H}}$.*

In the optimal augmented auction, customers with high waiting costs who would otherwise balk in a FIFO system may now join and participate in trading because this option to trade makes them better off than if they are served FIFO. On the other hand, as compared to the $\overline{H}$ auction, the pooling segment in the optimal mechanism diminishes the appeal of trading for customers with high waiting costs since they have to pay more to get the same priority; thus fewer customers join. The optimal mechanism has a lower arrival rate than the $\overline{H}$ auction, but it raises more

5 Trading Through an Intermediary

revenue, which must stem from a higher trade participation fee. This is summarized in Corollary 1.

Corollary 1 *The optimal trade participation fee in the augmented auction is strictly above $\overline{H}$, i.e., $H^* > \overline{H}$.*

Trade restriction resolves the intermediary's conundrum: it always charges strictly above $\overline{H}$, yet all joining customers choose to pay this trade participation fee. Combining Theorem 4, Proposition 3 and Corollary 1 shows that the gain from charging a higher trade participation fee above $\overline{H}$ in the augmented auction overshadows the cost of a resulting lower arrival rate for the intermediary.

5.5 The Value of Trading vs. FIFO

Now, we turn to the service provider's pricing decision in the presence of the intermediary. In a FIFO queue, the service provider would set a revenue-maximizing admission fee, p^F, as formalized in (2.4). We compare this to a setting where the service provider invites the revenue-maximizing intermediary to mediate the trading platform. The service provider is completely detached from the trading platform and does not contract with the intermediary due to technological reasons and reputational concerns discussed in Sect. 1. The service provider and the intermediary play a sequential game: the service provider first sets an admission fee p^T and then the intermediary's implements its optimal trading mechanism. Corollary 2 shows that the service provider is always better off by inviting the intermediary.

Corollary 2 *The intermediary running the trading platform strictly increases the service provider's revenue relative to FIFO.*

Next, we numerically quantify, under a variety of input parameters, how the intermediary's trading mechanism impacts the service provider's pricing decision in Table 2.4. We also compare the service provider's revenue with the intermediary's trading platform relative to a FIFO queue in Table 2.5. In all numerical trials, we fix the service rate to be 1 and the waiting cost to be uniformly distributed between 0 an 1 as in Table 2.1. We vary the service value V between 2 and 10, and the market size Λ between 0.1 and 3. Denote the percentage difference between the service provider's FIFO price, p^F, and price under trading, p^T, by Δ_p; the percentage difference between the service provider's revenue under FIFO, Π^F and revenue under trading, Π^T, by Δ_Π.

$$\Delta_p = \frac{p^T - p^F}{p^F} \times 100\%, \qquad \Delta_\Pi = \frac{\Pi^T - \Pi^F}{\Pi^F} \times 100\%.$$

Table 2.4 shows that it is in general ambiguous how the service provider should adjust its price when the intermediary implements the trading platform. Table 2.5 shows the service provider's revenue improvement. In terms of its pricing behavior,

Table 2.4 Percentage change in price Δ_p

Λ	V = 2	V = 3	V = 4	V = 5	V = 6	V = 7	V = 8	V = 9	V = 10
0.1	−0.73%	1.16%	0.76%	0.56%	0.45%	0.37%	0.32%	0.28%	0.25%
0.3	−1.49%	−1.73%	3.70%	2.66%	2.08%	1.71%	1.45%	1.26%	1.11%
0.5	−1.78%	−1.86%	−1.81%	−0.09%	6.39%	5.11%	4.26%	3.65%	3.19%
0.7	−1.86%	−1.78%	−1.60%	−1.42%	−1.19%	−0.98%	−0.82%	−0.59%	−0.09%
0.9	−1.83%	−1.63%	−1.39%	−1.01%	−0.87%	−0.57%	−0.50%	−0.29%	−0.23%
1.1	−1.76%	−1.68%	−1.31%	−0.87%	−0.52%	−0.34%	−0.18%	0.03%	0.13%
2	−1.59%	−0.73%	−0.32%	0.00%	0.38%	0.48%	0.65%	0.81%	0.87%
3	−0.79%	−0.15%	0.27%	0.50%	0.81%	0.87%	1.10%	1.20%	1.21%

Table 2.5 Percentage change in revenue Δ_Π

Λ	V = 2	V = 3	V = 4	V = 5	V = 6	V = 7	V = 8	V = 9	V = 10
0.1	1.65%	1.16%	0.76%	0.56%	0.45%	0.37%	0.32%	0.28%	0.25%
0.3	3.99%	5.21%	3.70%	2.66%	2.08%	1.71%	1.45%	1.26%	1.11%
0.5	5.55%	6.89%	7.82%	7.32%	6.39%	5.11%	4.26%	3.65%	3.19%
0.7	6.67%	7.97%	8.80%	9.36%	9.74%	10.01%	10.20%	10.33%	8.18%
0.9	7.49%	8.71%	9.42%	9.87%	10.15%	10.33%	10.45%	10.51%	10.55%
1.1	8.11%	9.22%	9.83%	10.18%	10.38%	10.49%	10.54%	10.56%	10.55%
2	9.64%	10.28%	10.51%	10.56%	10.53%	10.45%	10.35%	10.24%	10.13%
3	10.28%	10.55%	10.53%	10.40%	10.24%	10.07%	9.90%	9.73%	9.56%

the numerical instances can be divided into three cases. *Case 1*: In the top right corner of Table 2.4, when the service value is high and the market size is small, the service provider's price goes up. This corresponds to the case when the full market is captured in the FIFO queue. As we argued following Corollary 2, trading allows the service provider to raise its price. This can be verified by recognizing that in those instances the relative price change is equal to the relative revenue change shown in Table 2.5 as the arrival rate is unaffected. *Case 2*: In the bottom right corner of Table 2.4, when the service value is high and the market size is also large, the service provider's price rises again. However, in these instances, the system does not capture the full market, and the arrival rate is also changed as a result of trading. We observe that the revenue change is higher than the price change now, which implies that trading allows the service provider to both command a higher price and lure more customers. *Case 3*: In the rest of the instances, the service provider offers a price cut, so that the revenue increase is solely attributed to a higher arrival rate. Here the FIFO queue does not capture the full market. As Proposition 3 suggests, even if the service provider sticks to its original price, it will enjoy a higher revenue since more customers join when the trading platform is in place. However, the service provider responds by actually decreasing its price to get an even higher arrival rate. As we suggest in Sect. 4.2, a lower price might be more favorable to customers from a behavioral perspective, and this may facilitate the promotion of the intermediary's trading platform.

Somewhat strikingly, in our numerical study, when the market is not fully captured (cases 2 and 3), the magnitude of the price change is, in fact, quite small: less than 2% in all those instances; yet the revenue change is quite sizable by comparison (about 10% in many instances). The implication is that the intermediary's trading platform can potentially be a seamless built-in for the service provider: the service provider does not need to worry about running the auction itself; it does not even need to significantly alter its price as a response of the new platform (which is valuable especially when the menu cost is high). The bottom line is that the intermediary increases the service provider's revenue relative to a FIFO system, and improves system efficiency. These are the intermediary's value propositions to the service provider with either revenue or welfare considerations. Of course, there is a natural double marginalization problem in our setup where both the service provider and the intermediary are monopolists. Theoretically, the service provider would earn an even higher revenue if it operated the trading platform by itself as in Sect. 4.2. Practically, this may not be in the service provider's best interest for technological reasons and reputational concerns previously stated. Vertical integration would achieve the maximum joint revenue as in Sect. 4.2, but this usually involves efforts expended on negotiation, coordination and contracting. In this regard, an intermediary on a separate platform should probably be good enough in practice.

6 Conclusion Remarks

This chapter analyzes a congested service system in which customers are privately informed about their waiting cost and trade their waiting positions on a trading platform. We design the optimal mechanisms that maximize social welfare, the service provider's revenue, and the revenue of the intermediary that develops and manages the trading platform, respectively. We find that while both the social planner and the service provider want customers to trade as much as possible (inducing the $c\mu$ rule), the intermediary *restricts* trading among customers (pooling) to maximize its own revenue. In particular, a budget-balanced baseline auction leads to a higher arrival rate than is socially desirable and thus an admission fee must be levied to maximize social welfare. By comparison, the revenue-maximizing service provider would charge a higher admission fee than the social planner would. For practical reasons, the service provider may wish to delegate the trading platform to a revenue-maximizing intermediary. To that end, we propose an augmented auction with a trade participation fee *and* two trade restriction prices. Compared to the baseline auction with a trade participation fee only, the intermediary can charge a higher fee in the optimal auction and still have *all* joining customers voluntarily participate in trading. We show that the intermediary's trading mechanism always strictly improves the service provider's revenue relative to a FIFO system despite the intermediary's revenue-maximizing nature. This is a potentially powerful sales argument the intermediary can make to convince the service provider of installing the platform.

One practical concern for introducing the trading marketplace is the rise of speculative behavior. One is the arrival of "scalpers" who game the system by selling their spots for money without actually receiving the service. These customers are typically time-insensitive and ascribe low valuation to the service itself and thus would not join the system otherwise. We will study queue-scalping in Chap. 4. Another related phenomenon is "line-sitting" whereby real customers hire line-sitters to wait in line on their behalf and swap in only when line-sitters approach the head of the line. We will study line-sitting in Chap. 3. On the one hand, the presence of speculators does not violate other customers' property rights since such swaps are still one-to-one substitution. On the other hand, these customers are likely to renege before entering the service, appropriating pecuniary gains that might otherwise be captured by the service provider. In principle, the up-front trade participation fee in the intermediary's optimal auction should deter some speculative customers. Additionally, the platform can act as a gatekeeper that closely monitors any suspicious trading activities and bans unscrupulous customers from using the trading platform if necessary. This further justifies the importance of the trading platform (intermediary) in mediating transactions.

References

Bagnoli M, Bergstrom T (2005) Log-concave probability and its applications. Economic Theory 26(2):445–469
Cramton P, Gibbons R, Klemperer P (1987) Dissolving a partnership efficiently. Econometrica 55(3):615–632
El Haji A, Onderstal S (2019) Trading places: an experimental comparison of reallocation mechanisms for priority queuing. J Econ Manag Strateg 28(4):670–686
Gershkov A, Schweinzer P (2010) When queueing is better than push and shove. Int J Game Theory 39(3):409–430
Gray K (2009) Property in a queue. In: Alexander GS, Penalver EM (eds.) Property and community. Oxford University Press, New York, pp 165–195
Hassin R (1995) Decentralized regulation of a queue. Manag Sci 41(1):163–173
Katta A, Sethuraman J (2005) Pricing strategies and service differentiation in queues: a profit maximization perspective. Working paper, Columbia University, New York
Kleinrock L (1967) Optimum bribing for queue position. Oper Res 15(2):304–318
Lui FT (1985) An equilibrium queueing model of bribery. J Polit Econ 93(4):760–781
Mann L (1969) Queue culture: the waiting time line as a social system. Am J Sociol 75(3):340–354
Myerson RB, Satterthwaite MA (1983) Efficient mechanisms for bilateral trading. J Econ Theory 29(2):265–281
Naor P (1969) The regulation of queue size by levying tolls. Econometrica 37(1):15–24
Rosenblum DM (1992) Allocation of waiting time by trading in position on a G/M/S queue. Oper Res 40:S338–S342
Yang L, Debo L, Gupta V (2017) Trading time in a congested environment. Manag Sci 63(7):2377–2395

References

Open Access This chapter is licensed under the terms of the Creative Commons Attribution 4.0 International License (http://creativecommons.org/licenses/by/4.0/), which permits use, sharing, adaptation, distribution and reproduction in any medium or format, as long as you give appropriate credit to the original author(s) and the source, provide a link to the Creative Commons license and indicate if changes were made.

The images or other third party material in this chapter are included in the chapter's Creative Commons license, unless indicated otherwise in a credit line to the material. If material is not included in the chapter's Creative Commons license and your intended use is not permitted by statutory regulation or exceeds the permitted use, you will need to obtain permission directly from the copyright holder.

Chapter 3
Line-Sitting Services

1 Introduction

Queues are an integral part of many service systems. However, waiting in a long line is universally unpleasant. With the rise of the gig economy, line-sitting (i.e., customers hire a third-party line stander to sit in line on their behalf) has taken off and seeped into all kinds of waiting lines. Examples include queues for congressional hearings in DC, for buying Hamilton tickets and Cronuts in New York, for paying government bills in Italy, for seeing doctors in China, and for eating at trendy restaurants. Line-sitters have also appeared at passport/visa application lineups and COVID-19 testing sites all over the world.

The recent years have seen line-sitting morphing into a burgeoning business. Same Ole Line Dudes (SOLD), a New York City-based company, provides line-sitting services for customers buying Dominique Ansel cronuts or Hamilton tickets; Skip the Line, a Washington DC-based business, can save space at popular restaurants, museum exhibits, and shopping events; Washington DC Line Standing, another DC-based company, helps clients stand in line for Congressional hearings. These firms typically set an hourly rate for their line-sitting services, based on the nature of the lines. For instance, SOLD charges $10–$15 per hour; Skip the Line, a fee of $30 per hour; and Washington DC Line Standing, $40 per hour. Additionally, thanks to technological advances, various mobile-application startups have been launched to facilitate on-demand booking of line-sitters. Notable examples include *LineAngel* based in Los Angeles and *Placer* in New York City.

At first sight, one may be prone to the thought that line-sitting is a minor variant of the more traditional priority purchasing scheme which is widespread and extensively studied. After all, isn't it all about customers being able to pay extra for reduced physical wait? Yes and no. There are two key differences between line-sitting and priority purchasing. First, priority is sold by the service provider (e.g., Universal Studios selling Front-of-Line passes), whereas line-sitting is managed by an independent third-party company (e.g., SOLD). Second, a priority customer reduces her wait by bumping customers who opt out of the priority-upgrade option, whereas a line-sitting adopter skips wait by swapping position with the hired line-sitter when the line-sitter nears the front of the line without pushing back non-adopters. These two subtle distinctions not only lead to divergent customer behavior but also have rich revenue implications for the service provider and welfare implications for the customer population. As such, a game-theoretical queueing model was studied in Cui et al. (2020) to formally analyze the impact of line-sitting on the service provider's revenue and customer welfare.

Based on Cui et al. (2020), we employ a canonical first-in-first-out (FIFO) queueing model as a benchmark in which customers with heterogeneous waiting costs decide whether to join a service system or balk, based on the service reward, service fee, and the waiting cost. Next, we set up the model of line-sitting in which, in addition to joining themselves and balking, customers can also choose to hire a line-sitter to stand in the line at an hourly rate specified by the line-sitting firm. Furthermore, we formulate a model of priority purchasing, in which, besides joining a regular line and balking, customers can also choose to join the priority line by paying an additional priority premium set by the service provider. We fully characterize the equilibrium in each of the three schemes, namely, (1) FIFO without line-sitting or priority, (2) line-sitting, and (3) priority purchasing. We then perform pairwise comparisons of the three schemes in terms of the service provider's revenue and customer welfare. Finally, we combine the results from the pairwise comparisons to identify the optimal scheme out of the three that either maximizes the service provider's revenue or achieves the highest customer welfare, or both.

2 Model Preliminaries and FIFO Benchmark

Consider an $M/M/1$ service system with the first-in-first-out (FIFO) queue discipline. Customer needs for the service arise according to a Poisson process with rate Λ per hour. The service provider has an exponentially distributed service time with rate μ per hour. Let $\rho = \Lambda/\mu$ denote the potential workload of the system. If a customer joins the service system, she earns a service reward R and pays the service provider a base service fee B. The hourly customer waiting cost in the service system, c, is uniformly distributed over the interval $(0, \bar{c})$. The uniform distribution is assumed for tractability, while our key insights continue to hold under various forms of distributions, including the normal, beta, power, and triangular distributions. The arrival rate of potential customers Λ, service rate μ, service reward R, service fee B, and waiting-cost distribution are common knowledge. Customers do not observe the queue length when they make decisions but are privately informed of their individual waiting cost rate. We assume an unobservable queue because (1) customers typically decide whether to hire a line-sitter when their service needs arise, which tends to occur before they observe the queue length (we shall introduce the line-sitting model in Sect. 3), and (2) the unobservable model is more amenable to analysis. Customers do not renege if they join the service system.

2.1 FIFO Benchmark

We first set up a FIFO benchmark model without line-sitters. Each customer decides whether to join the system or balk when they experience a need for the service, in order to maximize their expected utility. Balking gives zero utility. For a customer with hourly waiting cost c, the expected utility from joining the queue $U^{FIFO}(c)$ given system throughput λ_e (or the effective joining rate) is equal to the service reward less the service fee less the expected waiting cost:

$$U^{FIFO}(c) = R - B - \frac{c}{\mu - \lambda_e}, \tag{3.1}$$

where $1/(\mu - \lambda_e)$ is the expected waiting time (including the time at service) in the $M/M/1$ queue. Because the expected utility function $U^{FIFO}(c)$ is decreasing in c, strategic customers will adopt a threshold joining strategy for any given throughput λ_e, i.e., there exists a cost threshold c^{FIFO} such that a customer with hourly waiting cost c joins the system if $c \leq c^{FIFO}$ and balks otherwise. Intuitively, this means that customers who are less sensitive to waiting would join, whereas those who are more sensitive to waiting choose to balk. In equilibrium, system throughput λ_e^{FIFO} must satisfy the condition that $\lambda_e^{FIFO} = \Lambda c^{FIFO}/\bar{c}$.

Given c^{FIFO} (and thus the equilibrium system throughput λ_e^{FIFO}), the service provider's revenue (rate) in the FIFO benchmark is the service fee times the system throughput, i.e., $B\lambda_e^{FIFO}$; customer welfare is equal to $\Lambda \int_0^{c^{FIFO}} U^{FIFO}(c)/\bar{c}\,dc$, where $U^{FIFO}(c)$ is specified in (3.1). For now, we treat the service fee B as given to obtain clean results; in Sect. 6, we shall find the revenue-maximizing B for the service provider under various schemes and demonstrate the robustness of our findings. For notational convenience, we define $\overline{R} = R\mu/\bar{c}$ and $\overline{B} = B\mu/\bar{c}$, i.e., $\overline{R}$ and $\overline{B}$ are the normalized service reward R and normalized service fee B, respectively. Thus, the FIFO benchmark can be fully described by $(\overline{R}, \overline{B}, \rho, \bar{c})$. We assume $\overline{R} - \overline{B} \geq 1$ throughout this chapter, which is equivalent to $R - B \geq \bar{c}/\mu$. It is without loss of generality because if the assumption was violated, then customers whose hourly waiting cost c falls within the interval $[\mu(R-B), \bar{c})$ would never join the service system even if there is no waiting at all, which implies that we can always scale $\bar{c}$ down to $\mu(R-B)$ to exclude those irrelevant customers. As a result, we can derive customers' equilibrium decisions (characterized by c^{FIFO}), the corresponding service provider's revenue Π^{FIFO}, and customer welfare CW^{FIFO}.

3 Line-Sitting

Building on the FIFO model, we now set up the line-sitting model. There is a third-party line-sitting firm that provides customers with line-sitting services for an hourly charge r. If a customer (she) uses the line-sitting service, a line-sitter (he) joins the queue and waits on behalf of her; her total payment to the line-sitting firm is the product of the hourly rate r and the amount of time he spends in the queue. We assume there are a sufficient number of line-sitters available to work whose hourly opportunity cost is normalized to zero. Line-sitting tasks are generic and do not involve specific skills; consequently, the supply of line-sitters may not be a grave concern. In Sect. 7, we show indeed that our insights continue to hold even when only finitely many line-sitters are available. The simplifying assumption that line-sitters have negligible opportunity costs may be considered a reasonable representation of practice to the extent that line-sitters have been reported to be students, stay-at-home moms, or low-income individuals.

When a need for the service arises, each risk-neutral, expected-utility-maximizing customer decides whether to (i) join the service system by hiring a line-sitter, (ii) join themselves, or (iii) balk (which gives zero utility). It is clear that a joining customer with hourly waiting cost c should use the line-sitting service only if c exceeds the hourly line-sitting rate r. Moreover, because both the total line-sitting payment and waiting cost are linear in time, each hiring customer finds it optimal to let the line-sitter stand in line as long as possible. That is, a hiring customer would ask the line-sitter to take over the entire wait in the queue. In real life, line-sitters can notify customers through text messaging or a mobile app when they move close to the front of the line. For simplicity, we assume that the hiring customer heads to the service system when she learns that her line-sitter is close to the front of the queue, and she is able to show up to take the line-sitter's spot when the service is about to start. Hence, for a customer with hourly waiting cost c, her expected utility for choosing to join the system by hiring a line-sitter (given system throughput λ_e), $U^{LS}(c)$, is equal to the service reward less the service fee less the expected waiting cost at service less the expected total payment for line-sitting:

$$U^{LS}(c) = R - B - \frac{c}{\mu} - \frac{r\lambda_e}{\mu(\mu - \lambda_e)}, \qquad (3.2)$$

where $\lambda_e/[\mu(\mu - \lambda_e)]$ is the expected waiting time in the queue (excluding the time at service) of an $M/M/1$ system or equivalently the line-sitter's expected duration of standing in line. In contrast, if a customer decides to join the service system by herself, her expected utility (given system throughput λ_e) is the same as $U^{FIFO}(c)$ which is already specified in (3.1). Finally, it is useful to point out that in our model while customers decide whether to hire a line-sitter when their service need arises, the total payment is not due until line-sitting is complete because the payment is based on the realized waiting time in the queue. In Sect. 8, we shall consider the impact of pre-commitment payment when customers pay a prespecified amount of fee for service even if the line-sitter's actual waiting time is less than the pre-committed wait.

Under the line-sitting setting, similar to $U^{FIFO}(c)$, the expected utility function $U^{LS}(c)$ is also decreasing in c; thus, strategic customers will adopt a double-threshold strategy (if $r < c^{FIFO}$), i.e., there exists a cost threshold c^{LS} such that a customer with hourly waiting cost c joins the service system by herself if $c < r$, joins by hiring a line-sitter if $c \in [r, c^{LS})$, and balks if $c > c^{LS}$. Intuitively, it means that customers who are relatively insensitive to waiting join the system by themselves; those who are intermediately sensitive to waiting join but hire line-sitters; and those who are highly sensitive to waiting balk. In equilibrium, system throughput λ_e^{LS} must satisfy the condition that $\lambda_e^{LS} = \Lambda c^{LS}/\bar{c}$. If $r \geq c^{FIFO}$, no customers will hire a line-sitter in equilibrium, and the system degenerates to the FIFO benchmark. In this case, only customers with $c > r \geq c^{FIFO}$ might potentially use line-sitting, but these customers either do not exist (if $c^{FIFO} = \bar{c}$) or would not join (if $c^{FIFO} < \bar{c}$) because their expected utility from joining would be negative even by hiring a line-sitter (since $U^{LS}(c) < U^{FIFO}(c^{FIFO}) = 0, \forall c > c^{FIFO}$).

The line-sitting firm sets the hourly rate r to maximize total revenue:

$$\max_{r \in (0,\bar{c})} r \cdot \frac{\Lambda(c^{LS} - r)}{\bar{c}} \cdot \frac{\lambda_e^{LS}}{\mu(\mu - \lambda_e^{LS})} \tag{3.3}$$

where $\lambda_e^{LS} = \Lambda c^{LS}/\bar{c}$. The total line-sitting revenue (per hour) in (3.3) is the product of three terms: (i) the hourly rate r; (ii) the expected number of arriving customers who choose to hire line-sitters per hour, $\Lambda(c^{LS} - r)/\bar{c}$; and (iii) the expected waiting time each line-sitter spends in the queue $\lambda_e^{LS}/[\mu(\mu - \lambda_e^{LS})]$. In Proposition 1, we solve for the line-sitting firm's optimal hourly rate r^*, and give the corresponding cost threshold c^{LS} and system throughput λ_e^{LS} in equilibrium.

Proposition 1 *The optimal hourly rate for the line-sitting firm, r^*, and the corresponding cost threshold c^{LS}, system throughput λ_e^{LS}, and fraction of joining customers who end up using the line-sitting service $(c^{LS} - r^*)/c^{LS}$ are given in Table* 3.1.

The cases presented in Proposition 1 are mutually exclusive and collectively exhaustive of the parameter space. In Cases (1) and (2), the potential workload of the system ρ is relatively small, and all customers join the service system in equilibrium. In the FIFO benchmark, the all-joining scenario occurs only when $\rho \leq (\overline{R} - \overline{B} - 1)/(\overline{R} - \overline{B})$. In the presence of the line-sitting firm, all customers would still join when this condition holds; even when it is violated, the all-joining scenario may still arise (note that, e.g., Case 1 subsumes $\rho \leq (\overline{R} - \overline{B} - 1)/(\overline{R} - \overline{B})$). This shows the value line-sitting brings to high-waiting-cost customers—a customer not patient enough to wait in a FIFO queue may now choose to join the system by hiring a line-sitter because doing so eliminates her waiting time in the queue at a price lower than her personal waiting cost.

Although Cases (1) and (2) have the same all-joining customer behavior, they differ in the line-sitting firm's pricing pattern. In Case (1), the optimal hourly rate r^* is flat in the potential workload ρ, whereas in Case (2), it is decreasing in ρ. The line-sitting firm trades off the hourly rate with the number of customers who use the line-sitting service and each customer's expected in-line waiting time in equilibrium. When the potential workload is small (Case (1)), the firm only needs to balance the

Table 3.1 Results of Proposition 1

Case	ρ	r^*	c^{LS}	λ_e^{LS}	$\frac{c^{LS}-r^*}{c^{LS}}$
(1)	$\rho \leq \frac{2(\overline{R}-\overline{B}-1)}{2(\overline{R}-\overline{B})-1}$	$\overline{c}/2$	$\overline{c}$	Λ	$1/2$
(2)-a	$\rho \in \left(\frac{2(\overline{R}-\overline{B}-1)}{2(\overline{R}-\overline{B})-1}, \frac{(\overline{R}-\overline{B})^2-1}{\overline{R}-\overline{B}}\right)$	$\frac{\overline{c}(\overline{R}-\overline{B}-1)(1-\rho)}{\rho}$	$\overline{c}$	Λ	$\frac{1+(\rho-1)(\overline{R}-\overline{B})}{\rho}$
(2)-b	$\rho \in \left(\frac{2(\overline{R}-\overline{B}-1)}{2(\overline{R}-\overline{B})-1}, 1\right)$				
(3)-a	$\rho \in \left[\frac{(\overline{R}-\overline{B})^2-1}{\overline{R}-\overline{B}}, \frac{\sqrt{5}+1}{2(\overline{R}-\overline{B})}\right]$	$\overline{c}\left(\frac{[2(\overline{R}-\overline{B})\rho+1]\sqrt{(\overline{R}-\overline{B})\rho+1}-[(\overline{R}-\overline{B})\rho+1]^2}{\rho[(\overline{R}-\overline{B})\rho+1]}\right)$	$\frac{\overline{c}(\overline{R}-\overline{B})}{\sqrt{(\overline{R}-\overline{B})\rho+1}}$	$\frac{\Lambda(\overline{R}-\overline{B})}{\sqrt{(\overline{R}-\overline{B})\rho+1}}$	$\frac{(\sqrt{(\overline{R}-\overline{B})\rho+1}-1)((\overline{R}-\overline{B})\rho+1)}{(\overline{R}-\overline{B})\rho}$
(4)-a	$\rho > \frac{\sqrt{5}+1}{2(\overline{R}-\overline{B})}$	0^+	$\overline{c}/\rho$	μ^-	1
(4)-b	$\rho \geq 1$				

Note. a: $\overline{R} - \overline{B} \in \left[1, \frac{1+\sqrt{5}}{2}\right]$; b: $\overline{R} - \overline{B} > \frac{1+\sqrt{5}}{2}$.

hourly rate and the number of line-sitting users without worrying about the expected waiting time since all customers join regardless of the line-sitting rate. However, when the potential workload gets relatively large (Case (2)), the third effect kicks in, i.e., an increase in the hourly rate would decrease not only the number of customers who use the line-sitting service but also the expected in-line waiting time (due to customer balking). Therefore, a larger potential workload would compel a lower hourly rate in order to prevent customers from balking.

When the potential workload ρ becomes even larger, heavy congestion makes customer balking inevitable, as shown in Cases (3) and (4) of Proposition 1. Similar to Case (2), we can show that the optimal hourly rate is decreasing in ρ also in Case (3). Notably, in Case (4) when the potential workload is sufficiently large, customer demand for line-sitting becomes so price-elastic that the line-sitting firm finds it optimal to keep lowering the hourly rate for more line-sitting users and longer in-line waiting times. As a result, the optimal hourly rate is set as low as possible (zero in this case but in general a value equal to the opportunity cost of the line-sitters if we had not normalized it to zero). The resulting expected line-sitting time tends to be very large (infinity in the zero-opportunity-cost case), making the total expected payment of each transaction a positive and finite amount, equal to $R - B - \bar{c}/\Lambda$.

Given the hourly rate r of the line-sitting firm, and the cost threshold c^{LS} (and thus throughput λ_e^{LS}), the service provider's revenue (rate) in the presence of the line-sitting firm is equal to $B\lambda_e^{LS}$; and customer welfare is given by

$$\Lambda \left[\int_0^r U^{FIFO}(c)/\bar{c}\, dc + \int_r^{c^{LS}} U^{LS}(c)/\bar{c}\, dc \right],$$

where $U^{FIFO}(c)$ and $U^{LS}(c)$ are specified in (3.1) and (3.2), respectively. We can then derive closed-form expressions for the service provider's revenue Π^{LS} and customer welfare CW^{LS} when the line-sitting firm charges the optimal hourly rate.

3.1 Comparison Between Line-Sitting and FIFO

We now investigate the impact of line-sitting on the service provider's revenue and customer welfare (at the optimal hourly line-sitting rate r^* set by the line-sitting firm).

Theorem 1 *The service provider receives a higher revenue in the presence of the line-sitting firm than in the FIFO benchmark, i.e., $\Pi^{LS} \geq \Pi^{FIFO}$.*

Theorem 1 is intuitive—the service provider increases revenue by accommodating line-sitting because some high-waiting-cost customers who would balk in the FIFO benchmark are now willing to join the system by hiring line-sitters (to stand in line on behalf of them). The line-sitting firm strictly increases the service provider's throughput when the potential workload of the system is large enough that not all potential customers join in the FIFO benchmark, i.e., when $\rho > (\overline{R} - \overline{B} - 1)/(\overline{R} - \overline{B})$. Because service fee B is fixed, a higher throughput translates into a higher revenue for the service provider. We refer to line-sitting's ability to increase system throughput as the *demand expansion* effect, which is at the heart of line-sitting.

If the service provider can adjust the service fee to the line-sitting firm's entry, its revenue will still be higher with line-sitting than without because adjusting the service fee will only further improve revenue, i.e., $\Pi^{LS}(B^{LS}) \geq \Pi^{LS}(B^{FIFO}) \geq \Pi^{FIFO}(B^{FIFO})$ if we use $\Pi^X(B^Y)$ to denote the service provider's revenue under setting X when it charges the optimal service fee for setting Y in B^Y. Thus, it would still be wise for a revenue-oriented service provider to accommodate line-sitting. In practice, however, it is not unusual for a service provider to prohibit line-sitting, possibly due to non-revenue-related factors which will be discussed in more detail in Sect. 9. Now that we have investigated the impact of line-sitting on the service provider's revenue, what is the effect on customer welfare? We provide the answer in the following Theorem 2.

Theorem 2 *Customer welfare in the presence of line-sitting, CW^{LS}, and customer welfare in the FIFO benchmark, CW^{FIFO}, compare as follows:*

(1) *if $\rho < 1 - \sqrt{3}/3$, $CW^{LS} > CW^{FIFO}$;*
(2) *if $\rho \in [1 - \sqrt{3}/3, 1)$, there exist two thresholds $\overline{R}_a$, $\overline{R}_b$ such that $CW^{LS} > CW^{FIFO}$ if and only if $\overline{R} < \overline{R}_a$ or $\overline{R} > \overline{R}_b$, where $\overline{R}_a = \overline{B} + \frac{2\rho - 1 + \sqrt{4\rho^2 + 1}}{2\rho}$ and $\overline{R}_b = \overline{B} + \frac{\rho^2 - 12\rho + 8 - \sqrt{\rho^4 + 8\rho(\rho^2 - 2\rho + 2)}}{8(\rho - 1)(2\rho - 1)}$;*
(3) *if $\rho \in [1, (\sqrt{5} + 1)/2]$, there exists a unique threshold $\overline{R}_c = \overline{B} + \frac{\sqrt{5}+1}{2\rho}$ such that $CW^{LS} > CW^{FIFO}$ if and only if $\overline{R} < \overline{R}_c$.*
(4) *if $\rho > (\sqrt{5} + 1)/2$, $CW^{LS} < CW^{FIFO}$.*

Theorem 2 presents precise conditions under which line-sitting has a positive (or negative) impact on customer welfare. The results are illustrated in Fig. 3.1. On the high level, line-sitting exerts three forces on customer welfare. First, line-sitting users can retain more surplus because they pay at an hourly rate lower than their own waiting cost rate; this puts an upward pressure on customer welfare. Second, the demand expansion effect distilled from Theorem 1 implies that line-sitting brings value to new customers who would not otherwise join the system, which also puts an upward pressure on customer welfare. Third, these additional customers nonetheless generate negative congestion externalities, which put downward pressure on customer welfare. Note that for customers who join by themselves, an increase in congestion can hurt them directly by exacerbating their waiting costs, whereas for line-sitting users, an increase in congestion can hurt them indirectly because line-sitters can pass it on to their users through a larger line-sitting bill.

When the potential workload ρ is small ($\rho < 1 - \sqrt{3}/3$), most customers, if not all, would join the service system under both FIFO and line-sitting due to light

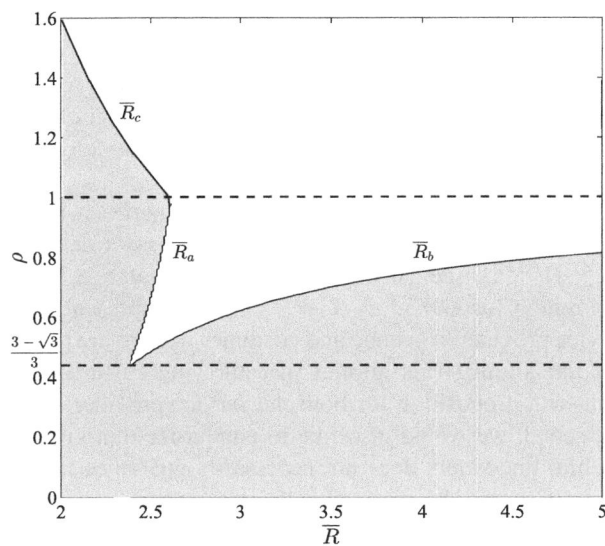

Note. The shaded area corresponds to the region for $CW^{LS} > CW^{FIFO}$ in the (R,ρ) space. $B=1$.

Fig. 3.1 Customer welfare comparison between line-sitting and FIFO

system congestion. The line-sitting option would reduce the cost of high-waiting-cost customers (those with $c \geq r^*$) without raising the congestion level dramatically. Hence, overall customer welfare improves.

Now consider intermediate values of the potential workload ($\rho \in [1-\sqrt{3}/3, 1)$). When the service reward is sufficiently small, i.e., $\overline{R} < \overline{R}_a$, customers do not have strong joining incentives; hence, there is light congestion under FIFO. The line-sitting option would prompt more customers to join the system, and since the system load is not too high, the extra service utility customers receive outweighs the extra negative congestion externalities, thereby improving customer welfare. When the service reward is sufficiently large, i.e., $\overline{R} > \overline{R}_b$, almost all potential customers join under both FIFO and line-sitting. Thus, line-sitting again only increases congestion slightly. However, when the service reward is intermediate, i.e., $R \in [\overline{R}_a, \overline{R}_b]$, the throughput increase creates more negative congestion externalities than positive service utilities, thus lowering customer welfare. Observe from Fig. 3.1 that welfare deterioration becomes more predominant (i.e., the interval $[\overline{R}_a, \overline{R}_b]$ expands) as ρ increases. This is because a higher workload amplifies the effect of congestion externalities.

Finally, consider a large potential workload ($\rho \geq 1$). When the service reward is small, i.e., $\overline{R} < \overline{R}_c$, customer welfare improves for similar reasons as discussed in the earlier $\overline{R} < \overline{R}_a$ case. In contrast, when the service reward is large, i.e., $\overline{R} > \overline{R}_c$, the line-sitting option would incentivize joining by a sizable amount, which considerably prolongs the system wait (in this case, recall from Proposition 1 that the line-sitting firm would set a low optimal hourly rate but charge each user for a long line-sitting time). As such, the line-sitting option creates too much congestion to compensate for the gains in service utilities, and hence customer welfare suffers. Observe from Fig. 3.1 that welfare deterioration becomes more predominant (i.e., the interval $(\overline{R}_c, \infty)$ expands) as ρ increases, similar to our earlier observation with an intermediate ρ. In particular, when $\rho > (\sqrt{5} + 1)/2$, line-sitting would harm customer welfare for any service reward.

We conclude with two remarks from the comparison between line-sitting and FIFO. First, because the service provider's revenue is always weakly higher with line-sitting ($\Pi^{LS} \geq \Pi^{FIFO}$; see Theorem 1), the shaded area in Fig. 3.1, which corresponds to the region for $CW^{LS} > CW^{FIFO}$, also represents the region in which both the service provider's revenue and customer welfare are (weakly) higher in the presence of line-sitting. This implies that allowing customers to use line-sitting can be a win-win proposition for both the service provider and customers, relative to FIFO. Second, we would also like to emphasize that giving customers an extra option to hire line-sitters does not necessarily guarantee improvement in customer welfare, because the decisions of self-interested customers can generate an overwhelming amount of negative congestion externalities in the system.

4 Accommodating Line-Sitting or Selling Priority?

Thus far, we have introduced the model of line-sitting based on a classical FIFO model, and showed that line-sitting improves the service provider's revenue because the high-waiting-cost customers, who would balk in the FIFO case, are now willing to join the system by paying a line-sitter to stand the line. The idea of paying a premium to skip the wait bears a resemblance to the well-established practice of priority queues (e.g., visitors to the London Eye in the UK can pay an extra £9, in addition to the base admission fee for an online Fast Track ticket. While a priority queue is typically managed by the same service provider, line-sitting is run by a third-party firm. The priority premiums go directly to the service provider, whereas the line-sitting payments do not. As such, wouldn't a service provider always favor implementing a priority purchasing scheme over accommodating a third-party line-sitting firm? And what about customer welfare? In this section, we seek to answer these questions by first setting up the model for priority purchasing.

4.1 Priority Purchasing

The model of priority purchasing is based on the FIFO benchmark introduced in Sect. 2. The service provider sets and collects a premium P for priority service. Each customer selects one of the three available options when their need for the service arises: (i) join the system as a regular customer, or (ii) join it as a priority customer, or (iii) balk (which gives zero utility). A priority customer obtains non-preemptive priority for service over regular customers (i.e., a regular customer who has started service will not be bumped by a priority customer), and the service disciplines within the regular line and within the priority line are both FIFO.

Given the expected waiting time in the regular line (denoted by w_1) and in the priority line (w_2) both including the time at service, for a potential customer with hourly waiting cost c, the expected utility from joining as a regular customer, $U^{REG}(c)$, and that as a priority customer, $U^{PRI}(c)$, are given by

$$U^{REG}(c) = R - B - cw_1 \quad \text{and} \quad U^{PRI}(c) = R - (B+P) - cw_2, \quad (3.4)$$

respectively, where a regular customer pays the (base) service fee B and expects a waiting time of w_1, whereas a priority customer pays a total of $B + P$ and expects a waiting time of w_2. It is rational for a joining customer with hourly waiting cost c to purchase priority if and only if her expected waiting-cost savings exceed the priority premium, i.e., $c(w_1 - w_2) \geq P$.

Because the expected utility functions $U^{REG}(c)$ and $U^{PRI}(c)$ are both linearly decreasing in c and $U^{REG}(c)$ is decreasing at a larger rate than $U^{PRI}(c)$, strategic customers will follow a double-threshold strategy, i.e., there exist two cost thresholds (c_a^{PRI}, c_b^{PRI}) such that customers with waiting cost $c \leq c_a^{PRI}$ choose to join the system as regular customers; those with waiting cost $c \in (c_a^{PRI}, c_b^{PRI}]$ join as priority customers, and those with waiting cost $c > c_b^{PRI}$ balk. rst in, rst out rm's revenue in Gavirneni and Kulkarni's (2016) case, Let $q = (c_b^{PRI} - c_a^{PRI})/c_b^{PRI}$ denote the fraction of joining customers who purchase priority. Given system throughput λ_e and priority purchase fraction q, it is well-known that w_1 and w_2 can be derived as follows (see, e.g., Chapter 33 of Harchol-Balter 2013):

$$w_1(\lambda_e, q) = \frac{\lambda_e}{(\mu - \lambda_e)(\mu - \lambda_e q)} + \frac{1}{\mu}, \quad w_2(\lambda_e, q) = \frac{\lambda_e}{\mu(\mu - \lambda_e q)} + \frac{1}{\mu}.$$

In equilibrium, the effective joining rate (system throughput) must satisfy the condition $\lambda_e^{PRI} = \Lambda c_b^{PRI}/\bar{c}$, and $w_1(\lambda_e^{PRI}, q)$ and $w_2(\lambda_e^{PRI}, q)$ must be consistent with (c_a^{PRI}, c_b^{PRI}) in that $q = (c_b^{PRI} - c_a^{PRI})/c_b^{PRI}$, $c_a^{PRI} = P/(w_1 - w_2)$ and $c_b^{PRI} = (R - B - P)/w_2$ (if c_a^{PRI} and c_b^{PRI} are less than $\bar{c}$). For given priority premium P, we can characterize the customer equilibrium (c_a^{PRI}, c_b^{PRI}) in closed form. The service provider sets priority premium P to maximize total revenue:

$$\max_{P \geq 0} \lambda_e^{PRI}(B + qP). \quad (3.5)$$

The service provider's revenue (rate) in (3.5) consists of the base service fee collected per hour, $\lambda_e^{PRI} B$ and the priority premium collected per hour $\lambda_e^{PRI} q P$. As before, we continue to treat the base service fee B as given, and leave the joint optimization of the base service fee and the priority premium to Sect. 6. Customer welfare in this setting can be written as

$$\Lambda \left[\int_0^{c_a^{PRI}} U^{REG}(c)/\bar{c}\,dc + \int_{c_a^{PRI}}^{c_b^{PRI}} U^{PRI}(c)/\bar{c}\,dc \right],$$

where $U^{REG}(c)$ and $U^{PRI}(c)$ are specified in (3.4). We can derive closed-form expressions for the service provider's optimal priority premium P^*, the corresponding revenue of the service provider Π^{PRI}, and customer welfare CW^{PRI} under P^*.

4.2 Comparison Between Priority and FIFO

We benchmark the priority model against FIFO in the following Theorem 3, similar to what was done for the line-sitting case in Sect. 3.1. Doing so will facilitate the formal comparison between priority purchasing and line-sitting in Sect. 4.3.

Theorem 3 *The service provider obtains a higher revenue in the priority purchasing scheme than in the FIFO benchmark, i.e., $\Pi^{PRI} > \Pi^{FIFO}$, but it results in lower customer welfare, i.e., $CW^{PRI} < CW^{FIFO}$.*

The service provider can boost its revenue by selling priority to customers because doing so is essentially a practice of price discrimination that takes advantage of customers' heterogeneous waiting costs. If the priority premium is zero, all joining customers will choose to upgrade, and no one would receive any actual priority. On the other hand, if the priority premium is prohibitively high, none of the customers will upgrade and the priority model again degenerates into the FIFO case. The optimal priority premium is such that only a fraction of joining customers opt into priority, making the service provider strictly better off. Customer welfare, however, is compromised, in part, because the priority purchasing scheme allows the service provider to appropriate more surplus value from customers.

4.3 Comparison Between Line-Sitting and Priority

This subsection compares line-sitting and priority purchasing in terms of the service provider's revenue and customer welfare. Recall from Theorems 1 and 3 that either accommodating line-sitting or implementing priority would benefit a FIFO service provider. One might expect the service provider to benefit more from introducing a priority purchasing scheme than permitting line-sitting, because the priority premium contributes directly to the service provider's revenue, whereas the line-sitting business is run by a third-party company. Somewhat surprisingly, Theorem 4 reveals that this is not always the case.

4 Accommodating Line-Sitting or Selling Priority?

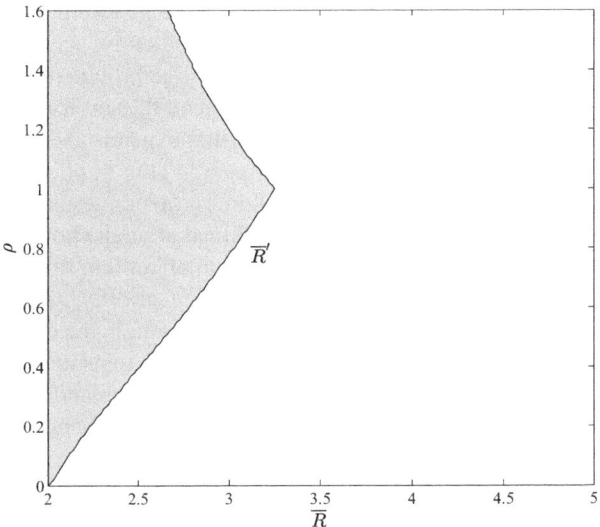

Note. The shaded area corresponds to the region $\Pi^{LS} > \Pi^{PRI}$ in the $(\overline{R}, \rho)$ space. $\overline{B} = 1 > (\sqrt{1+\rho}-1)/(1+\rho), \forall \rho$.

Fig. 3.2 The service provider's revenue comparison between line-sitting and priority

Theorem 4 *If $\overline{B} \leq (\sqrt{1+\rho} - 1)/(1+\rho)$, the service provider's revenue in the priority purchasing scheme, Π^{PRI}, is higher than that in the line-sitting scheme, Π^{LS}, i.e., $\Pi^{PRI} > \Pi^{LS}$. Otherwise, there exists an $\overline{R}'$ such that $\Pi^{LS} > \Pi^{PRI}$ if and only if $\overline{R} < \overline{R}'$, where $\overline{R}'$ is unimodal in ρ.*

The results of Theorem 4 are illustrated in Fig. 3.2. The two practices help improve the service provider's revenue (relative to FIFO) by different means: the priority system improves revenue by charging high-waiting-cost customers a priority premium, i.e., price discrimination, whereas line-sitting does so by increasing system throughput, i.e., demand expansion (see Theorem 1). When the service fee B is too low, i.e., when $\overline{B} \leq (\sqrt{1+\rho} - 1)/(1+\rho)$, the additional throughput brought by the line-sitting firm, compared to FIFO, only translates into limited extra revenue for the service provider, and therefore, implementing the priority purchasing scheme is always superior.

However, when the base service fee is not too low, i.e., $\overline{B} > (\sqrt{1+\rho} - 1)/(1+\rho)$, the priority system is better than line-sitting for the service provider only when the service reward R is sufficiently large, i.e., when the condition $\overline{R} > \overline{R}'$ is satisfied. A large service reward would justify joining for those high-waiting-cost customers that have a stronger willingness to pay for priority than their low-waiting-cost counterparts. On the other hand, when the service reward is not large enough, only customers with relatively low waiting costs find it worthwhile to join the service system (in the priority model), which circumscribes the service provider's ability to profit from implementing priority; in the meantime, the demand expansion effect from line-sitting becomes particularly effective in luring high-waiting-cost customers who would not otherwise join, and consequently, accommodating line-sitting becomes more revenue-improving for the service provider.

Interestingly, Theorem 4 further reveals the range of the service reward for which line-sitting generates more revenue than priority first expands and then shrinks with the potential workload ρ, as illustrated by Fig. 3.2. This implies that for a fixed service reward, accommodating line-sitting is more favorable than selling priority when ρ is intermediate. When the potential workload is small enough, all customers join under either scheme, so the demand expansion effect that line-sitting relies on for increasing revenue is mute, which makes selling priority more desirable. On the other hand, when the potential workload is large enough, the demand expansion effect realizes its full potential by bringing the throughput to its upper limit—system capacity μ; an even higher load will not further expand demand in the line-sitting scheme but can still boost the revenue from selling priority; hence, selling priority also becomes superior. Consequently, for the service provider, accommodating line-sitting works best when ρ is intermediate.

We should mention one key driver of line-sitting's potential revenue dominance is that it introduces an extra source of cost reduction by shifting a portion of customers from waiting in the physical queue to an "offline" channel. The priority purchasing scheme does not enjoy this cost advantage since all customers, regardless of their priority status, must wait in the physical queue themselves. Such a cost advantage renders the possibility of line-sitting outperforming priority in its revenue contribution to the service provider. Next, we examine in Theorem 5 how customer welfare in the priority purchasing scheme compares with that of the line-sitting scheme.

Theorem 5 *Customer welfare in the line-sitting scheme, CW^{LS}, and customer welfare in the priority purchasing scheme, CW^{PRI}, compare as follows: there exists $\rho' > 1 - \sqrt{3}/3$ such that*

(1) *if $\rho < \rho'$, $CW^{LS} > CW^{PRI}$;*
(2) *if $\rho \in [\rho', 1)$, there exist two thresholds $\overline{R}'_a \leq \overline{R}'_b$ such that $CW^{LS} \geq CW^{PRI}$ if and only if $\overline{R} \leq \overline{R}'_a$ or $\overline{R} \geq \overline{R}'_b$;*
(3) *if $\rho \geq 1$, there exists $\overline{R}'_c$ such that $CW^{LS} > CW^{PRI}$ if and only if $\overline{R} < \overline{R}'_c$.*

The results of Theorem 5 are illustrated in Fig. 3.3: the shaded area below the solid curve represents circumstances under which customer welfare is higher in line-sitting than in priority, i.e., $CW^{LS} > CW^{PRI}$, whereas the area under the dotted curve corresponds to circumstances under which line-sitting achieves higher customer welfare in priority than in FIFO, i.e., $CW^{LS} > CW^{FIFO}$ (a reproduction of Fig. 3.1 from Sect. 3.1). Figure 3.3 suggests that the region corresponding to $CW^{LS} > CW^{PRI}$ actually contains that corresponding to $CW^{LS} > CW^{FIFO}$ and this is consistent with the finding that $CW^{PRI} < CW^{FIFO}$ (Theorem 3).

Given our detailed explanation of customer-welfare comparison between line-sitting and FIFO in Theorem 2, and given that customer-welfare comparison between line-sitting and priority yields qualitatively similar results, we do not

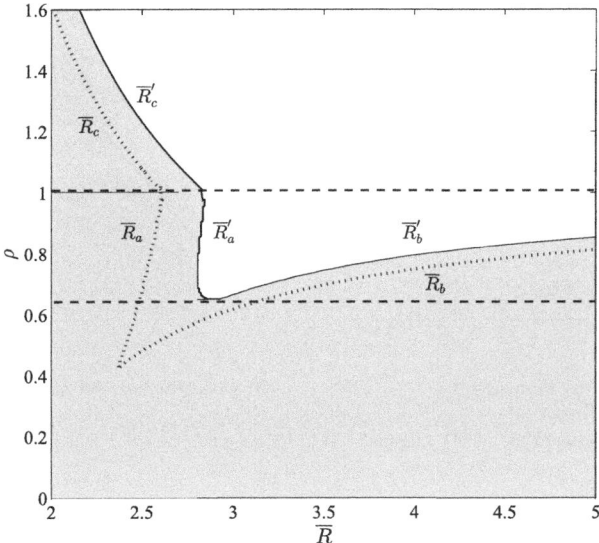

Note. The shaded area corresponds to the region $CW^{LS} > CW^{PRI}$ in the $(\overline{R}, \rho)$ space. $\overline{B} = 1$.

Fig. 3.3 Customer welfare comparison between line-sitting and priority

discuss Theorem 5 at length besides highlighting the white region in Fig. 3.3, which shows $CW^{LS} < CW^{PRI}$. In this region, the potential workload ρ is high and service reward R is large. In this case, the line-sitting firm charges a low hourly rate (see Proposition 1) to induce excessive line-sitting time (and effectively, large customer payment), making line-sitting even worse than priority from a customer-welfare standpoint.

5 Three-Way Comparison

We focus on studying the new business practice of line-sitting in this chapter. Thus far, we have set up a line-sitting model based on FIFO in Sect. 2, and also compared it with a priority purchasing scheme in Sect. 4 as a more traditional approach for customers to pay and skip wait. Building on the pairwise comparisons of the three schemes (FIFO, line-sitting, priority) in Sects. 3.1, 4.2, and 4.3, we now proceed to conduct a three-way comparison to identify the service scheme that delivers the maximum revenue for the service provider and/or maximum customer welfare, i.e., finding $\arg\max_s \Pi^s$ and $\arg\max_s CW^s$ for $s \in \{FIFO, LS, PRI\}$. Figure 3.4a illustrates the outcome. Note that it is created simply by combining Fig. 3.1 from Sect. 3.1 and Fig. 3.2 from Sect. 4.3.

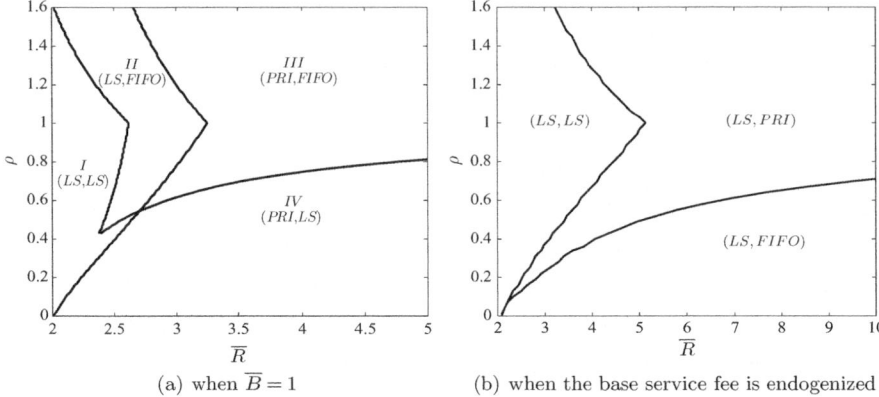

Fig. 3.4 Optimal schemes in terms of the service provider's revenue and customer welfare

From Fig. 3.4a, it is evident that the FIFO system is never revenue-maximizing for the service provider (Theorems 1 and 3), whereas the priority purchasing scheme is not welfare-maximizing for customers (Theorem 3). However, line-sitting can be optimal at the same time for both the service provider and the customers (see Region *I* in Fig. 3.4a), and it is the only scheme out of the three that can be simultaneously optimal for both. In addition, line-sitting is by construction the only model that also benefits the line-sitting company. As a result, it can create a win-win-win situation for the service provider, customers, and the line-sitting company. Therefore, albeit a contentious issue, line-sitting should be viewed as a value-generating business under appropriate circumstances.

6 Endogenizing Service Fee B

The base service fee B and the corresponding $\overline{B}$ are given in our base models and do not vary across the three schemes under comparison. In the short run, the service provider may not be able to adjust its price to various schemes, e.g., due to menu costs. Our preceding results are best applicable to those settings in which the base service fee is not scheme-specific. In the long run, the service provider may be able to change the service fee in response to the scheme being used. This section investigates such endogenous service fees.

Let B^{FIFO}, B^{LS}, and B^{PRI} denote the optimal service fees the service provider charges under FIFO, line-sitting, and priority, respectively, i.e., $B^s = \arg\max_{B} \Pi^s$ for $s \in \{FIFO, LS, PRI\}$. We can explicitly characterize these optimal service fees, based on which, we conduct numerical experiments to find the schemes that achieve the highest server revenue and greatest customer welfare, respectively. The results are illustrated in Fig. 3.4b. We observe that consistent with Fig. 3.4a which fixes the service fee, the line-sitting scheme still dominates the left corner of the $(\overline{R}, \rho)$ space and remains the only scheme that can be simultaneously optimal for both the service provider and customers. We also observe that when the base service fee is endogenized, accommodating line-sitting dominates selling priority for the service provider.

7 Finitely Many Line-Sitters

In the base model, we have assumed a sufficient supply of line-sitters such that there is always a line-sitter available to work upon customer request. In this subsection, we consider a line-sitting firm that organizes N line-sitters. The main complication is that when a customer wishes to hire a line-sitter, none would be available if all of the N line-sitters are currently standing in line on behalf of other customers. If this occurs, then a joining customer must wait herself regardless of her line-sitting preference. Hence, the line-sitters' availability creates an additional level of heterogeneity among customers. Let the probability that all line-sitters are busy be π_b; the joining threshold when all line-sitters are busy, c^{FIFO} (similar to the FIFO benchmark); and the joining threshold when at least one line-sitter is available, c^{LS} (similar to the base model of line-sitting). Thus, the system throughput λ_e is given by

$$\lambda_e = \Lambda \left[(1 - \pi_b) c^{LS}/\bar{c} + \pi_b c^{FIFO}/\bar{c} \right]. \quad (3.6)$$

To obtain π_b, recognize that given system throughput λ_e, joining threshold c^{LS}, and hourly rate r, the probability that none of the N line-sitters is available is equal to the blocking probability of an *Erlang loss system* with N servers, Poisson arrival rate $\lambda' = \Lambda(c^{LS} - r)/\bar{c}$, and mean service time $\tau = \lambda_e [\mu(\mu - \lambda_e)]^{-1}$. Hence,

$$\pi_b = \frac{(\lambda' \tau)^N / N!}{\sum_{i=0}^{N} (\lambda' \tau)^i / i!}. \quad (3.7)$$

For any hourly rate r, on the one hand, given conjectured joining thresholds c^{FIFO} and c^{LS}, the throughput and blocking probability, (λ_e, π_b), are jointly determined by (3.6) and (3.7); on the other hand, given conjectured throughput λ_e, joining thresholds c^{FIFO} and c^{LS} can be found by the usual best-response argument as in our FIFO benchmark and the base model of line-sitting. In equilibrium, $(\lambda_e, \pi_b, c^{FIFO}, c^{LS})$ must be self-consistent.

Given N, the line-sitting firm sets the hourly rate r to maximize total revenue:

$$\max_{r\in(0,\bar{c})} r \cdot \frac{\Lambda(c^{LS}-r)}{\bar{c}} \cdot (1-\pi_b) \cdot \frac{\lambda_e}{\mu(\mu-\lambda_e)}.$$

We run numerical experiments and find that our qualitative insights are preserved even when only a single line-sitter is available ($N = 1$) and that with five available line-sitters, the directional impact of line-sitting on the service provider's revenue and customer welfare is already reasonably similar (in terms of the parameter space partitioning) to the infinite supply case in the base model.

8 Pre-commitment Payment

In our base model, the line-sitting fee is paid at the completion of service, which can be referred to as the *post-payment* scheme. Nevertheless, could the line-sitting firm benefit from the *pre-commitment* payment scheme, in which the customer still pays a prespecified fee for service even if the line-sitter's actual waiting time is less than the pre-committed wait? In this section, we compare the two payment schemes in Wang and Wang (2019). For tractability, we assume that balking or reneging is not allowed, and the effective arrival rate satisfies $\lambda < \mu$ to ensure system stability.

Under the pre-commitment payment scheme, a customer decides how long she wants a line-sitter to wait in line on behalf of her, denoted by t, a quantity that she commits before the waiting time in line is realized. Define w as the actual waiting time in line. If $w \leq t$, the customer still needs to pay the line-sitting the pre-specified amount payment among $r \cdot t$. The hiring customer shows up to take the line-sitter spot when the service is about to start. Otherwise, if $w > t$, the customer swaps with the line-sitter after time t and waits in line herself for the rest of the wait in line (i.e., $w - t$). As such, customers can be regarded as newsvendors who determine the optimal time t to maximize their utilities. Anticipating that, the line-sitting firm needs to adjust the optimal service rate r to maximize its revenue.

In an $M/M/1$ queue with arrival rate λ and service rate μ, the probability that the server is busy upon the arrival of a customer is $\rho = \lambda/\mu$. Conditioned on the server being busy, the waiting time in the queue (W_b) is exponentially distributed with rate $\mu - \lambda$. Thus, a joining customer with delay sensitivity c chooses t to maximize her expected utility:

$$U^{PC}(c) = \max_t \left[-rt - \frac{c}{\mu} - c\rho E[\max\{W_b - t, 0\}] - c(1-\rho) \cdot 0 \right],$$

$$= \max_t \left[-rt - \frac{c}{\mu} - c\rho \int_0^\infty \max\{T-t, 0\}(\mu-\lambda)e^{-(\mu-\lambda)T} dT \right],$$

where rt is the customer's up-front line-sitting payment; c/μ is the expected waiting cost in service; and $c\rho E[\max\{W_b - t, 0\}]$ is the expected waiting cost for the customer spent in the queue. Waiting time reduction is positive if and only if the server is busy upon arrival (otherwise there is no wait), which occurs with probability ρ. Conditioned on a positive waiting time reduction, the amount of waiting time for the customer is $\max\{W_b - t, 0\}$, where W_b is exponentially distributed with rate $\mu - \lambda$. The customer's optimal line-sitting time, $t^*(c)$, follows the newsvendor solution:

$$e^{-(\mu-\lambda)t^*(c)} = \frac{r}{c\rho},$$

which leads to $t^*(c) = \frac{\ln(c\rho/r)}{\mu-\lambda}$ for $c > r/\rho$. The expression of $t^*(c)$ shows that the customers would purchase a positive amount of line-sitting time if and only if their delay sensitivity satisfies $c > r/\rho$. Additionally, customers with a higher c would purchase a longer time because $t^*(c)$ is increasing in c. This is different from the post-payment case where the expected line-sitting time customers pay for would be $\frac{\lambda}{\mu(\mu-\lambda)}$ if $c > r$, and customers with delay sensitivity $c \leq r$ would not purchase the line-sitting service. That is, the threshold of purchasing the line-sitting service under the post-payment scheme (i.e., r) is lower than that under the pre-commitment payment scheme (i.e., r/ρ).

When the optimal quantity $t^*(c)$ is adopted, the expected utility of a customer with delay sensitivity c under the pre-commitment payment scheme is given by

$$U^{PC}(c) = \begin{cases} -\frac{c}{\mu-\lambda}, & \text{if } 0 \leq c \leq r/\rho; \\ -r\frac{\ln(c\rho/r)}{\mu-\lambda} - \frac{r}{\mu-\lambda} - \frac{c}{\mu}, & \text{if } r/\rho < c \leq \bar{c}, \end{cases}$$

and we compare it with the expected utility of the same customer under the post-payment scheme, denoted by $U^{LS}(c)$, in the following proposition.

Proposition 2 *For any given line-sitting rate r, we have $U^{PC}(c) \leq U^{LS}(c)$.*

Proposition 2 reveals that when the same line-sitting rate r is adopted, customers under the pre-commitment payment scheme receive a lower utility. This is because when the pre-commitment time is higher than the actual waiting time in line, customers are overpaying the line-sitters. On the other hand, if the pre-commitment time is lower than the actual waiting time in line, customers have to stand in line for a portion of the time by themselves, incurring a larger waiting cost. Therefore, customers' utility is reduced either way under the pre-commitment payment scheme.

8.1 Revenue of the Line-Sitting Firm

Under the optimal strategy of the customers, the line-sitting firm's revenue is

$$\pi^{PC}(r) = \frac{\lambda r}{\bar{c}} \int_{r/\rho}^{\bar{c}} \frac{\ln(c\rho/r)}{\mu - \lambda} dc.$$

After some algebraic manipulation, we have:

$$\pi^{PC}(r) = \frac{\lambda r}{\bar{c}(\mu - \lambda)} \int_{r/\rho}^{\bar{c}} \ln(c\rho/r) dc = \frac{\rho r[r/\rho - \bar{c} + \bar{c}\ln(\bar{c}\rho/r)]}{\bar{c}(1-\rho)},$$

and we compare it with the line-sitting firm's revenue under the post-payment scheme, denoted by $\pi^{LS}(r)$ in the following result.

Proposition 3 *There exists a unique $\bar{r} \in (0, \bar{c}\rho)$ such that $\Pi^{PC}(r) \geq \Pi^{LS}(r)$ if and only if $r \leq \bar{r}$.*

Under the same line-sitting rate, Proposition 3 shows that the line-sitting firm's revenue is higher under the pre-commitment payment scheme if and only if r is small. This is because when r is small (resp., large), the total line-sitting time purchased by customers under the pre-commitment payment scheme exceeds (resp., falls short of) that under the post-payment scheme. Next, denote by r^{PC} and r^{LS} the optimal line-sitting rates under the two payment schemes, and Π^{PC} and Π^{LS} the line-sitting firm's (optimal) revenue when r^{PC} and r^{LS} are adopted, respectively. We have the following result.

Proposition 4 $r^{PC} < r^{LS}$ *and* $\Pi^{PC} < \Pi^{LS}$.

Somewhat surprisingly, Proposition 4 shows that the line-sitting firm's optimal revenue is actually lower under the pre-commitment payment scheme than under the post-payment scheme. This is because the post-payment scheme saves customers' money, so they hire the line-sitters more often, leading to higher revenue for the line-sitting firm.

8.2 Welfare Implications

Finally, we investigate how the pre-commitment payment scheme affects customer welfare as well as social welfare. We have the following result.

Proposition 5 $CW^{PC} > CW^{LS}$ *but* $SW^{PC} < SW^{LS}$.

Proposition 5 shows that the pre-commitment payment scheme can improve customer welfare. This is counterintuitive at the first sight because we have shown earlier that customers are worse off under the pre-commitment payment scheme compared to the post-payment scheme (Proposition 2). However, Proposition 2 holds only for a fixed line-sitting rate. Because customers are more reluctant to use the line-sitting service under the pre-commitment payment scheme, it is optimal for the line-sitting firm to lower the line-sitting rate (Proposition 4). As a result, customers are actually better off under the pre-commitment payment scheme compared to the post-payment scheme under the optimal line-sitting rates for both schemes. Finally, from social welfare's perspective, the line-sitting fee is an internal transfer between the customers and the line-sitting firm. The reason why the post-payment scheme achieves higher social welfare is that customers (with high delay sensitivity) who hire line-sitters do not have to wait in line at all, reducing customers' total waiting costs.

9 Concluding Remarks

This chapter covers the booming business of line-sitting in congestion-prone service systems and explores its economic impact. In the presence of a line-sitting firm, customers with high waiting costs are willing to pay to get a line-sitter in line for them. We first examine how line-sitting impacts the service provider's revenue and customer welfare (relative to a FIFO queue without line-sitting). In the light of the similarity between line sitting and priority purchasing—both enable customers to skip physical wait with an extra payment—we then investigate whether the service provider should accommodate line-sitting or sell priority, and how these two schemes differ in customer welfare.

We find that, like selling priority, allowing line-sitting always improves the service provider's revenue, relative to FIFO. Yet, the revenue improvement is made possible by different means. Selling priority increases revenue through price discrimination, whereas allowing line-sitting increases revenue through demand expansion. This distinction leads to a divergence of the two schemes in customer welfare: higher revenue from implementing priority tends to come at the expense of customer welfare, whereas line-sitting can lead to a win-win situation for both the service provider and the customers. However, demand expansion can be a double-edged sword: while customer welfare improves with line-sitting in some cases, it can also deteriorate in others, particularly when both the service reward and the potential system workload are high, due to the negative congestion externalities introduced by the extra demand.

One major difference between line-sitting and priority purchasing is that they are managed by different parties—the line-sitting business is run by a third-party company, whereas priority is sold directly by the service provider. It is thus tempting to believe that selling priority is more lucrative than accommodating line-sitting for the service provider who acquires the priority premium but not the line-sitting payment. On the other hand, line-sitting has a cost advantage in diverting its clients to an offline channel. Hence, it is unclear a priori which scheme performs better. Interestingly, we find that the latter force (line-sitting being cost advantageous) can outweigh the former (selling priority being a direct revenue stream). Not only can line-sitting be more favorable for the service provider, it is also the only scheme among the three (FIFO, line-sitting, and priority) that can potentially be optimal for the service provider and customers alike.

Despite its potential contributions to the service provider's revenue and customer welfare, line-sitting may raise fairness concerns among customers. One phenomenon that may trigger strong customer reaction is the instance of a single line-sitter holding a place for a group of many. In fact, this is the primary reason some service providers cite when banning line-sitting. However, if one-to-one-substitution is followed (the case in our model), we suspect that the associated fairness concerns may be less protruding than those with priority purchasing because; in the former, line-sitting users only swap positions with line-sitters who are already in the system without affecting other customers' queue positions, whereas, in the latter, priority customers can cut the line to bump regular customers. Moreover, customer complaints, if any, are less likely to be directed to service providers because the line-sitting proceeds do not accrue to them. We refer interested readers to Althenayyan et al. (2022) which provide an experimental investigation on the fairness concerns of line-sitting. Another follow-up work is Zhao and Wang (2023), who study a setting where customers waiting for service in one line can hire a line-sitter to stand in the line of a second server who offers identical service. Any hiring customer can receive service from the first available server.

References

Althenayyan A, Cui S, Ulku S, Yang L (2022) Not all lines are skipped equally: an experimental investigation of line-sitting and express lines. In: Working paper

Cui S, Wang Z, Yang L (2020) The economics of line-sitting. Manag Sci 66(1):227–242

Harchol-Balter M (2013) Performance modeling and design of computer systems: queueing theory in action. Cambridge University Press, Cambridge

Wang Z, Wang J (2019) Pre-commitment or post-payment: which worsens a line-sitting firm's revenue? Oper Res Lett 47(5):447–451

Zhao C, Wang Z (2023). The impact of line-sitting on a two-server queueing system. Eur J Oper Res 308(2):782–800

Open Access This chapter is licensed under the terms of the Creative Commons Attribution 4.0 International License (http://creativecommons.org/licenses/by/4.0/), which permits use, sharing, adaptation, distribution and reproduction in any medium or format, as long as you give appropriate credit to the original author(s) and the source, provide a link to the Creative Commons license and indicate if changes were made.

The images or other third party material in this chapter are included in the chapter's Creative Commons license, unless indicated otherwise in a credit line to the material. If material is not included in the chapter's Creative Commons license and your intended use is not permitted by statutory regulation or exceeds the permitted use, you will need to obtain permission directly from the copyright holder.

Chapter 4
Queue Scalping

1 Introduction

In recent years, enabled by technological advances, queue-scalping has turned into a booming business. One noticeable example is in the context of telephone queues. A technology startup named EnQ constantly makes outgoing calls to the Internal Revenue Service's (IRS) contact centers to save spots near the front of the line. A customer who wishes to get tax resolution from the IRS more quickly can instead call EnQ for a fee, and EnQ would use its patented call-bridging technology to swap the customer's incoming call with its existing call already on hold, enabling the customer to bypass the long IRS hold time. Tomlinson (2016) illustrates how it works: a caller who directly calls the IRS is estimated to wait 55 min, but if she calls EnQ and pays $8, her wait will be brought down to approximately 3 min. Washington Post (2016) refers to EnQ as a "time-scalper." Queue-scalping also emerges in many public hospitals in China where patients seeking doctor consultation must get a registration ticket that secures them a spot on the doctor's waitlist (known as *Guahao* in Chinese). Such speculative behavior has garnered widespread attention. While queue-scalping often engenders a public outcry, many also recognize it as a "necessary evil," attributing its occurrence to a shortage of staff and medical facilities and the lack of capacity.

Despite the growing presence of queue-scalping, little is known about its operational and economic characteristics in the literature. To fill this gap, we build a queueing-game-theoretic model to study queue-scalping in Yang et al. (2021). In particular, a profit-maximizing queue-scalping firm determines whether to enter the queue of a service system and, if so, the number of scalpers to dispatch and the queue-scalping price to charge. A special case of this general model is a single scalper's entry and pricing problem, which is the starting point of our analysis. Customers are delay- and price-sensitive. They have a common valuation of service but differ in their delay cost per unit time. When a need for service arises, each customer decides whether to join the queue and transact with the queue-scalping firm, or join the tail of the queue without purchasing, or balk. If a customer chooses to purchase, she swaps positions with the foremost scalper (closest to the head of the queue), while, in the meantime, the scalper who gives away his spot rejoins the tail of the queue in anticipation of the next selling opportunity. That is, scalpers perceptually circulate in the queue. We characterize the dynamics of scalpers' movement, the strategic joining and purchasing behavior of customers, the sizing and pricing decisions of the queue-scalping firm, and the primary service provider's long-run capacity decision.

Our work on queue-scalping builds on the ticket-scalping literature. Karp and Perloff (2005) assume that scalpers can perfectly price-discriminate, and conclude that the original seller may benefit from the entry of scalpers. Su (2010) captures the effect of demand uncertainty and capacity constraints; the author finds that the presence of scalpers can increase the original seller's profit from static pricing and mimic the outcome of dynamic pricing. More recently, Courty (2019) proposes a simple mechanism to eliminate scalping in ticket resale. Hakimov et al. (2021) model the existing first-come-first-served online booking system and propose an alternative batch system, which makes scalping unprofitable. *One major difference between ticket-scalping and queue-scalping is that capacity in the former case is perishable whereas capacity in the latter is available on an ongoing basis.* As a result, the operational intricacy of queue-scalping (specifically, the strategic interactions it introduces among customers) significantly distinguishes it from ticket-scalping.

2 Model Description

We model the service system as an $M/M/1$ queue. Customers arrive according to a Poisson process with rate Λ, where Λ is henceforth referred to as the "demand volume." The service time for each customer is i.i.d. exponentially distributed with mean $1/\mu$, where μ is the capacity of the system. Upon arrival, each customer decides whether to join or balk to maximize her expected utility. If she balks, her utility is zero. Otherwise, she joins the tail of the queue, i.e., she waits behind all the other existing customers. Customers are served in the order of their queue positions. Customers do not renege after joining. Each customer's delay cost per unit time c is an i.i.d. random draw from a continuous probability distribution over the support $[0, \bar{c}]$ with cumulative distribution function (CDF) F. The probability density function (PDF) f satisfies $f(c) > 0, \forall c \in (0, \bar{c})$. Customers have common valuation V for receiving service. To exclude triviality, we assume $V > \bar{c}/\mu$. The model primitives, including Λ, μ, V, and the delay-cost distribution F, are common knowledge, yet each customer is privately informed of their individual delay-cost rate c. Customers do not observe the queue length or their queue positions. We let $\rho = \lambda/\mu$ denote the capacity utilization. Since the expected utility is a decreasing function of delay cost c, rational customers must follow a threshold joining strategy:

2 Model Description

there exists a unique cutoff value c^F such that customer c joins if and only if $c \leq c^F$. The equilibrium FIFO throughput is therefore $\lambda^F \triangleq \Lambda F(c^F)$.

Our queue-scalping model builds on the FIFO model. A queue-scalping firm dispatches N queue-scalpers to the service system; N is a decision variable of the queue-scalping firm, with $N = 0$ corresponding to a no-entry decision. For each unit of time a scalper spends in the system, it costs the queue-scalping firm k. Each time an arriving customer transacts with the queue-scalping firm, she exchanges positions with the *foremost* queue-scalper (the one closest to the server among all the queue-scalpers) at the moment of the transaction and the queue-scalping firm charges her price P. After the transaction, the buying customer takes the foremost scalper's position and the scalper rejoins the tail of the queue. As such, scalpers perpetually circulate in the queue, taking advantage of every possible selling opportunity. Perpetual circulation captures the case of scalping on a *repeated* basis, which is vital for companies like EnQ to sustain its business. To this end, our focus is on professional scalpers who can have a lasting and considerable impact on the service system as opposed to one-off scalpers with a temporary and limited effect. The transaction and reordering of the queue are assumed to be instantaneous, and clearly, they do not affect any other customers' waiting positions.

Each queue-scalper waits in the queue as if he were an ordinary customer but never enters service. The service provider cannot distinguish scalpers from ordinary customers. Likewise, the queue-scalpers' information structure is also no different than that of ordinary customers, i.e., the queue is unobservable to ordinary customers and queue-scalpers alike. Each scalper must run into one of the following two scenarios: (1) he sells his spot before advancing to the head of the queue; or (2) he advances to the foremost position of the queue and is summoned to service before his spot is sold. In the latter case, we further consider two ramifications:

1. *Head-queueing rule*: Holding his spot in the front of the queue, but letting customers behind access service, until his position is purchased by a customer;
2. *Tail-queueing rule*: Forgoing his position and rejoining the tail of the queue.

The head-queueing rule is amenable to analysis and yields sharp analytical results. The tail-queueing rule precludes explicit analytical characterization, but fits settings in which scalpers do not have the authority to hold spots. It is apparently less favorable to scalpers and thus would not be chosen by them unless forced to. The commonality of both rules, however, is that queue-scalpers do not consume capacity or hold up the line to deny other customers' access to service. We shall demonstrate that our main insights are robust to these two variations.

Upon arrival, each customer is informed of the queue-scalping price P, the expected delay (including the service time) W_1^N if she transacts with the queue-scalping firm, and the expected delay (including the service time) W_2^N if she does not, and decides whether to balk, join and purchase from the queue-scalping firm, or join without purchase, to maximize her expected utility:

$$U(c) \triangleq \max \begin{cases} V - cW_1^N - P, & \text{(join and buy);} \\ V - cW_2^N, & \text{(join and not buy);} \\ 0, & \text{(balk).} \end{cases}$$

From the specification of the expected utility $U(c)$, a joining customer with delay-cost rate c buys from the queue-scalping firm if and only if $V - cW_1^N - P \geq V - cW_2^N$, or $c(W_2^N - W_1^N) \geq P$, i.e., her expected delay-cost reduction exceeds the queue-scalping price. Moreover, the expected utility in either of the joining cases is decreasing in c. Thus, it follows that customers adopt a double-threshold strategy: there exist cutoff values $\tilde{c}$ and c^S such that those with low delay-cost rate $c \in [0, \tilde{c})$ join the tail of the queue; those with intermediate delay-cost rate $c \in [\tilde{c}, c^S]$ join and purchase from the queue-scalping firm; and those with high delay-cost rate $c \in (c^S, \bar{c}]$ balk. In particular, customer $\tilde{c}$ is indifferent between buying and not buying, i.e., $\tilde{c}(W_2^N - W_1^N) = P$.

Hence, given cutoff values $\tilde{c}$ and c^S, the system throughput λ is equal to $\Lambda F(c^S)$, and the fraction of joining customers who purchase from the queue-scalping firm, or the purchase rate, denoted by q, is equal to $(F(c^S) - F(\tilde{c}))/F(c^S)$. The expected delays W_1^N and W_2^N determine cutoff values $\tilde{c}$ and c^S (through customers' expected-utility maximization), and they are, in turn, determined by system throughput λ and purchase rate q (through queueing dynamics). In the equilibrium of this customer game, λ and q must be internally consistent with $\tilde{c}$ and c^S.

For a given N, let $W_1^N(\lambda, q)$ and $W_2^N(\lambda, q)$ be the expected delays for buying and non-buying customers, respectively, under system throughput λ and purchase rate q. The queue-scalping firm determines the number of scalpers N and price P to maximize its long-run average profit (rate) subject to equilibrium conditions, i.e.,

$$\max_{N \in \mathbb{N}_0, P \geq 0} P\lambda q - Nk, \tag{4.1a}$$

$$\text{s.t.} \quad U(c^S) = V - c^S W_1^N(\lambda, q) - P \geq 0, \quad (\bar{c} - c^S)U(c^S) = 0, \tag{4.1b}$$

$$P = \tilde{c}[W_2^N(\lambda, q) - W_1^N(\lambda, q)], \tag{4.1c}$$

$$\lambda = \Lambda F(c^S), \quad q = \frac{F(c^S) - F(\tilde{c})}{F(c^S)}. \tag{4.1d}$$

In the profit function (4.1a), $P\lambda q$ is the revenue (rate) from scalping, and Nk is the cost (rate) of maintaining N scalpers. Given N and P, Conditions (4.1b) and (4.1c) determine the cutoff values c^S and $\tilde{c}$, respectively, as a function of the throughput λ and the purchase rate q, whereas Condition (4.1d), in turn, determines λ and q as a function of c^S and $\tilde{c}$. Thus, Conditions (4.1b) through (4.1d) jointly pin down $(\lambda, q, c^S, \tilde{c})$ in equilibrium for a given set of N and P. We henceforth use $\lambda^S \triangleq \Lambda F(c^S)$ to denote the equilibrium system throughput in the presence of queue-scalping.

3 Analysis of the Single-Scalper Model

To build intuition and establish sharp analytical results, we first consider in this section a single scalper who decides whether to enter the queue and, if so, the optimal queue-scalping price to charge. That is, we restrict $N \in \{0, 1\}$ in problem (4.1a)–(4.1d). If the scalper does not enter the queue, i.e., $N = 0$, then his profit is trivially zero. If the scalper enters, i.e., $N = 1$, then a key determinant in the queue-scalper's pricing problem is the expressions of the expected delays $W_1^I(\lambda, q)$, $W_2^I(\lambda, q)$, induced by the queue-scalping dynamics. We establish them in Lemma 1. All the analytical results in this section are subject to the head-queueing rule.

Lemma 1 *In the presence of a queue-scalper, given system throughput λ, purchase rate q, and capacity utilization $\rho = \lambda/\mu$, the expected delay for customers who purchase from the queue-scalper, $W_1^I(\lambda, q)$, and that for non-purchasing customers, $W_2^I(\lambda, q)$, are given by*

$$W_1^I(\lambda, q) = \frac{1}{\mu - \lambda} - \frac{\rho^2(1-q)}{\mu - \lambda + \lambda q}, \quad W_2^I(\lambda, q) = \frac{1}{\mu - \lambda} + \frac{\rho^2 q}{\mu - \lambda + \lambda q}.$$

Customers who purchase from the queue-scalper jump ahead in line, and thus their expected delay is shorter than the mean delay of a FIFO system (with the same throughput), $1/(\mu - \lambda)$. As a consequence, non-buying customers expect a longer delay than they would from a FIFO system. Note from Lemma 1 that the increase in non-buying customers' expected delay is smaller than the mean service time, $1/\mu$, i.e., $W_2^I(\lambda, q) < 1/(\mu - \lambda) + 1/\mu$. When a non-buying customer joins the queue, the queue-scalper must wait ahead of her and may sell his spot before she enters service; therefore, she may need to wait for the service completion of at most one additional actual customer (who overtakes her by taking the queue-scalper's spot) than she would in the absence of the queue-scalper. A non-buying customer can be overtaken at most once because after an overtaking instance, the queue-scalper would join the tail of the queue behind her, and thus she would not be impacted by any future queue-scalping transactions.

Queue-scalping can be broadly seen as decentralized (partial) priority provision. The amount of priority a buying customer can gain depends on where the scalper is placed in the queue, which, in turn, depends on other customers' purchasing behavior. It is well-established in the literature that rational customers in a standard pay-for-priority scheme would be more prone to purchase priority and had more other customers purchased; in other words, customers exhibit "follow-the-crowd" (FTC) purchasing behavior (Hassin and Haviv 2003, Chapter 4, §2).

Would customers be subject to a similar behavioral pattern when they decide whether to acquire the queue-scalper's spot? It boils down to studying whether the difference in the expected delays of buying and non-buying customers, $D^I(q) \triangleq W_2^I(\lambda, q) - W_1^I(\lambda, q)$, is increasing (which corresponds to FTC) or decreasing (which corresponds to "avoid-the-crowd," or ATC) in the purchase rate q.

Proposition 1 *In the presence of a single queue-scalper, customers follow the ATC behavior, i.e., $D^I(q)$ is decreasing in $q \in [0, 1]$.*

Proposition 1 follows from Lemma 1. It shows that customers evince ATC behavior in the presence of a single queue-scalper, which contrasts how they would behave in a standard priority queue. Two forces govern how an increase in other customers' purchase rate affects a focal customer. On the one hand, as more (future) customers buy, a focal customer who does not buy is more likely to encounter and get overtaken by a buying customer before she completes service, which puts an upward pressure on the focal customer's buying incentive. On the other hand, as more (previous) customers buy, the scalper will be further pushed to the tail of the queue, which reduces how much a focal customer can skip if she buys, creating a downward pressure on her buying incentive. Thus, it is unclear a priori which force dominates.

3.1 What Queues Are Susceptible to Scalping?

In this subsection, we analyze the scalper's entry and pricing decision, based on which, we examine which types of queues are the most susceptible to scalping. We first derive the maximum revenue the scalper could achieve if he were to enter, and then weigh it against the entry cost k to determine whether he should enter. All the results in the remainder of this section are established under a uniform delay-cost distribution, but they can be generalized. Proposition 2 characterizes the optimal (revenue-maximizing) price the queue-scalper would charge if he were to enter and how it would vary with the demand volume.

Proposition 2 *Suppose the delay-cost distribution is uniform over $[0, 1]$. The queue-scalper's optimal price P^* if he enters is characterized as follows: $P^* = \frac{\Lambda(\sqrt{\mu} - \sqrt{\mu - \Lambda})}{\mu^2 \sqrt{\mu - \Lambda}}$ if $\Lambda \leq \mu - 1/V$ and $P^* = \frac{\Lambda V^2 (\sqrt{\Lambda V + 1} - 1)}{(\Lambda V + 1)^2}$ if $\Lambda > \mu - 1/V$; the optimal price P^* is unimodal in Λ.*

When the demand volume is small ($\Lambda \leq \mu - 1/V$), all arriving customers join, and we can show that the queue-scalper should charge a higher price with a larger demand volume. Intuitively, a larger demand volume increases system congestion, stimulating the need for a shorter wait, which, in turn, enables the scalper to raise his price. When the demand volume is large ($\Lambda > \mu - 1/V$), however, some arriving customers balk, and Proposition 2 shows that a larger demand volume can compel the queue-scalper to charge a lower price. While the upward pressure on the optimal price is still present, a larger demand volume would also drive away more delay-sensitive customers (i.e., c^S would get smaller); as a result, the queue-scalper can only sell his spot to customers who are less willing to pay for a shorter delay, which puts a downward pressure on the optimal price he can charge. Proposition 3 builds on Proposition 2 and characterizes the impact of the demand volume on the queue-scalper's revenue if he enters.

Proposition 3 *Suppose the delay-cost distribution is uniform over* $[0, 1]$. *The queue-scalper's revenue* Π *if he enters is unimodal in* Λ. *Specifically, there exists a unique* $\Lambda^* \geq \mu - 1/V$ *such that* Π *is increasing in* Λ *for* $\Lambda \leq \Lambda^*$ *and decreasing in* Λ *for* $\Lambda > \Lambda^*$.

When the demand volume is small, an increase in the demand volume leads to higher revenue for the queue-scalper, as expected, but surprisingly, Proposition 3 also reveals that when the demand volume is large, this prediction is reversed: an increase in the demand volume reduces the scalper's revenue. To understand why, note that a larger demand volume creates two competing forces that influence revenue: it brings in more purchasing customers for the queue-scalper, but also compels a lower price when the demand volume is already large (Proposition 2). The arrival rate of purchasing customers is naturally bounded by the system throughput (the arrival rate of all joining customers), which is further bounded by system capacity (because of the system stability induced in equilibrium). Thus, when the demand volume is large, increasing it even further would increase the arrival rate of purchasing customers only marginally (because it may already be close to capacity), making the price cut a dominant force that pushes down revenue.

4 Analysis of the Multi-Scalper Model

In this section, we generalize our results to the case of a queue-scalping firm that manages *multiple* queue-scalpers. Lemma 2 gives the expected-delay expressions for $W_1^N(\lambda, q)$ and $W_2^N(\lambda, q)$ when N scalpers are present. Again, unless otherwise specified, the results in this section are subject to the head-queueing rule.

Lemma 2 *In the presence of the queue-scalping firm utilizing N queue-scalpers, given system throughput λ, purchase rate q, and capacity utilization $\rho = \lambda/\mu$, the expected delay for purchasing customers,* $W_1^N(\lambda, q) = \frac{1}{\mu - \lambda} - \frac{\rho(1-q)}{\mu q}x$, *and the expected delay for non-purchasing customers,* $W_2^N(\lambda, q) = \frac{1}{\mu - \lambda} + \frac{\rho}{\mu}x$, *where* $x = \mathbf{1}_{N-1}\mathbf{A}_{N-1}\boldsymbol{\beta}_{N-1} + \frac{\lambda q}{\mu - \lambda + \lambda q}$; $\mathbf{1}_{N-1} = (1, 1, \ldots, 1) \in \mathbb{R}^{1 \times (N-1)}$ *is a row vector* of ones; $\mathbf{A}_{N-1} \in \mathbb{R}^{(N-1)\times(N-1)}$ is a lower triangular matrix with

$$\mathbf{A}_{N-1}[1,1] = \frac{\lambda q}{\mu - \lambda + \lambda q}, \quad \mathbf{A}_{N-1}[n,k] = 0, \quad 1 \leq n < k \leq N-1,$$

$$\mathbf{A}_{N-1}[n,1] = \sum_{i=1}^{n-1} \mathbf{A}_{N-1}[n-1,i]\left(\frac{\mu}{\mu + \lambda q}\right)^i \left(\frac{\lambda q}{\mu - \lambda + \lambda q}\right),$$
$$2 \leq n \leq N-1,$$

$$\mathbf{A}_{N-1}[n,k] = \sum_{i=k-1}^{n-1} \mathbf{A}_{N-1}[n-1,i]\left(\frac{\mu}{\mu + \lambda q}\right)^{i-(k-1)} \left(\frac{\lambda q}{\mu + \lambda q}\right),$$
$$2 \leq k \leq n \leq N-1,$$

and $\boldsymbol{\beta}_{N-1} = (\beta_1, \ldots, \beta_{N-1})^\top \in \mathbb{R}^{(N-1)\times 1}$ is a column vector with $\beta_n = 1 - \left(\frac{\mu}{\mu+\lambda q}\right)^n \frac{\mu - \lambda}{\mu - \lambda + \lambda q}$, $1 \leq n \leq N-1$.

The expressions of $W_1^N(\lambda, q)$ and $W_2^N(\lambda, q)$ in Lemma 2 are in closed form, but are generally quite complex for large N, and the matrix notation is a compact form of representation. Lemma 2 generalizes Lemma 1 from $N = 1$ to general N. As N increases, we can show from Lemma 2 that $W_2^N(\lambda, q)$ increases; $W_1^N(\lambda, q)$ decreases, and the gap between $W_1^N(\lambda, q)$ and $W_2^N(\lambda, q)$ widens. Intuitively, given throughput λ and purchase rate q, more scalpers would imply that the foremost scalper is closer to the head of the queue, enabling a buying customer to save more waiting time; more scalpers would also imply a non-buying customer being overtaken by potentially more future-arriving buying customers, which prolongs her wait. The limiting case of $N = \infty$ effectively corresponds to a standard non-preemptive priority queue. Non-buying customers in the queue would always wait behind a "cluster" of infinitely many queue-scalpers, whereas a buying customer could jump ahead of all non-buyers by taking the position of the foremost queue-scalper.

Now, in the presence of N queue-scalpers, do customers exhibit ATC or FTC behavior? Recall that customers avoid the crowd in the presence of a single queue-scalper, but follow the crowd in the priority queue (effectively the case of infinitely many queue-scalpers). Figure 4.1 supplements Lemma 2 by plotting $D^N(q) = W_2^N(\lambda, q) - W_1^N(\lambda, q)$ under various N.

We have four observations. First, with a small number of queue-scalpers, $D^N(q)$ is largely decreasing in q, and customers mostly exhibit ATC behavior, similar to the single-queue-scalper case. Second, with a large number of queue-scalpers, $D^N(q)$ is largely increasing in q and customers mostly exhibit the FTC behavior, mimicking the priority-queue case. Third, with an intermediate number of queue-scalpers, $D^N(q)$ is increasing in q (FTC) when q is small and decreasing in q (ATC) when q is large. This non-monotonicity result implies that as the number of scalpers increases, the FTC behavior first starts to kick in when only a few customers

Fig. 4.1 ATC/FTC behavior for different N Note. $\mu = 2, \lambda = 1.8$. The horizontal axis is purchase rate q; the vertical axis is $D^N(q) = W_2^N(\lambda, q) - W_1^N(\lambda, q)$

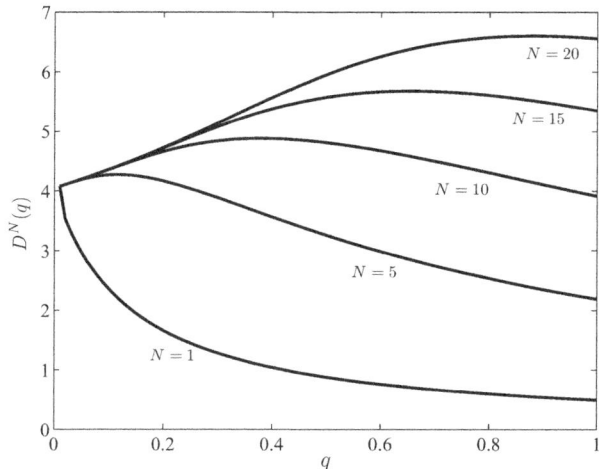

purchase (i.e., q being small). In such a case, the scalpers mostly scatter around the head of the queue, and an uptick in customer purchase would not push the scalpers toward the tail much, and therefore, customers are more sensitive to the upward pressure from being overtaken than the downward pressure of overtaking others; hence, FTC crops up. Fourth, we observe that in general, as N increases, customer behavior under queue-scalping shifts away from ATC (as in the single-scalper case) to FTC (as in the priority-queue case).

4.1 What Queues Are Susceptible to Scalping?

In this subsection, we address the question of what queues are the most susceptible to scalping; in particular, we are interested in how the nature of the queue (in terms of the demand volume) determines the extent of scalping (in terms of the number of scalpers that enter the queue). In Proposition 4, we first examine the impact of the demand volume on the queue-scalping firm's revenue for a fixed number of scalpers.

Proposition 4 *For any finite N, the queue-scalping firm's revenue is not monotonically increasing in demand volume Λ under either (head- or tail-) queueing rule.*

The result shown in Proposition 4 for multiple scalpers is qualitatively similar to the one demonstrated in Proposition 3 for a single scalper. To supplement Proposition 4, we have performed numerical experiments and found that the queue-scalping firm's revenue is unimodal in the demand volume for various values of N under the head-queueing rule and a uniform delay-cost distribution, reminiscent of the revenue property characterized in Proposition 3 for the case of a single scalper.

The key to establishing Proposition 4 is that a non-buying customer can be overtaken only a finite number of times, specifically, by at most N buying customers when N queue-scalpers are present. Similar to the single-queue-scalper case, this limits how much customers are willing to pay for the queue-scalping option; as a result, when the demand volume is already large such that customers balk, an even larger demand volume would compel a lower price (because the downward pressure from customer balking overshadows the upward pressure from increased congestion) and subsequently lead to lower revenue. While the preceding analysis focuses on the revenue of the queue-scalping firm and keeps the number of queue-scalpers N fixed, Theorem 1 shows that the optimal profit of the queue-scalping firm that endogenizes the number of scalpers N still preserves the non-monotonicity property.

Theorem 1 *Under either (head- or tail-) queueing rule, the optimal profit of the queue-scalping firm and the optimal number of scalpers N^* are both non-monotone in demand volume Λ unless $N^* \equiv 0$ for all Λ. Moreover, if $\Lambda \leq \mu\sqrt{k}/(\sqrt{k}+\sqrt{c})$ or $\Lambda \geq \mu/F(k)$, $N^* = 0$, i.e., a queue with a very small or very large demand volume is impervious to scalping.*

When a service system has a small demand volume, it is intuitive that the revenue from scalping due to light congestion is too modest to cover its cost, and therefore, such a queue is immune to scalping. When a service system has a large demand volume, since the scalping revenue is low for any fixed number of scalpers (by Proposition 4), populating the queue with more scalpers would boost revenue only marginally and thus would not justify the scalpers' additional costs; therefore, such a queue is also (surprisingly) impervious to scalping.

Figure 4.2 supplements Theorem 1 by numerically showing that the queue-scalping firm's profit, the number of scalpers it dispatches, and the price it charges are all (mostly) unimodal in the demand volume, under the head-queueing rule and a uniform delay cost distribution. Consistent with our theoretical result, the figure shows that when a queue's demand volume is sufficiently small, no scalping would be witnessed; when a queue's demand volume is large, although scalping still exists, it only has a limited presence, and therefore may not be vastly disruptive. Notably, scalping is the most rampant in queues with non-extreme demand volume. Such a queueing setting is expected to see the most scalpers, the highest queue-scalping

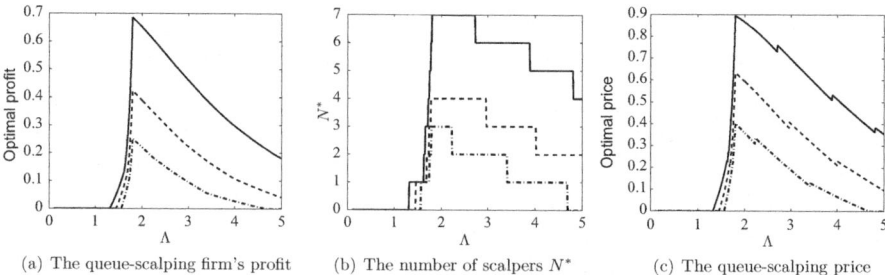

(a) The queue-scalping firm's profit (b) The number of scalpers N^* (c) The queue-scalping price

Fig. 4.2 The impact of demand volume Λ on queue-scalping *Note.* $V = 5$, $\mu = 2$, $F(c) = c$ for $c \in [0, 1]$. The solid line: $k = 0.15$; the dashed line: $k = 0.2$; the dot-dashed line: $k = 0.25$

price, and the greatest profit for the queue-scalping firm. Thus, service providers facing such an environment should be particularly alert to the potential presence of scalpers. One important implication of our results is that an expansion in capacity may only lead to the presence of more scalpers. The lack of capacity is often cited as a reason for the presence of scalping. As a result, the service provider may be prompted to improve their cost efficiency and consequently expand capacity. Doing so is often assumed to mitigate scalping, but as we have shown, it may only spur scalping, especially in a plausible situation where capacity is tight before the expansion.

In sum, the main driving forces for our non-monotonicity results are twofold: (1) a non-buying customer can only be overtaken finitely many times; (2) a large demand volume turns away customers with high delay sensitivity. These two features do not rely on the single-server assumption or the exponential-service-time assumption, and therefore, our qualitative results hold even for a multi-server queueing system with non-exponential service times.

5 Impact of Queue-Scalping

In this section, we examine how the presence of queue-scalpers impacts the system throughput (in Sect. 5.1), consumer surplus (in Sect. 5.2), and social welfare (in Sect. 5.3). We focus on the nontrivial cases in which some scalpers enter the queue. If no scalpers are present, the system throughput, consumer surplus, and social welfare will trivially be unchanged. The analytical results in this section hold for both the head- and tail-queueing rules.

5.1 System Throughput

Recall from Sect. 2 that the FIFO system throughput in the absence of scalping is $\lambda^F = \Lambda F(c^F)$ and the system throughput in the presence of scalping is $\lambda^S = \Lambda F(c^S)$. The goal of this subsection is to compare λ^F and λ^S. To facilitate our analytical development, we define a property of probability distributions called *elasticity*.

Definition 1 The elasticity ϵ of probability distribution F (with density f) is defined as $\epsilon(x) \triangleq xf(x)/F(x)$. If $\epsilon(x) > 1$ for all x, then F is elastic; if $\epsilon(x) \leq 1$ for all x, then F is inelastic.

Theorem 2 *The presence of queue-scalping increases the system throughput, (i.e., $\lambda^S \geq \lambda^F$) if the delay-cost distribution F is inelastic and reduces it (i.e., $\lambda^S \leq \lambda^F$) if F is elastic.*

Inelastic and elastic distributions are both common. Examples of inelastic distributions include exponential, (half-)normal, standardized versions of logistic, Laplace, Gumbel, and power distributions $F(x) = x^\alpha$ with $\alpha \in (0, 1]$. Distributions with a decreasing PDF are inelastic, whereas those with an increasing PDF are elastic. Thus, a beta distribution with PDF $f(x) = \frac{x^{\alpha-1}(1-x)^{\beta-1}}{B(\alpha,\beta)}$ is elastic if and only if $\alpha \geq 1 \geq \beta$ and inelastic if and only if $\alpha \leq 1 \leq \beta$. The uniform distribution is a special case of beta, with $\alpha = \beta = 1$, which implies that its elasticity is a constant equal to one, and therefore, by Theorem 2, the presence of queue-scalping does not affect the system throughput.

In general, however, the presence of queue-scalping is a double-edged sword for system throughput. On the one hand, it presents an opportunity to delay-sensitive customers who would otherwise balk to join the queue without undergoing a long wait. This puts an upward pressure on system throughput. On the other hand, purchasing scalpers' spots creates negative externalities among customers as they wish to overtake and dread being overtaken by each other.

5.2 Consumer Surplus

Consumer surplus in a FIFO queue without scalping, CS^F, is defined as

$$CS^F = \Lambda \int_0^{c^F} \left(V - \frac{c}{\mu - \lambda^F} \right) dF(c). \tag{4.2}$$

Consumer surplus in the presence of scalping, CS^S, is defined as

$$CS^S = \Lambda \left[\int_0^{\tilde{c}} \left(V - cW_2^N \right) dF(c) + \int_{\tilde{c}}^{c^S} \left(V - cW_1^N - P \right) dF(c) \right].$$

The goal of this subsection is to compare CS^F and CS^S. To facilitate our analytical development, we define the failure rate of probability distributions.

Definition 2 The failure rate (or hazard rate) h of probability distribution F (with density f) is defined as $h(x) \triangleq f(x)/[1 - F(x)]$. If $h(x)$ is weakly increasing in x for all x, then F has an increasing failure rate (IFR).

Theorem 3 *When the delay-cost distribution F is IFR, the presence of queue-scalping decreases consumer surplus, i.e., $CS^S < CS^F$.*

Many common distributions are IFR, such as those mentioned after Theorem 2: uniform, exponential (which has a constant failure rate), half-normal, logistic, Laplace, Gumbel, and power, among others. Consumer surplus is an aggregate measure of customer utility. Customers can be divided into three segments in terms of how their utility changes after the entry of the queue-scalping firm (see Fig. 4.3

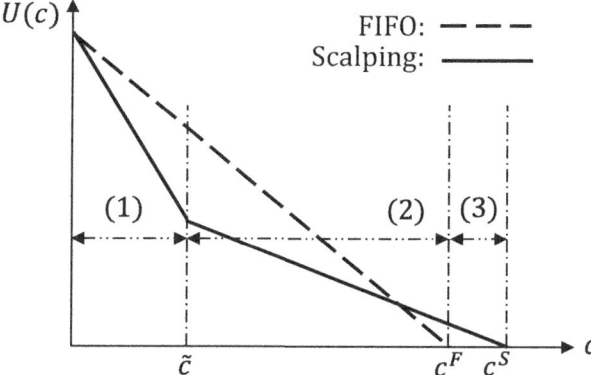

Fig. 4.3 Illustration of customer utility as a function of delay sensitivity under FIFO and queue-scalping

for an illustration): (1) those with low delay sensitivity who join either way but do not buy from the queue-scalping firm after it enters; (2) those with intermediate delay sensitivity who join either way and buy afterward; and (3) those with high delay sensitivity who do not join before but do so afterward. Customers in segment (1) are worse off as a result of queue-scalping because they bear the risk of being overtaken by buying customers who would otherwise wait behind them. Customers in segment (3) are better off because their expected utility changes from zero to positive due to the scalping option now available.

It is a priori unclear how customers in segment (2) will be affected. On the one hand, their delay is shortened; on the other hand, they pay the queue-scalping price. Indeed, Fig. 4.3 illustrates an instance in which some customers in segment (2) are better off and some are worse off (because, as stated earlier, the act of overtaking other customers creates negative externalities). In general, downward pressure tends to dominate, causing consumer surplus to fall. The queue-scalping firm extracts surplus from customers as it pits them against each other for scalpers' front spots in the line. Such surplus extraction may be a reason why scalping often sparks customer outrage.

5.3 Social Welfare

Social welfare in a FIFO queue without scalping, SW^F, is equal to consumer surplus CS^F defined in (4.2) because there are no monetary transfers. Social welfare in the presence of scalping, SW^S, is defined as

$$SW^S = \Lambda \left[\int_0^{\tilde{c}} \left(V - cW_2^N \right) dF(c) + \int_{\tilde{c}}^{c^S} \left(V - cW_1^N \right) dF(c) \right].$$

Proposition 5 *There exists $\epsilon > 0$ such that if $\lambda^S \in (\lambda^F - \epsilon, \lambda^F + \epsilon)$, then the presence of queue-scalping increases social welfare, i.e., $SW^S > SW^F$. In particular, $SW^S > SW^F$ if the delay-cost distribution is uniform.*

Proposition 5 shows that queue-scalping increases social welfare as long as the throughput change due to queue-scalping is not too dramatic. For instance, if the demand volume Λ is small, all customers join regardless of whether scalpers are present, which implies that scalping does not change throughput and thus must increase social welfare. Further, if the delay-cost distribution is uniform, then the presence of scalpers does not affect the throughput for any demand volume (see our discussion after Theorem 2), and thus, social welfare always increases in that case. If the system throughput is changed by queue-scalping under a nonuniform delay-cost distribution, it is analytically difficult to pin down the directional change of social welfare, but to the extent such a change is small, social welfare still increases. Intuitively, queue-scalping introduces service differentiation that prioritizes those who are more delay-sensitive, which tends to improve social efficiency. However, as shown by Theorem 3, this efficiency gain is often not captured by customers, but, rather, siphoned off by the queue-scalping firm.

6 The Long-Run Capacity Response

Thus far, we have implicitly assumed that the primary service provider is inactive and the capacity level is exogenously fixed. In this section, we introduce how queue-scalping impacts the primary service provider's long-run capacity decision. In light of our motivating examples from public services (e.g., tax offices and public hospitals), we focus on the case where the service provider's operating objective is to maximize social welfare.

We assume that maintaining capacity μ costs the service provider $\omega\mu^2/2$ per unit time (the capacity cost is a cost term in social welfare). The quadratic capacity cost is the simplest way to capture a convex increasing capacity cost. Let μ^{FIFO} denote the socially optimal capacity in a FIFO queue without scalpers, and μ^{QS}, the socially optimal capacity in a queue with scalpers. In the model, the welfare-maximizing service provider first determines the capacity, and the profit-maximizing queue-scalping firm then determines the queue-scalping price and the number of scalpers to dispatch. To enable sharp analytical characterization, we set the scalping cost to zero such that the queue-scalping firm would insert an infinite number of scalpers, resulting in a full-priority queue.

Proposition 6 *Suppose the delay-cost distribution is uniform and scalping cost $k = 0$. If $\omega < \underline{\omega} \triangleq \frac{\Lambda V^3}{2\bar{c}^2(\Lambda V/\bar{c}+1)^2}$, then $\mu^{QS} < \mu^{FIFO}$. If $\omega > \bar{\omega} \triangleq \frac{\Lambda V^3}{2\bar{c}^2(\Lambda V/\bar{c}+1)}$, then $\mu^{QS} > \mu^{FIFO}$.*

6 The Long-Run Capacity Response

According to Proposition 6, when it is cheap to scale capacity, the FIFO capacity is high, and the presence of queue-scalping prompts the service provider to dial back capacity, which implies that priority provision and capacity investment are strategic substitutes in this case. However, when it is expensive to scale capacity, the FIFO capacity is low, and the service provider responds to queue-scalping by expanding capacity, making priority provision and capacity investment strategic complements. Since the service provider has a tendency to adjust capacity toward an intermediate level, we refer to it as a "pull-to-center" effect.

Let λ^{FIFO}, CS^{FIFO}, and SW^{FIFO} denote the system throughput, consumer surplus, and social welfare, respectively, under the socially optimal FIFO capacity; let λ^{QS}, CS^{QS}, and SW^{QS} denote their respective counterparts under the socially optimal capacity in response to queue-scalping. Proposition 7 characterizes how these performance metrics compare under endogenous capacity.

Proposition 7 *Suppose the delay-cost distribution is uniform and scalping cost is $k = 0$. Under endogenous capacity:*

(i) $SW^{QS} > SW^{FIFO}$;
(ii) If $\omega < \underline{\omega}$, then $\lambda^{QS} = \lambda^{FIFO} = \Lambda$; If $\omega > \bar{\omega}$, then $\lambda^{QS} > \lambda^{FIFO}$;
(iii) If $\omega < \underline{\omega}$ or $\omega > \bar{\omega}$, then $CS^{QS} < CS^{FIFO}$.

Since social welfare increases in the presence of queue-scalping even if capacity is fixed (Proposition 5), optimally adjusting capacity will only further improve social welfare. The change in system throughput is driven by the capacity change. When scaling capacity is expensive, the service provider expands capacity (see Proposition 6), luring more customers and thus increasing system throughput. When scaling capacity is cheap, ample capacity is supplied to capture all potential customer demand under either FIFO or queue-scalping, and thus system throughput is unaffected. For consumer surplus, recall from Theorem 3 that it falls in the presence of queue-scalping under fixed capacity; if the socially optimal capacity also falls (which occurs when scaling capacity is cheap; see Proposition 6), then consumer surplus unequivocally falls. If the socially optimal capacity rises (which occurs when scaling capacity is expensive), then the secondary effect of faster service puts an upward pressure on consumer surplus, contrasting the downward pressure from the primary effect of queue-scalping (under fixed capacity). We show that in this case, the primary downward pressure outweighs the secondary upward pressure, causing consumer surplus to decline as a result of queue-scalping. Nevertheless, one caveat for this result is our assumption of full priority (for tractability). We shall see momentarily that in the case of partial priority (due to a finite number of scalpers)—which eases the primary downward pressure—the reverse can be true.

7 Comparison with Line-Sitting

The mechanisms behind line-sitting and queue-scalping are notably different. We elaborate on the major differences between the two below. Table 4.1 gives a synopsis.

First, a line-sitting firm essentially exploits an arbitrage opportunity from the delay-cost difference between line sitters and customers. While such a cost difference is also critical to queue-scalping, a queue-scalping firm additionally exploits customers' fear of being bumped if they do not purchase from scalpers.

The two schemes also differ in handoffs (position swapping). In queue-scalping, the handoff is straightforward for customers: the swap occurs as soon as a customer arrives. However, in line-sitting, the swap occurs when line-sitters move sufficiently close to the head of the queue, and the inherent stochasticity of service systems makes the timing of handoffs tricky in practice. It may not be easy for line-sitters to determine when to contact their clients: if they call them too early, then their clients have to wait themselves and line-sitters forgo potential earnings; if they call them too late, then they may run the risk of losing their hard-earned spots by the time their clients arrive. This issue is exacerbated in virtual queues where line-sitters do not observe the system state and cannot accurately estimate how close they are to the head of the queue.

Due to the above structural differences, the two schemes differ in the service settings to which they are applicable. The handoff difficulty implies that line-sitting works best for settings where the service itself can be delegated to a third party (in addition to the wait). This may explain why line-sitters are commonly hired for iPhone and Cronut purchases. By contrast, the ease of handoffs in queue-scalping combined with the fact that waiting is still not completely eliminated even after the swap makes queue-scalping a good fit for tax or medical services that must be completed by customers in person (which justifies the wait after the swap).

Moreover, line-sitting lends itself to physical queues as it brings value to customers by transferring them from, say, standing in line outside an iPhone store (a high-cost undertaking) to, say, waiting from the comfort of their home (a low-cost activity). Line-sitting may be less suited for virtual queues, such as telephone queues, whereby the difference between waiting offline and waiting on hold may be too marginal to make a case for monetizing line-sitting by directly charging

Table 4.1 Differences between queue-scalping and line-sitting

	Queue-scalping	Line-sitting
Service order	Priority	FIFO
Value proposition	Waiting-time reduction	Waiting-cost reduction
Provision mode	Perpetual circulation (MTS)	Entry upon request (MTO)
Handoffs	Straightforward	Timing can be tricky
Service delegation	Ideal for self-service	Ideal for delegated-service
Physical or virtual queue	Primarily virtual	Primarily physical

customers. Moreover, the aforementioned handoff difficulty can hamper the use of line-sitting. By contrast, queue-scalping is more compatible with virtual queues. For one thing, it does not suffer from tricky handoff issues; for the other, it brings the tangible benefit of waiting-time reduction. Nevertheless, it may be difficult for queue-scalping to make its way into physical queues. On the one hand, having to physically stand in line to hold one's spot limits a queue-scalper's ability to find a potential buyer. On the other hand, to find a buyer, a queue-scalper must hawk his spot, and doing so can easily get him identified. Further, the fact that a queue-scalper must tirelessly stand in the queue without any guarantee of sales makes it an overwhelmingly risky prospect.

8 Effect of Queue Information

Our base model assumes that the real-time queue length is unobservable to arriving customers, who have to make decisions based on their anticipated delays. This section introduces the observable case and investigates the effect of information on customer behavior and the pricing strategy of a queue-scalper. For tractability, we consider a single scalper and assume that all customers have the same delay sensitivity C.

We define the position of the queue-scalper to be (i, j) if the queue-scalper is in the i-th position, and there are j customers behind him. It should be noted that i cannot be 1 if $j \geq 1$, because the queue-scalper has no interest in receiving service and when he is at the head of the line, he would spontaneously swap position with the customer behind him. Thus, the state set of the queue-scalper should be $\Omega = \{(1,0) \bigcup (i,j) | i \geq 2, j \geq 0\}$. When the position of the queue-scalper is found to be (i, j), the expected cost an arriving customer would incur from buying the spot is $P + iC/\mu$. However, if she does not purchase the queue-scalping service, her expected cost is $C \left(\frac{i+j}{\mu} + \frac{1-\Pr[i,j+1]}{\mu} \right)$, where $\Pr[i, j+1]$ is the probability that the customer would not be overtaken by any future arriving customers before her service starts when she is currently in the $(i + j + 1)$-th position and the queue-scalper is in the i-th position. Let $n_e \equiv \lfloor v_P \rfloor = \lfloor \mu P / C \rfloor$ denote the normalized price of the queue-scalping service. Lemma 3 gives a customer's equilibrium strategy.

Lemma 3 *For an arriving customer who finds the position of queue-scalper (i, j), the equilibrium strategy is a double-threshold strategy $[m_e, n_e]$:*

(1) If $j \geq n_e + 1$, she would buy the queue-scalper's position;
(2) If $j \leq n_e - 1$, she would never buy the queue-scalper's position;
(3) If $j = n_e$, there exists a unique threshold m_e such that she would purchase if and only if $i \geq m_e + 1$.

To determine threshold m_e, it suffices to derive the probability $\Pr[2, n_e + 1]$. To simplify the notations, we define $\overline{p} = \lambda/(\lambda+\mu) = \rho/(1+\rho)$ and $\overline{q} = \mu/(\lambda+\mu) =$

$1/(1+\rho)$. The following theorem characterizes the explicit equilibrium strategy of customers.

Theorem 4 *In the observable case, the equilibrium of customers $[m_e, n_e]$ is given as follows: $n_e = \lfloor v_P \rfloor$, and $m_e = 2$ if $\phi(\overline{p}, \overline{q}) \leq 1$; otherwise, if $\phi(\overline{p}, \overline{q}) > 1$, $m_e = \lceil \frac{\ln(1+\rho)\phi(\overline{p},\overline{q})}{\ln(1+\rho)} \rceil$, where*

$$\phi(\overline{p}, \overline{q}) \equiv \frac{\overline{p}^{n_e+1}\left[1 + (n_e - 4)\overline{q} - 2(n_e - 1)\overline{q}^2 + \overline{q}(2\overline{q})^{n_e+1}\right]}{(1 - 2\overline{q})^2}.$$

First, it is intuitive to find that n_e is independent of ρ as well as the decimal part of v_P (i.e., the value of $v_P - \lfloor v_P \rfloor$). However, for any given v_P, threshold m_e is weakly decreasing in ρ, which indicates that customers are more inclined to buy the position when the system is more congested. Additionally, for a fixed $\lfloor v_P \rfloor$, m_e is also weakly increasing in the decimal part of v_P. That is, customers are more hesitant to buy the position when the price increases (with fixed $\lfloor v_P \rfloor$). Interestingly, we can verify that m_e is not necessarily increasing in $\lfloor v_P \rfloor$. This is because when v_P increases, a larger n_e is induced, which makes the system more congested, and motivates more customers to purchase (i.e., $m_e \downarrow$). In equilibrium, the profit of the queue-scalper can be expressed as

$$\Pi^{ob}(P) = \lambda P \left(\sum_{j \geq n_e+1, i \geq 2} \pi^{ob}(i, j) + \sum_{i \geq m_e+1} \pi^{ob}(i, n_e) \right),$$

where $\pi^{ob}(i, j)$ is the steady-state probability of the system at state (i, j) and is derived in Wang and Wang (2021).

Let $\Pi^{un}(P)$ denote the profit of the scalper in the unobservable case. We compare the queue-scalper's profit under two information levels numerically in Fig. 4.4. We let $\mu = C = 1$. We denote by Π^{un} and Π^{ob} the maximal profit rate of the scalper in the unobservable case and the observable case, respectively, by selecting the optimal price. In Fig. 4.4, we first plot $\Pi^{ob}(P)$ (and $\Pi^{un}(P)$) as a function of price P. In particular, three different workloads are considered: $\rho = 0.6$, $\rho = 0.8$, $\rho = 0.96$.

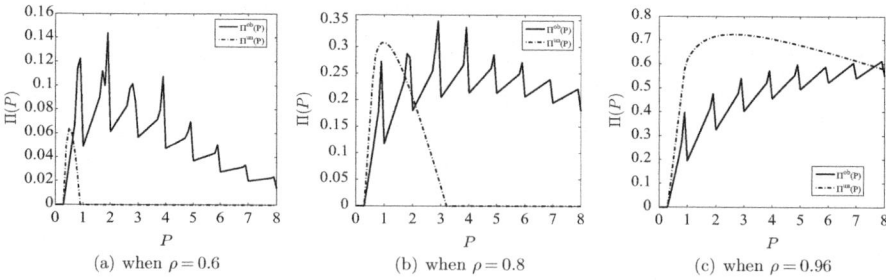

Fig. 4.4 Queue-scalper's profit in observable [Ob] and unobservable [Un] cases vs. P

Note that $\Pi^{ob}(P)$ is piecewise in P because the equilibrium of customers $[m_e, n_e]$ is not continuous in P. When ρ is small ($\rho = 0.6$), we have that $\Pi^{un}(P) < \Pi^{ob}(P)$ for most prices (and $\Pi^{un} < \Pi^{ob}$) because in the unobservable case, customers anticipate a short expected waiting time and find it not necessary to purchase the queue-scalper's spot. However, in the observable case, customers make state-dependent decisions. They are always willing to buy the queue-scalping service with a higher price when the system reaches higher states. Therefore, when ρ is small, the queue-scalper should encourage the customers to purchase by disclosing the system information. When ρ increases, the advantage of information transparency decreases, and more customers prefer to purchase when the system information is concealed; see Fig. 4.4b (i.e., when $\rho = 0.8$). Finally, when the system has heavy traffic (e.g., $\rho = 0.96$), the advantage of information is reversed, and we have $\Pi^{un}(P) > \Pi^{ob}(P)$ for most prices and $\Pi^{un} > \Pi^{ob}$ in particular. This is because when the system is congested, most customers are more inclined to buy the queue-scalping service in the unobservable case while fewer customers tend to purchase in the observable queue as there are times when the system will still be in low states.

9 Concluding Remarks

This chapter takes a first cut at systematically understanding the economic and operational characteristics of queue-scalping. We now discuss some modeling assumptions, alternative perspectives, and future research directions. While we have presented how a welfare-maximizing service provider should respond to queue-scalping through capacity adjustment, it may also be of interest to explore how a revenue-maximizing service provider sets the base service fee in response to queue-scalping and specifically how this form of decentralized priority provision contrasts centralized priority provision where the service provider charges for both base and priority services.

We treat the queue-scalping firm as a local monopoly capable of setting the queue-scalping price in a given queue. This assumption seems a reasonable fit for the queue-scalping practice as it is rarely seen that queue-scalpers engage in cut-throat competition in the same queue. This can be due to nontrivial technological hurdles to entry (as in the example of EnQ), or the ease with which incumbents can identify and deter entrants (as in the example of hospital queue-scalping). Incorporating competition will not affect our results regarding the impact of scalping on system throughput and consumer surplus, and may only strengthen our results that queues with a non-extreme demand volume can be the most susceptible to scalping because even when the collective revenue is increasing, each individual scalper's share of the revenue can still decrease if a larger demand volume lures more scalpers to enter and compete against each other.

The queue-scalping firm in our model charges a uniform price and sells the position of the foremost queue-scalper in each transaction. When multiple queue-scalpers ($N \geq 2$) are operated, one could presumably offer a menu of queue-scalping options by charging N prices for the different positions of the queue-scalper. Doing so would arguably increase the queue-scalping firm's revenue but create implementation complexity in practice.

References

Courty P (2019) Ticket resale, bots, and the fair price ticketing curse. J Cult Econ 43(3):345–363

Hakimov R, Heller C, Kübler D, Kurino M (2021) How to avoid black markets for appointments with online booking systems. Am Econ Rev 111(7):2127–51

Hassin R, Haviv M (2003) To queue or not to queue: equilibrium behavior in queueing systems. Kluwer Academic Publishers, Boston

Karp L, Perloff JM (2005) When promoters like scalpers. J Econ Manag Strateg 14(2):477–508

Su X (2010) Optimal pricing with speculators and strategic consumers. Manag Sci 56(1):25–40

Tomlinson K (2016) Taking cuts in the IRS line. Archer Security Group (17 February 2016), http://www.archerenergysolutions.com/taking-cuts-in-the-irs-line/

Wang Z, Wang J (2021) The effect of information on queue-scalping service systems. Oper Res Lett 49(4):485–491

Washington Post (2016) Waiting for the IR$. (25 February 2016). https://www.washingtonpost.com/lifestyle/magazine/gene-weingarten-waiting-for-the-ir/2016/02/24/1a2a6afc-cb51-11e5-a7b2-5a2f824b02c9_story.html

Yang L, Wang Z, Cui S (2021) A model of queue scalping. Manag Sci 67(11):6803–6821

Open Access This chapter is licensed under the terms of the Creative Commons Attribution 4.0 International License (http://creativecommons.org/licenses/by/4.0/), which permits use, sharing, adaptation, distribution and reproduction in any medium or format, as long as you give appropriate credit to the original author(s) and the source, provide a link to the Creative Commons license and indicate if changes were made.

The images or other third party material in this chapter are included in the chapter's Creative Commons license, unless indicated otherwise in a credit line to the material. If material is not included in the chapter's Creative Commons license and your intended use is not permitted by statutory regulation or exceeds the permitted use, you will need to obtain permission directly from the copyright holder.

Chapter 5
Referral Priority Programs

1 Introduction

Many technology companies are breaking new ground today as they introduce sign-up wait lists for a limited release of their products to eager customers before a mass-market launch. Notable examples include Dropbox, a file-hosting service; Mailbox, an email inbox-management application; and Robinhood, a mobile application for commission-free stock trading. These companies have enjoyed such sensational success that they are forced to create sign-up wait lists to ensure that everyone has a fantastic, reliable experience. Today's apps and services are increasingly relying on massive cloud backends, which makes scaling capacity particularly challenging at the initial stage, so companies use wait lists as a buffer to clear technological hurdles based on feedback from real users. Thus, customer activation, i.e., taking customers off the wait lists and letting them access the product, can only be done cautiously at a limited rate, which may cause nontrivial wait times for later arriving customers.

Recognizing this situation, some of these firms embrace a novel mechanism that allows customers to shorten their wait times and move up in line if they invite their friends to also sign up on the wait list. For instance, Robinhood's confirmation email reads, "Interested in priority access? Get early access by referring your friends. The more friends that join, the sooner you will get access." Robinhood is by no means alone. This referral scheme has enjoyed such widespread popularity that companies like Waitlisted.co—a third-party startup specialized in helping hundreds of client companies build wait lists—made it a standard built-in feature; more than 99% of Waitlisted.co's clients have integrated this scheme into their wait lists. Like Waitlisted.co, many other growth-hacking companies jump on the bandwagon and support customer referrals on wait lists, such as Kickoff Labs, Maitre, and Prefinery, just to name a few. We call this emerging business practice the *referral priority program*.

The ingenuity of the referral priority program is that it cleverly leverages customers' dislike of waiting to create an incentive for spreading positive word of mouth and acquiring new customers on behalf of the firm. Unlike the traditional referral reward program, which offers monetary compensation to motivate referrals, the referral priority program "recruits" existing customers as sales agents without the firm incurring any explicit costs or proactively designing reward payments. Integrating such a free and hands-off referral program into a wait list holds immense appeal, especially for startup firms whose tight budget constraints prohibit the use of monetary rewards. However, the referral incentive in this setting is intricate because it is generated by the interactions among customers on the wait list. A customer's spot in line is relative, and non-referring customers could move backward when referring customers are granted priority access. Thus, the amount of priority one obtains with a successful referral depends on others' referral behavior. Moreover, as referrals bring in new customers, the system could suffer more congestion, which may, in turn, diminish customers' willingness to sign up.

The growing adoption of the referral priority program combined with the intricate nature of customer incentives and system dynamics begs an important question: is this scheme truly effective? We tackle this issue in Yang and Debo (2019) by carefully modeling customers' strategic joining and referral behavior. In doing so, we investigate the effectiveness of the program as a marketing tool for the firm (measured by system throughput, the rate of customer acquisition) and as an operational choice for customers (measured by customer welfare).

2 Model

We model the sign-up wait list of a firm as a single-server queueing system. The service time is exponentially distributed with mean $1/\mu$, where μ is the service rate. *Base customers*, denoted by "B," arrive to the system according to a Poisson process with rate Λ. These customers are aware of the service and arrive organically (not from referrals). We call Λ the base market size.

All customers have a common waiting cost per unit time c and a valuation for service v drawn from a uniform distribution over $[0, \bar{V}]$. Upon arrival, each customer decides whether to join the queue. Upon joining, each customer may make one referral. *Referred customers*, denoted by "R," arrive *instantaneously* upon receiving referral requests, and also decide on joining and referring. The same process continues for a friend's friend and so on. Customers incur a referral cost c_r if they decide to invite a friend. In case a referral is successful, i.e., the referred customer joins, the referring customer joins the priority class (Class 1). If a customer does not refer or if her referral is unsuccessful, she joins the regular class (Class 2). Class 1 customers are served with preemptive priority over Class 2 customers. Within each class, customers are served FIFO (first in, first out). Figure 5.1 illustrates the model.

The model primitives, Λ, μ, c, c_r, and the valuation distribution (including $\bar{V}$), are common knowledge. A customer's information set consists of her valuation and type (whether she is a base customer or a referred one), (v, χ), where $v \in$

2 Model

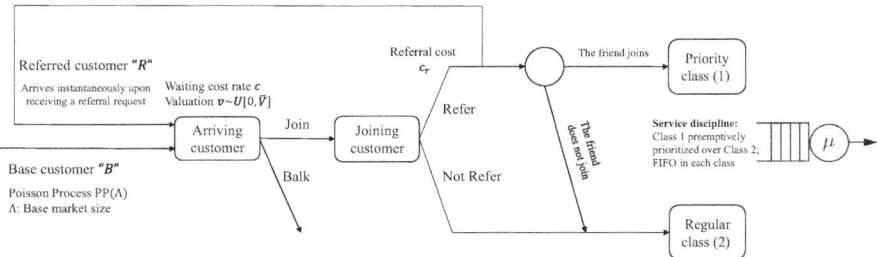

Fig. 5.1 Schematic illustration of the model *Note.* Because all referred customers *arrive* upon referral requests regardless of their joining decision, the arc for referred customers emanates from the point of a referral

$[0, \bar{V}]$, $\chi \in \{B, R\}$. That is, (i) an individual customer's valuation for service v is private information not known by other customers; (ii) a customer knows her own type, but a referred customer does not know the type of her referrer, or of her referrer's referrer and so on. Of course, by definition, a friend any customer refers is a referred customer. We assume customers do not observe the queue length of either class.

Customers make rational joining-referral decisions at the time of arrivals, knowing the existence of the referral priority program just described (e.g., customers may learn about the referral priority program through word of mouth). To decide whether to join or refer, a customer must form beliefs about the expected delay she is subject to in each of the priority classes and the probability that her friend joins (because she does not observe her friend's valuation). Upon arrival, each customer chooses a pair of actions (j, r), where $j \in \{0, 1\}$ indicates whether the customer joins ($j = 1$ for joining), and $r \in \{0, 1\}$ indicates whether the customer refers ($r = 1$ for referring). The action space is $A = \{(0, 0), (1, 0), (1, 1)\}$. A pure strategy is a mapping $\sigma(v, \chi) : [0, \bar{V}] \times \{B, R\} \mapsto A$, specifying an action given customer valuation v and customer type χ (base or referred). Let the strategy space be Σ.

Given everyone else's strategy σ, let $W_i^\chi(\sigma)$ be the induced steady-state expected delay (including time spent at service) in Class $i = 1, 2$ for customer type $\chi \in \{B, R\}$, and let $\alpha(\sigma) \in [0, 1]$ be the conversion rate induced by σ, or the probability that a referred customer joins. If everyone else plays strategy σ, a customer playing strategy $\sigma'(v, \chi) = (j', r'), \forall (v, \chi) \in [0, \bar{V}] \times \{B, R\}$ yields an expected utility:

$$U_{\sigma', \sigma}(v, \chi) = \begin{cases} 0, & (j', r') = (0, 0) \\ v - cW_2^\chi(\sigma), & (j', r') = (1, 0) \\ v - c_r - c[\alpha(\sigma)W_1^\chi(\sigma) + (1 - \alpha(\sigma))W_2^\chi(\sigma)], & (j', r') = (1, 1) \end{cases}.$$

(5.1)

If a customer does not join, her utility is normalized to zero. If a customer joins and does not refer, she joins Class 2 and expects a delay $W_2^\chi(\sigma)$, and, therefore, her expected utility is service value v less the expected waiting cost $cW_2^\chi(\sigma)$. If a customer joins and refers, with probability $\alpha(\sigma)$, her friend joins, and she advances to Class 1 that has expected delay $W_1^\chi(\sigma)$; with probability $1 - \alpha(\sigma)$, her friend does not join, and she still joins Class 2 with expected delay $W_2^\chi(\sigma)$. Hence, the expected utility for a customer who joins and refers is service value v less referral cost c_r and the expected waiting cost $c[\alpha(\sigma)W_1^\chi(\sigma) + (1 - \alpha(\sigma))W_2^\chi(\sigma)]$. Note that at the moment a customer decides to refer, she does not observe her friend's valuation, so conversion is probabilistic.

In a Bayesian Nash equilibrium, customers form beliefs over the expected delay and the response of their friends (in terms of the conversion rate). Given these beliefs, they choose actions to maximize their expected utility, and these actions result in the expected delay and conversion rate consistent with initial beliefs. A pure strategy Bayesian Nash equilibrium $\sigma \in \Sigma$ satisfies:

$$U_{\sigma,\sigma}(v, \chi) \geq U_{\sigma',\sigma}(v, \chi), \quad \forall (v, \chi) \in [0, \bar{V}] \times \{B, R\}, \sigma' \in \Sigma.$$

Given other customers' strategy, the optimal referral action for a joining customer of type χ is independent of v. Hence, customer χ joins if and only if her valuation is weakly above a certain cutoff value $v^\chi \in [0, \bar{V}]$. That is, a random base customer joins with probability $\beta \triangleq \mathbb{P}(v \geq v^B)$; a random referred customer joins with probability $\alpha \triangleq \mathbb{P}(v \geq v^R)$, which, by definition, is the conversion rate of any referral. Because customer valuation is uniformly distributed over $[0, \bar{V}]$, we have $v^B = \bar{V}(1 - \beta)$, $v^R = \bar{V}(1 - \alpha)$. Thus, an equilibrium is more conveniently characterized by a tuple $s = (\beta, \alpha, r^B, r^R)$, where $\beta, \alpha \in [0, 1]$ are just as defined, and $r^B, r^R \in \{0, 1\}$ dictate whether joining base and referred customers refer, respectively. More generally, customers could play a mixed referral strategy. This possibility can be easily accommodated by modifying the interpretation of $r^\chi \in [0, 1]$ to be the probability that customer χ refers a friend, $\chi \in \{B, R\}$. For the ease of exposition, we henceforth express expected delays W_i^χ as a function of s.

2.1 Queueing Preliminaries

By the simplifying assumption of instantaneous referral conversion, customer arrivals no longer follow a Poisson process in general but rather a compound Poisson process, otherwise known as *batch arrivals*. A batch forms at the instant of a base customer's arrival, because a sequence of referred customers would come successively until a customer stops referring or fails to refer successfully. Thus, given equilibrium conjecture s, the effective arrival rate is $\Lambda\beta$; the batch size N is a

2 Model

random variable following a modified geometric distribution:

$$\mathbb{P}(N=1) = 1-q, \quad \mathbb{P}(N=k) = q(1-p)p^{k-2}, k \geq 2, \quad \mathbb{E}[N] = \frac{1+q-p}{1-p}, \tag{5.2}$$

where $q \triangleq r^B \alpha$ is the unconditional probability that a joining base customer brings in a friend, which occurs if the base customer refers (with probability r^B) and the referral recipient joins (with probability α); and $p \triangleq r^R \alpha$ is the unconditional probability that a joining referred customer brings in a friend, which occurs if the referred customer refers (with probability r^R) and the referral recipient joins (also with probability α). The *system throughput* is thus $\Lambda\beta(1+q-p)/(1-p)$.

Notice that here, because all customers who refer successfully join Class 1, the first $N-1$ customers in the batch join Class 1, and the last customer in the batch joins Class 2. Moreover, a base customer (the first one in a batch) expects a different delay than referred customers (subsequent ones in a batch) in joining a given priority class, which is why our model stipulates that a customer's information set should include her type. Here, the implicit (yet reasonable) assumption is that customers are aware of whether they arrive organically or from referrals, but referred customers do not possess information about their own positions in the batch.

Our queueing system has a Poisson arrival rate $\lambda \triangleq \Lambda\beta$, and an arrival batch size following a modified geometric distribution as specified in (5.2); if the total batch size is N, the first $N-1$ customers in the batch join the priority class (Class 1), and the last customer joins the regular class (Class 2). System stability requires $\mu > \lambda(1+q-p)/(1-p)$. We operate under this assumption.[1] Lemma 1 gives closed-form expressions of expected delays $W_i^\chi(s), i=1,2, \chi \in \{B, R\}$.

Lemma 1 *Given equilibrium conjecture* $s = (\beta, \alpha, r^B, r^R)$, $W_i^\chi(s) = \omega_i^\chi(\Lambda\beta, r^B\alpha, r^R\alpha)$, *where*

$$\omega_1^B(\lambda, q, p) = \frac{\mu(1-p)^2 + \lambda pq}{\mu(1-p)(\mu(1-p) - \lambda q)},$$

$$\omega_1^R(\lambda, p, q) = \omega_1^B(\lambda, q, p) + \frac{1}{\mu(1-p)},$$

$$\omega_2^B(\lambda, q, p) = \frac{\mu(1-p)^2 + \lambda q}{[\mu(1-p) - \lambda q][\mu(1-p) - \lambda(1+q-p)]},$$

$$\omega_2^R(\lambda, q, p) = \omega_2^B(\lambda, q, p) + \frac{1}{\mu(1-p) - \lambda q}.$$

---

[1] In our referral-joining game, stability will always be endogenously satisfied in equilibrium due to customers' rational joining behavior.

Lemma 1 shows that referred customers expect a longer delay than base customers in a given priority class. This is because the base customer is the first in the batch. To exclude trivial cases in which referred customers will never join, we assume $\bar{V} > 2c/\mu$.

3 Equilibrium

In this section, we characterize the equilibria of the referral-joining game. First, in Sect. 3.1, we present possible forms of referral strategies that may arise in equilibrium. We then establish the existence of equilibria and some structural properties in Sect. 3.2.

3.1 Equilibrium Referral Strategies

Equipped with the expected delay expressions in Lemma 1 for a given equilibrium conjecture, we now turn to the characterization of the equilibrium. We start with customers' best response in referrals. From the utility functions in (5.1), customer χ refers (given others' strategy $s = (\beta, \alpha, r^B, r^R)$) if and only if

$$v - c_r - c[\alpha W_1^\chi(s) + (1-\alpha)W_2^\chi(s)] \geq v - cW_2^\chi(s).$$

Rewriting terms yields:

$$c_r \leq c\alpha[W_2^\chi(s) - W_1^\chi(s)]. \tag{5.3}$$

The left-hand side (LHS) of (5.3) is the cost of referring a friend, and the right-hand side (RHS) of (5.3) is the expected benefit of a referral. It shows that the referral incentive is driven by two factors: (i) the incentive to gain priority, determined by the relative difference in expected delays of two classes, and (ii) the likelihood that a friend joins. Factor (ii) highlights the distinction between the incentive to refer and the incentive to gain priority. If the conversion rate α is low, referrals may not be justified even when joining the priority class confers a substantial delay reduction. Note that condition (5.3) does not vary across customer valuation v but differs between base and referred customers.

Corollary 1 *$W_2^B(s) - W_1^B(s) \leq W_2^R(s) - W_1^R(s)$ with equality at $r^B = 0$. Therefore, in equilibrium, $r^B \leq r^R$ with equality at $r^B = r^R = 0$ or $r^B = r^R = 1$.*

Corollary 1 directly follows from Lemma 1 and suggests that given any equilibrium conjecture, referred customers expect a larger difference in expected delays of the two priority classes than base customers. Thus, from (5.3), it follows that referred customers have a greater incentive to refer. The intuition is as follows.

3 Equilibrium

From Lemma 1, referred customers would expect a longer delay in either class than base customers. Their longer delay in the regular class will be further exacerbated because more time spent there engenders more chances of being overtaken by future customers. Hence, referred customers are worse off than base customers in joining the regular class relative to the priority class. Referred customers' greater incentive to refer rules out the possibility of equilibria in which base customers refer while referred customers do not. It is also impossible that both base and referred customers play a mixed referral strategy (in which case Condition (5.3) would be an equality) because doing so would imply these two types of customers enjoy the same expected benefit of referrals (equal to c_r). Thus, we are left with four possible forms of referral strategies as follows:

(i) *Strict Non-referral Equilibrium* $(r^B, r^R) = (0, 0)$: neither base nor referred customers refer.
(ii) *All-Referral Equilibrium* $(r^B, r^R) = (1, 1)$: both base and referred customers refer.
(iii) *Weak Non-referral Equilibrium* $(r^B, r^R) = (0, \kappa)$, $\kappa \in (0, 1]$: base customers do not refer; referred customers randomize.
(iv) *Partial-Referral Equilibrium* $(r^B, r^R) = (\kappa, 1)$, $\kappa \in (0, 1)$: base customers randomize; referred customers refer.

3.2 Existence of Equilibria and Structural Results

Proposition 1 establishes structural properties of the all-referral equilibrium. We define a cutoff market size $\bar{\Lambda}$ to be used in Proposition 1 and results to follow:

$$\bar{\Lambda} \equiv \mu \frac{\bar{V}(\bar{V} - 2c/\mu)}{(\bar{V} - c/\mu)c/\mu}. \tag{5.4}$$

Proposition 1 *If and only if $\Lambda < \bar{\Lambda}$ and $c_r \in [0, c_r^l]$ (where $c_r^l > 0$ is a unique cutoff referral cost), there exists a unique all-referral equilibrium $(r^B, r^R) = (1, 1)$. Furthermore, the equilibrium joining probabilities of base and referred customers (β, α) and the system throughput are all decreasing in $c_r \in [0, c_r^l]$.*

Results in Proposition 1 are consistent with intuition. All customers refer if the referral cost is sufficiently small. Moreover, further decreasing the referral cost makes joining more attractive for both base and referred customers, and therefore, the equilibrium β and α increase, leading to a higher throughput. This equilibrium would arise under some c_r if the base market size Λ is smaller than $\bar{\Lambda}$. If Λ is too large, the expected delay in the system would be too overwhelming for referred customers to even join, and referrals would be futile due to non-conversion. Thus, the all-referral equilibrium would no longer be sustained. We note that for $c_r \in [0, c_r^l]$, although there exists a unique all-referral equilibrium, equilibria of other forms may also exist. Leveraging the structural result in Proposition 1, we formally establish the existence of equilibria in Theorem 1.

Theorem 1 *There always exists an equilibrium $(\beta, \alpha, r^B, r^R)$. Specifically, if $\Lambda \geq \underline{\Lambda}$, there exists a unique strict non-referral equilibrium $(r^B, r^R) = (0, 0)$ under any c_r; otherwise, unique c_r^l, c_r^m, c_r^h ($c_r^m < c_r^h$) can be found such that there exists:*

- *a unique strict non-referral equilibrium $(r^B, r^R) = (0, 0)$ if and only if $c_r \geq c_r^h$;*
- *a unique weak non-referral equilibrium $(r^B, r^R) = (0, \kappa)$ if and only if $c_r \in [c_r^m, c_r^h)$;*
- *a unique all-referral equilibrium $(r^B, r^R) = (1, 1)$ if and only if $c_r \in [0, c_r^l]$;*
- *a partial-referral equilibrium $(r^B, r^R) = (\kappa, 1)$ if $c_r \in (\min\{c_r^l, c_r^m\}, \max\{c_r^l, c_r^m\})$.*

Theorem 1 shows the form of the equilibrium referral strategies crucially depends on the magnitude of the referral cost c_r. Intuitively, the smaller the referral cost, the more inclined customers are to refer. This intuition largely holds, as shown by different segments of c_r corresponding to different equilibrium forms in Theorem 1, but these segments may overlap, suggesting the possibility of multiple equilibria of different forms. Except for the pair $(0, 0)$ and $(0, \kappa)$ (the two forms of non-referral equilibria), all other pairs of the four equilibrium forms can coexist. Moreover, for a given set of model primitives, there may exist multiple partial-referral equilibria, whereas any other form of equilibrium is unique. Sometimes, there may even exist multiple equilibria of three different forms.

Corollary 2 *In any equilibrium, the joining probability of referred customers is lower than that of base ones ($\alpha < \beta$).*

Corollary 2 points out that a random referred customer is less likely to join than base customers, whereas conditional on joining, referred customers are more eager to make referrals (Corollary 1). This demonstrates distinct characteristics of joining and referral incentives. Joining is driven by the *absolute* magnitude of the expected delays. The larger the delay, the less likely one would join. By contrast, referrals are driven by the *relative* difference between the expected delays in the two classes. The larger the difference, the more likely one would refer.

4 Effectiveness of the Referral Priority Program

This section studies when the referral priority program is (in)effective as a marketing tool for the firm, measured by system throughput, and as an operational choice for customers, measured by customer welfare. Specifically, we examine when customers would refer and when referrals would (dis)improve system throughput and customer welfare.

4 Effectiveness of the Referral Priority Program

4.1 Analytic Results

We first study when the referral priority program generates referrals, i.e., inducing a (partial- or all-) referral equilibrium.

Proposition 2 *There exist $\tilde{V}, \hat{V}, \tilde{\Lambda}_l, \tilde{\Lambda}_h, \hat{\Lambda}_l$ with $\tilde{\Lambda}_l < \tilde{\Lambda}_h$ such that a referral equilibrium ($r^R \geq r^B > 0$) is sustained if $\bar{V} > \tilde{V}$ and $\Lambda \in (\tilde{\Lambda}_l, \tilde{\Lambda}_h)$; only if $\bar{V} > \hat{V}$ and $\Lambda \in (\hat{\Lambda}_l, \bar{\Lambda})$ (where $\bar{\Lambda}$ is defined in Eq. (5.4)).*

Proposition 2 shows that if the customer population has a low valuation for service (the uniform distribution with a higher $\bar{V}$ stochastically dominates the one with a lower $\bar{V}$), customers do not refer regardless of the base market size. If the customer population has a high enough valuation for service, customers refer as long as the base market size Λ is intermediate. Higher service valuation is conducive to referrals because it would attract more to join, thereby increasing the conversion rate and stimulating the need for priority. As for the base market size, if it is too small, the benefit of gaining priority is incremental because there is not much congestion in the first place. Thus, customers would refrain from referrals. Following this logic, one would expect a larger base market size to be always conducive to referrals. Nevertheless, when the base market size is too large, referred customers would be overwhelmed by heavy congestion and decide not to join. Therefore, a low conversion rate under a large base market size would, again, diminish the incentive to refer.

Now, we turn to examine the equilibrium outcome when referrals are generated in a referral priority program, and compare it with the FIFO benchmark. We denote base customers' joining probability and the system throughput in a referral equilibrium by β^R and λ^R, respectively. We denote customers' joining probability and the system throughput in a FIFO non-referral benchmark equilibrium by β^F and λ^F, respectively.

Proposition 3 (Demand Cannibalization) *In any all-referral or partial-referral equilibrium, base customers join with a lower probability than they would under FIFO ($\beta^R < \beta^F$).*

Proposition 3 reveals that in the referral priority program, the demand generated from referred customers cannibalizes the demand from base customers who would otherwise join in the absence of the program. These base customers balk because their expected delay in the system is prolonged by the referral priority program. This phenomenon is somewhat intriguing considering that the referral program provides customers with an extra option, which should make joining more valuable. However, as more customers take up this option by bringing in their friends (who arrive in batch), the system becomes more congested than before, which, in turn, makes joining less attractive with this additional option. To this end, customers are "obliged" to refer not so much because they desire a shorter delay than they would get under FIFO, but rather because they simply wish to avoid the even longer delay in the regular class.

This result exposes a potential misconception about the referral priority program: it does not merely acquire more customers for free, but rather changes the mix of customers that adopt the service. On one hand, some base customers are lost (the effective arrival rate is lower). On the other hand, new customers are brought to the system (the batch size may be more than 1). These two opposing forces make it unclear how the throughput would change. Next, we derive verifiable conditions on the model primitives to address this question.

4.1.1 System Throughput

Recall that our model is fully described by parameters Λ, μ, $\bar{V}$, c, and c_r. Theorem 2 provides a necessary condition on Λ, μ, $\bar{V}$, and c under which the referral priority program could backfire for some referral cost c_r.

Theorem 2 *The referral priority program induces an equilibrium that reduces the throughput relative to FIFO ($\lambda^R < \lambda^F$) only if $\Lambda \in (\mu/(2 - c/(\mu \bar{V})), \bar{\Lambda})$ and $\bar{V} > (3 + \sqrt{3})c/(2\mu)$.*

Only when the base market size is relatively large will the downward pressure on system throughput from losing base customers potentially outweigh the upward pressure from acquiring referred customers. In other words, when the base market size is small relative to the capacity, the referral priority program may either not generate any referrals (and thus retain the FIFO throughput) or generate referrals that strictly increase the throughput relative to FIFO.

While Theorem 2 provides a necessary condition under which the referral priority program could backfire for some referral cost c_r, Theorem 3 complements Theorem 2 by providing a sufficient condition on Λ, μ, $\bar{V}$, and c under which the referral priority program backfires for some value of c_r. Of course, as customers do not refer for high values of c_r, the values of c_r for which the referral priority program backfires in Theorem 3 must be low enough. Later, in Proposition 4, we revisit this question with one particular value of c_r in mind: $c_r = 0$.

Theorem 3 *The referral priority program induces an equilibrium that reduces the throughput relative to FIFO ($\lambda^R < \lambda^F$) under some positive c_r if $\bar{V} > 5c/(2\mu)$ and $\Lambda \in (\underline{\Lambda}, \bar{\Lambda})$, where $\underline{\Lambda} = \frac{y\mu\bar{V}-c}{y(1-y)\bar{V}}$, and $y \in (c/(\mu\bar{V}), 1 - c/(\mu\bar{V}))$ uniquely solves*

$$-2\mu^2\bar{V}^2 y^3 + 7c\mu\bar{V}y^2 - y\left(5c^2 + 3c\mu\bar{V}\right) + c^3/(\mu\bar{V}) + c^2 + c\mu\bar{V} = 0.$$

Moreover, $\underline{\Lambda} \leq \mu(3\bar{V})/[2(\bar{V} + 2c/\mu)]$.

Theorem 3 indicates that when the base market size is sufficiently large ($\Lambda > \underline{\Lambda}$) but not large enough to dissuade referrals altogether ($\Lambda < \bar{\Lambda}$) (recall from Proposition 1 that $\bar{\Lambda}$ is the upper bound on the base market size to generate referrals), implementing the referral priority program is detrimental to the system throughput (for at least some positive referral cost), i.e., the downward pressure from the balking of base customers overshadows the upward pressure from the joining of referred customers. This phenomenon could occur in a partial- or all-referral equilibrium.

Here is the intuition behind why the referral priority program may backfire and reduce the system throughput. In essence, as customers refer, they arrive one after another, which renders the arrival process more *bursty*. In our model, referrals give rise to a compound Poisson arrival process, which is more bursty than the plain Poisson process without referrals. Such burstiness prolongs delay, and this effect becomes particularly significant when the base market size gets relatively large, turning away so many base customers that the gain of referred customers will no longer make up for the loss of base ones. As a matter of fact, referral-induced bursty arrivals could result in lower throughput yet longer expected delay, which, in turn, deters further joining and thus sustains lower throughput in equilibrium. This suggests that referral incentives—endogenously generated by customers' own interactions and not controlled by the firm—can defeat the very purpose of the referral priority program.

The condition in Theorem 3 reveals the referral priority program may backfire under some positive c_r. It remains unclear whether the system throughput in the referral priority program will always be higher than the FIFO throughput when customers face sufficiently small referral cost. The following result shows this is not true.

Proposition 4 *For any $\bar{V} > 3c/\mu$, there exists a sufficiently small $\epsilon > 0$ such that under $\bar{\Lambda} - \epsilon$ and $c_r = 0$, the referral priority program reduces the throughput relative to FIFO ($\lambda^R < \lambda^F$).*

Intuitively, less costly referrals would make joining more attractive, and thus lure more customers. Indeed, Proposition 1 suggests the all-referral equilibrium achieves the highest throughput when $c_r = 0$. However, Proposition 4 shows that even when referrals are hassle-free, the referral priority program may still reduce the throughput, at a large base market size. Given the referral cost may be partially influenced by the firm (e.g., providing easily accessible referral links through multiple social media channels), this result implies that the firm might partially circumvent the decline in throughput by making referrals easier, but would generally not eradicate the problem.

4.1.2 Customer Welfare

Next, we study the welfare implications of introducing the referral priority program. Denote the expected utility of a joining customer with valuation v under equilibrium $s = (\beta, \alpha, r^B, r^R)$ by

$$u^\chi(v, s) = v - r^\chi \left(c\alpha W_1^\chi(s) + c(1-\alpha) W_2^\chi(s) + c_r \right)$$
$$- \left(1 - r^\chi\right) c W_2^\chi(s), \quad \chi \in \{B, R\}.$$

We define aggregate customer welfare:

$$CW(s) = \Lambda \left\{ \int_{\bar{V}(1-\beta)}^{\bar{V}} u^B(v,s) \frac{1}{\bar{V}} dv + \frac{\beta r^B}{1-r^R\alpha} \int_{\bar{V}(1-\alpha)}^{\bar{V}} u^R(v,s) \frac{1}{\bar{V}} dv \right\}.$$

Define individual joining customer welfare:

$$ICW(s) = \frac{CW(s)}{\Lambda\beta \left[1 + \frac{r^B\alpha}{1-r^R\alpha}\right]}.$$

Proposition 5 *Customer welfare has the following properties:*

(i) *Individual joining customer welfare ICW under the referral priority program is always weakly lower than that under FIFO;*
(ii) *If the referral priority program' throughput is lower than that under FIFO, so is its aggregate customer welfare CW.*

The result in Proposition 5 is surprising in the sense that customers are presented with an additional option (refer to gain priority), yet having this option may only make them worse off. This is akin to Braess's paradox. Once referrals are generated, individual joining customer welfare is always lower than FIFO. This result is a consequence of demand cannibalization (Proposition 3) and weaker joining incentives of referred customers (Corollary 2). Demand cannibalization suggests joining is less attractive to base customers, and therefore, the expected utility of an average base customer is lower. Because referred customers have even lower joining incentives, the expected utility of an average referred customer is thus also lower than what an average customer would gain from a FIFO system. These two forces together imply lower *individual* joining customer welfare. As a result, in which direction *aggregate* customer welfare moves is unclear, depending also on whether the market expands, i.e., whether the system throughput increases. This implies that it is even more difficult for the referral priority program to improve aggregate customer welfare than to increase throughput. In particular, the sufficient conditions in Theorem 3 carry over here and are also sufficient conditions for customer welfare to deteriorate when the referral priority program is launched. Under these circumstances, the referral priority program will be a *lose-lose*: it fails both as a marketing tool for the firm and as an operational choice for customers.

In addition to the commonly acknowledged waiting externalities self-interested customers ignore when they join, in our model, they also ignore two sources of externalities when making referral decisions. The first source is a negative one because bringing friends to the queue increases system congestion. (A referring customer partially internalizes the extra waiting costs imposed on the customers she overtakes by incurring a referral cost.) The second source is a positive one because bringing in new customers who would not otherwise join the system generates value for the new customers. These two sources of externalities prevent self-interested customers from making the most collectively desirable decisions.

4 Effectiveness of the Referral Priority Program

4.2 Summary

Figure 5.2 encapsulates much of the insights from the analytical results established. Fixing parameters $c = 1$, $\mu = 1$, $c_r = 0.2$, we can partition the $(\bar{V}, \Lambda)$ space into three regions when evaluating the referral priority program's impact on throughput. In Region I, the program does not generate referrals and maintains the FIFO throughput. Region II represents a particularly pessimistic scenario: the program generates referrals but reduces the throughput relative to the FIFO system. Region III is the only region in which the referral priority program is effective: it generates referrals and increases the throughput relative to FIFO.

As shown in Fig. 5.2a, when customer population's valuation for the service is low (manifested by a small $\bar{V}$), customers do not generate referrals under any base market size. When the customer population's valuation is relatively high, customers' referral decision depends on the base market size. Customers do not refer if the base market size is either too small or too large. When the base market size is intermediate, customers generate referrals, but the resulting throughput will be higher than FIFO only when the base market size is intermediately small.

Note in Fig. 5.2a that a higher valuation by the customer population tends to expand the referral region (combining Regions II and III) and the region in which referrals increase throughput (Region III). Whereas a large base market size usually induces a low conversion rate, a high service valuation by the customer population entices customers and thus induces a high conversion rate, countervailing the congestion effect caused by a large base market size. Therefore, the referral priority program is effective in boosting the system throughput when the customer population has high valuation toward the service, and when the base market size is intermediately small.

Figure 5.2b is a zoom-in view of Fig. 5.2a and shows the impact of the referral priority program on both system throughput and customer welfare. Region II is a lose-lose: both system throughput and aggregate customer welfare are lower under the referral priority program than under FIFO. Region III-a is a win-lose: system throughput is higher but aggregate customer welfare is lower. Region III-b is a win-win: the referral priority program improves both system throughput and aggregate customer welfare relative to FIFO.

Figure 5.2 fixes referral cost c_r at 0.2. We have also conducted more numerical experiments to examine the impact of referral cost. We find that in general, with a larger referral cost, Regions II and III combined tend to shrink, suggesting that customers refer more rarely; Region III tends to shrink, suggesting that it is less often for referrals to increase system throughput; Region III-(b) tends to shrink, suggesting that customer welfare improves under stricter conditions.

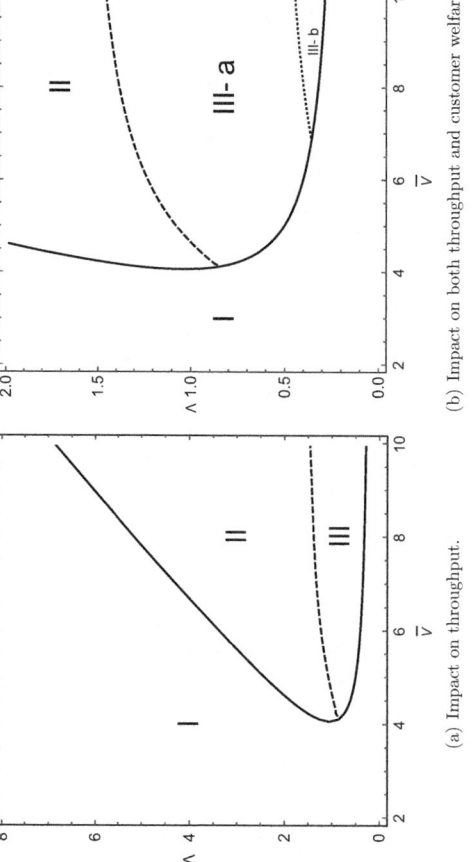

(a) Impact on throughput.   (b) Impact on both throughput and customer welfare.

Note. $c = 1$, $\mu = 1$, $c_r = 0.2$. Region I: no referrals, the same throughput and customer welfare as FIFO: Region II: referrals generated, lower throughput and lower customer welfare than FIFO; region III: referrals generated, higher throughput than FIFO: region III-a (b): customer welfare lower (higher) than FIFO. There may exist multiple equilibria, and the one with the lowest throughput is chosen to generate the plot. Numerically, we only observe multiple equilibria when Λ is small (around the boundary of Regions I and III). Other equilibrium selection criteria would not change the qualitative characteristics of the plot in general.

Fig. 5.2 The impact of the referral priority program on system throughput and customer welfare

5 Extensions

Yang and Debo (2019) study two natural extensions. One extension allows for multiple referral and, consequently, multiple priority classes. The other extension relaxes the assumption of instantaneous arrivals of referred customers by incorporating a time lag in referral conversion.

In the multi-referral extension, each customer may make at most D referrals, where D can be interpreted as the number of friends each customer has. A customer making k successful referrals receives preemptive priority over customers who make less than k successful referrals, and joins priority class k. Thus, there are at most $D + 1$ priority classes, with Class D being of the highest priority and Class 0 being of the lowest priority. In this extended model, each time a base customer joins, a batch of customers is generated according to a (modified) Galton-Watson *branching process* that starts with one root individual (the base customer). The extinction of the branching process marks the end of the batch generation. While the branching process gives rise to a more complicated batch-size distribution, the multi-referral model preserves the batch-arrival structure. Yang and Debo (2019) show that the key insights remain valid.

In the time-lag extension, there is a time lag, exponentially distributed with mean $1/\gamma$, between when a referral link is sent and when the referred customer arrives. Thus, each base arrival is followed by a (modified) geometrically distributed sequence of referred customers' arrivals, spaced out by an exponentially distributed inter-arrival time. This arrival process is in the spirit of a *Markov-modulated Poisson process* (MMPP). Like a compound Poisson process, an MMPP is a more *bursty* arrival process than Poisson process. As we explained in Sect. 4, such burstiness is at the heart of referrals and the key driver for our results. Yang and Debo (2019) demonstrate the robustness of the results to this extension through simulation.

6 Optimal Pricing, Referral Reward Program, and Comparison

In previous sections, we focused on the analysis of the referral priority program itself, assuming customers obtain free access to the wait list. In this section, we include the firm's optimal pricing decision as a monopolist to maximize the expected profit when it runs the referral priority program. Incorporating optimal pricing provides a fair basis for profit comparison between the referral priority program and the referral *reward* program (see, e.g., Biyalogorsky et al. 2001) in which the firm motivates word of mouth by offering a monetary reward for a successful referral.

In Sect. 6.1, we introduce the referral reward program and the firm's joint optimization problem of the admission price[2] and referral reward. Section 6.2 reports a numerical study that compares the two programs' profit performance; we will show the percentage change of profit in both programs relative to the FIFO (non-referral) benchmark as formulated in (5.5a)–(5.5b):

$$\max_{P \geq 0,\ \beta \in [0,1]} P \Lambda \beta \tag{5.5a}$$

$$\text{s.t.} \quad \bar{V}(1-\beta) - P - \frac{c}{\mu - \Lambda \beta} = 0, \tag{5.5b}$$

where P and $\Lambda\beta$ are the optimal monopoly price and the concomitant system throughput, respectively, in the FIFO benchmark.

Another natural benchmark for theoretical comparison is the pay-for-priority scheme,[3] in which the firm optimally sets prices P_1 and P_2 for the priority class and regular class, respectively. We establish in Proposition 6 that the pay-for-priority scheme always has the same revenue performance as the FIFO pricing scheme (because customers have identical waiting cost rate c in our model), and thus considering the FIFO benchmark suffices.

Proposition 6 *The maximum revenue in the pay-for-priority scheme is equal to that of the FIFO benchmark specified in* (5.5a)–(5.5b).

6.1 Pricing in the Referral Reward Program

The firm charges an admission price P for access to the service. Customers are served according to FIFO. In the referral reward program, no priority is credited toward referrals, but each customer who successfully brings in a friend receives a reward $\Delta \geq 0$ set by the firm. We adopt the same modeling assumption about referrals as in the referral priority program of Sect. 2 (e.g., at most one referral, the referred customer arrives immediately, etc). It is immediate that the referral reward program's expected profit is at least as high as that of the optimal FIFO benchmark (5.5a)–(5.5b) because the firm can always set $\Delta = 0$ to shut down referrals. The same cannot be said about the referral priority program, because the firm does not directly control referrals.

---

[2] In this section, we consistently assume that customers pay an admission price upon joining the queue. In practice, customers joining the wait list may not be committed to purchase, which we leave for future research.

[3] We note that in practice, the pay-for-priority scheme may arise in a very different context, and the practice of price differentiation may not be favored by startup firms whose main objective is to grow the market size.

6 Optimal Pricing, Referral Reward Program, and Comparison

Given admission price P and referral reward Δ, the equilibrium can be characterized by (β, α, κ), where, as before, β and α are the probability that a base and referred customer joins, respectively, and κ is the probability that a customer refers. Recall from the referral priority program that in general, base customers may follow a different referral strategy than referred customers. However, in the referral reward program, they would not because both types of customers are incentivized by the same reward Δ. Hence, κ applies to both types of customers. On the other hand, they would still adopt different joining strategies because their expected delays remain different. Specifically, referred customers would expect a longer expected delay than base ones (as we will see in Lemma 2). Let $W^\chi(\alpha, \beta, \kappa)$, $\chi \in \{B, R\}$ be the expected delays for base and referred customers, respectively, for a given equilibrium conjecture (β, α, κ). The resulting queueing system is a batch-arrivals queue with arrival rate $\Lambda\beta$ and batch size following a geometric distribution with mean $1/(1 - \kappa\alpha)$.

Lemma 2 *In the referral reward program, given equilibrium conjecture (β, α, κ):*

$$W^B(\alpha, \beta, \kappa) = \frac{\mu(1 - \kappa\alpha)^2 + \Lambda\beta\kappa\alpha}{\mu(1 - \kappa\alpha)[\mu(1 - \kappa\alpha) - \Lambda\beta]}, \quad W^R(\alpha, \beta, \kappa) = W^B(\alpha, \beta, \kappa)$$
$$+ \frac{1}{\mu(1 - \kappa\alpha)}.$$

6.2 Numerical Comparison

We conduct a numerical study to compare the profit performance of the two referral programs. Table 5.1 tabulates the two programs' percentage change in profit relative to the non-referral FIFO benchmark for different base market size Λ and different maximum service valuation $\bar{V}$, fixing c, μ, c_r. Table 5.1 can be partitioned into three regimes in terms of profit comparison. In Regime 1, both programs achieve the same profit equal to the non-referral FIFO benchmark (the lower-left cells, demarcated by the dashed lines). In Regime 2, the referral priority program outperforms the referral reward program (cells in the middle right, demarcated by the solid lines). In Regime 3, the referral priority program earns a lower profit than the referral reward program (upper-left and lower-right cells). We obtain the following observations from Table 5.1.

Observation 1 Customers do not refer in either program when the base market size is large and the service valuation is low (Regime 1). In both schemes, a large base market size deters referrals, whereas a high service valuation stimulates referrals.

Observation 2 When the base market size is intermediately small and the service valuation is relatively high (Regime 2), the referral priority program is favored over the referral reward program. In this regime, both referral programs generate referrals

Table 5.1 Percentage change in profit (%) of the referral priority program (first) and the referral reward program (second) relative to the non-referral FIFO benchmark

Λ	$\bar{V} = 5$	$\bar{V} = 7.5$	$\bar{V} = 10$	$\bar{V} = 12.5$	$\bar{V} = 15$	$\bar{V} = 17.5$	$\bar{V} = 20$
0.1	(0, 6.47)	(0, 26.81)	(0, 41.02)	(5.49, 51.93)	(33.38, 60.76)	(51.82, 68.16)	(64.87, 74.50)
0.3	(0, 2.25)	(0, 19.48)	(26.88, 31.57)	(40.56, 40.86)	(48.42, 48.39)	(54.76, 54.71)	(60.19, 60.12)
0.5	(0, 0.27)	(4.97, 13.41)	(23.27, 23.59)	(31.43, 31.40)	(37.8, 37.74)	(43.14, 43.05)	(47.72, 47.62)
0.7	(0, 0)	(3.60, 8.58)	(17.09, 17.09)	(23.66, 23.61)	(28.97, 28.89)	(33.43, 33.33)	(37.25, 37.13)
0.9	(0, 0)	(0.78, 4.86)	(11.97, 11.95)	(17.43, 17.36)	(21.83, 21.74)	(25.52, 25.41)	(28.69, 28.57)
1.1	(0, 0)	(0, 2.12)	(8.02, 7.99)	(12.55, 12.48)	(16.19, 16.10)	(19.23, 19.13)	(21.84, 21.73)
1.3	(0, 0)	(0, 0.61)	(5.03, 4.99)	(8.81, 8.73)	(11.82, 11.73)	(14.33, 14.23)	(16.48, 16.37)
1.5	(0, 0)	(0, 0.03)	(2.79, 2.75)	(5.97, 5.90)	(8.49, 8.40)	(10.58, 10.48)	(12.35, 12.25)
1.7	(0, 0)	(0, 0)	(1.06, 1.20)	(3.84, 3.77)	(5.97, 5.89)	(7.72, 7.63)	(9.20, 9.11)
1.9	(0, 0)	(0, 0)	(0, 0.36)	(2.24, 2.17)	(4.07, 3.99)	(5.56, 5.47)	(6.81, 6.72)
2.1	(0, 0)	(0, 0)	(0, 0.02)	(1.03, 1.04)	(2.62, 2.55)	(3.91, 3.83)	(4.99, 4.91)
2.3	(0, 0)	(0, 0)	(0, 0)	(0.12, 0.37)	(1.52, 1.45)	(2.65, 2.57)	(3.59, 3.51)
2.5	(0, 0)	(0, 0)	(0, 0)	(−0.47, 0.06)	(0.67, 0.69)	(1.68, 1.60)	(2.51, 2.44)
2.7	(0, 0)	(0, 0)	(0, 0)	(−0.29, 0)	(0.02, 0.24)	(0.92, 0.87)	(1.67, 1.60)
2.9	(0, 0)	(0, 0)	(0, 0)	(−0.13, 0)	(−0.49, 0.04)	(0.33, 0.39)	(1.00, 0.94)
3.1	(0, 0)	(0, 0)	(0, 0)	(−0.03, 0)	(−0.89, 0)	(−0.14, 0.12)	(0.47, 0.47)

$c = 1$, $\mu = 1$, $c_r = 0.2$.

and achieve a higher profit than the non-referral FIFO benchmark. However, in this case, the referral priority program is more efficient in generating referrals, because it relies on customers' incentive to gain priority and does not require monetary compensation on the part of the firm. With a higher service valuation, the referral priority program outperforms the referral reward program for a wider range of base market sizes, which is reminiscent of the shape of Region III in Fig. 5.2.

Observation 3 The referral reward program is superior to the referral priority program when the base market size is either small or intermediately large (Regime 3). When the base market size is small, the two programs would beget opposite referral outcomes: the referral reward program encourages referrals, whereas the referral priority program fails to generate referrals. Hence, the referral reward program is more profitable. On the other hand, when the base market size is intermediately large, referrals in the referral priority program reduce the system throughput relative to FIFO, keeping the price fixed (as our analysis in Sect. 4 demonstrates), and sometimes optimally adjusting the price may not fully counteract this adverse effect, as illustrated in those cells with boldfaced, negative profit changes (reminiscent of the shape of Region II in Fig. 5.2). We should note that even when the referral priority program generates referrals and improves profit over FIFO, it may still be dominated by the referral reward program. This dominance typically occurs when the base market size is small or intermediately large. In the former case, the firm must charge a low enough price to create congestion and an incentive for priority, which makes referrals less efficient. In the latter case, the firm must use the price lever to combat the adverse effect of referrals (either a lower price to improve the conversion rate or a higher price to follow a margin strategy), which again makes the referral priority program inferior to the referral reward program.

7 Optimal Scheduling in Referral Priority Programs

The referral priority program studied so far gives referring customers *full priority* in the sense that a customer with one successful referral skips over all non-referring customers. This is indeed Robinhood's approach. However, other companies run their referral programs differently. For instance, x.ai, which offers artificial-intelligence-powered email scheduling services, gives the following account of its referral program: "Hang Tight. We appreciate your patience. Want to jump the line? Share below and move on up." They specify that a customer can move up by two spots for each successful referral. In essence, x.ai's referral program is one of *partial priority*, i.e., a referring customer can overtake some of the non-referring customers but not all of them. Still, other twists exist. Some companies, such as Dropbox and Mailbox, simply run a FIFO wait list without a referral priority program, whereas Waitlisted.co, a third-party wait-list-management tool that enables customization of referral priority programs, supports a function to artificially augment the queue size, which could be a means to implement *strategic delay*.

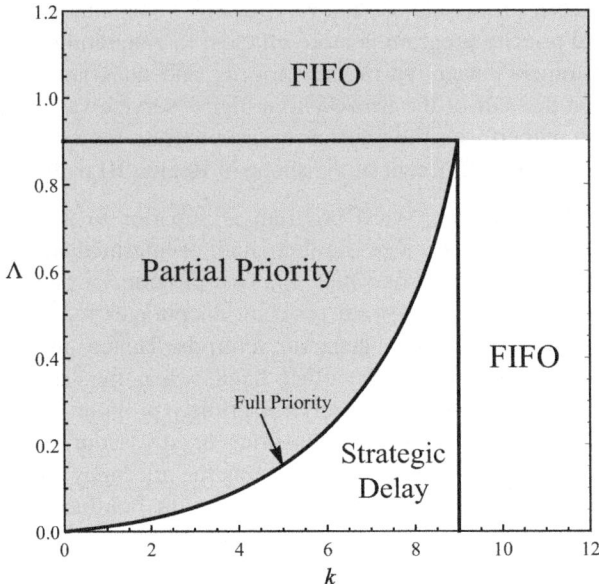

Note. $\mu = 1$, $c = 1$, $V = 10$. In the shaded (unshaded) area, the second best achieves (does not achieve) the first best.

Fig. 5.3 The structure of the optimal mechanism

The presence of all these variations begs the question of what should be the *optimal* referral priority program for customer acquisition. This is the research question tackled in Yang (2021), who takes a mechanism-design approach and identifies the optimal scheduling rule that maximizes throughput of referral priority programs. In the model of Yang (2021), the referral cost is denoted by k, and customers all have the same valuation V of the service. The structure of the optimal mechanism is summarized by Fig. 5.3.

As illustrated by Fig. 5.3, the firm should turn off any referral program and run a FIFO queue if the base market size is large or if the referral cost is large; in the former case, the first best (in which the firm ignores customers' referral incentives) is achieved, but not necessarily in the latter. If the referral cost is small and the base market size is intermediate, a partial-priority referral scheme is optimal and achieves the first best. If both the referral cost and the base market size are small, then the firm should insert strategic delay to the queue to motivate referrals, but it does not achieve the first best. At the boundary base market size that demarcates the previous two cases, a full-priority referral scheme is the most desirable. Moreover, this boundary base market size is increasing in the referral cost, suggesting that strategic delay should be more widely adopted as the optimal mechanism and partial priority less so as the referral cost increases.

Table 5.2 The comparison of different schemes in Example 1

	Throughput	r	α	W_1	W_0
FIFO	0.85	0	1	6.667	6.667
Full priority	0.763	1	0.473	2.968	12.516
Optimal (partial priority)	0.8938	0.049	1	8	10

The optimal mechanism is partial priority; it achieves the first best. The full-priority referral scheme leads to a system throughput even lower than FIFO

7.1 Numerical Illustrations

To explain the results above, we present three numerical examples that compare the optimal mechanism, the FIFO scheme, and the full-priority referral scheme. For each mechanism, we report equilibrium throughput, referral effort r, joining probability α, the expected delay for referring customers W_1, and that for non-referring customers W_0.

Example 1 $\mu = 1, c = 1, V = 10, k = 2, \Lambda = 0.85$. See Table 5.2.

In Example 1, under the optimal mechanism, customers expend only a slight referral effort ($r = 0.049$), and all arriving customers join ($\alpha = 1$), as in the FIFO case. Referrals strictly improve the system throughput over FIFO. The optimal mechanism is a partial priority scheme as customers who refer successfully enjoy a modest delay reduction relative to their non-referring counterparts ($W_1 = 8$ versus $W_0 = 10$). By contrast, the improvement in delay is more drastic in the full-priority scheme if one makes a successful referral ($W_1 = 2.968$ versus $W_0 = 12.516$). Such a sharp difference in expected delays prompts a strong referral incentive: customers in the full-priority scheme exert the maximum referral effort ($r = 1$). Nevertheless, the strong referral incentive undermines the joining incentive: only a fraction of arriving customers choose to join ($\alpha = 0.473 < 1$). This leads to an unintended consequence: the full-priority scheme in this example is not only suboptimal but even falls short of the FIFO throughput.

Yang and Debo (2019) show that a referral program which grants full priority to customers with a successful referral can backfire in the sense that launching such a program may harm the system throughput. Since Yang and Debo (2019) only compare the full-priority scheme with the non-referral FIFO case, their recommendation in this situation is simply to forsake referrals altogether. By contrast, a carefully calibrated partial-priority referral scheme—as a middle ground between FIFO and full priority—can improve the FIFO system throughput and achieve the first best, despite the undesirable performance of the full-priority referral scheme.

Example 2 $\mu = 1, c = 1, V = 10, k = 2, \Lambda = 0.7$. See Table 5.3.

However, the full priority scheme may also improve the FIFO throughput under other circumstances, as shown in Example 2. Similar to Example 1, the optimal

Table 5.3 The comparison of different schemes in Example 2

	Throughput	r	α	W_1	W_0
FIFO	0.7	0	1	3.33	3.33
Full priority	0.742	1	0.515	3.335	12.948
Optimal (partial priority)	0.871	0.196	1	8	10

The optimal mechanism is partial priority; it achieves the first best. The full-priority referral scheme leads to a system throughput higher than FIFO

Table 5.4 The comparison of different schemes in Example 3

	Throughput	r	α	W_1	W_0
First-best	0.0763	0.869	1	–	-
FIFO	0.01	0	1	1.01	1.01
Full priority	0.01	0	1	1.01	1.01
Optimal (strategic delay)	0.0748	0.866	1	8	10

The optimal mechanism is strategic delay. It does not achieve the first best but results in a higher throughput than FIFO. The full-priority scheme cannot generate referrals and thus reduces to FIFO

mechanism in Example 2 also calls for a partial-priority scheme which achieves the first best, but different from Example 1, both the (optimal) partial-priority and full-priority schemes induce a higher system throughput than FIFO in Example 2. The full-priority scheme here acquires referred customers also at the expense of some base customers (i.e., $\alpha < 1$), but the gain in referred customers outweighs the loss of base customers, so the overall throughput is still enhanced. By comparison, the optimal partial-priority scheme seizes referred customers without sacrificing base customers, and the resulting system throughput is even higher.

Example 3 $\mu = 1, c = 1, V = 10, k = 2, \Lambda = 0.01$. See Table 5.4.

In Example 3, the optimal mechanism of strategic delay exhibits a huge throughput improvement over FIFO (by a factor of 7). It still falls short of the first best, albeit only marginally in this case. By contrast, the full-priority scheme cannot stimulate referrals and results in the same equilibrium outcomes as FIFO. That the full-priority referral scheme's failure to generate referrals when the base market size is too small is a key insight of Yang and Debo (2019). However, instead of concluding referrals are out of the question, Yang (2021) shows that under those circumstances, a carefully designed referral program that involves strategic delay can still motivate referrals.

7.2 Capacity Implications

Yang (2021) also endogenizes the service capacity of the firm along with the scheduling rule. It is found that referrals prompt the firm to build more capacity, but in order to incentivize referrals, the firm in the second best may refrain from serving customers as fast as it would in the first best. Interestingly, since running the referral program motivates the firm to maintain a larger capacity, it can surprisingly shorten the average delay on the wait list even though more customers sign up and strategic delay is sometimes inserted.

8 Concluding Remarks

As an emerging business practice, the referral priority program has been quickly adopted by a growing number of technology companies that need to wait-list customers. In such a referral priority program, customers on a wait list can gain priority access if they successfully invite a friend to join the wait list. This is an appealing value proposition because the firm may attract more customers without providing any monetary reward (unlike the classical referral reward program).

Our model highlights the advantages/disadvantages of the referral priority program. When deciding whether and how to introduce the referral priority program, firms should exercise discretion and conduct careful market research to understand the underlying business environment. Moreover, we also provide prescriptive guidelines for how to optimize the referral priority program. Given the growing availability of supporting tools like Waitlisted.co and the simplicity in crediting referrals (no financial transactions involved), the referral priority program may be a favorable alternative both in profitability and implementability.

References

Biyalogorsky E, Gerstner E, Libai B (2001) Customer referral management: optimal reward programs. Mark Sci 20(1):82–95

Yang L (2021) Invite your friend and you'll move up in line: optimal design of referral priority programs. Manuf Serv Oper Manag 23(5):1139–1156

Yang L, Debo L (2019) Referral priority program: leveraging social ties via operational incentives. Manag Sci 65(5):2231–2248

Open Access This chapter is licensed under the terms of the Creative Commons Attribution 4.0 International License (http://creativecommons.org/licenses/by/4.0/), which permits use, sharing, adaptation, distribution and reproduction in any medium or format, as long as you give appropriate credit to the original author(s) and the source, provide a link to the Creative Commons license and indicate if changes were made.

The images or other third party material in this chapter are included in the chapter's Creative Commons license, unless indicated otherwise in a credit line to the material. If material is not included in the chapter's Creative Commons license and your intended use is not permitted by statutory regulation or exceeds the permitted use, you will need to obtain permission directly from the copyright holder.

Chapter 6
Distance-Based Service Priority

1 Introduction

The basic idea of the distance-based service priority policy covered in this chapter is to reduce service waiting time for customers who have to travel farther for the service by giving them higher service priority. The inspiration of the policy first occurred to us when one of us was seeking service from the Chinese Embassy in the United States. In the U.S., the Chinese Embassy is located in Washington D.C. and there are five additional Chinese Consulates-General located in New York City, Chicago, San Francisco, Los Angeles and Houston. Each of these six consulates provides service to a specific U.S. region, that is, a customer who seeks any in-person service needs to visit the consulate that holds jurisdiction over the region in which the customer resides in. For example, customers who reside in D.C., Delaware, Idaho, Kentucky, Maryland, Montana, Nebraska, North Carolina, North Dakota, South Carolina, South Dakota, Tennessee, Utah, Virginia, West Virginia and Wyoming can only seek in-person service from the Embassy in Washington D.C. To alleviate the travel hassle (driving or flying) of customers living in states far away from D.C., the Embassy has unwritten rules for those customers to receive service priorities upon their arrival over others who live closer. It helps the long-distance customers obtain service during a day trip without having to stay overnight in D.C. which would otherwise be impractical given the long wait time to obtain service at the Embassy.

We thought the policy could potentially increase the business for a congestion-prone service provider. This is because under the ordinary first-in-first-out (FIFO) service scheme also known as first-come-first-served, customers who live far away from the service location would have little or no interest in a service that requires a long wait due to their already significant travel costs. Service priority reduces the wait time to obtain the service once they arrive at the service location, thereby providing distant customers with a new incentive to seek service. Nevertheless, the policy de-prioritizes service requests of customers who live near the service location and the extra wait time could disincentivize them to continue to seek service. As a result, the system throughput can go down if additional service seekers contributed by distant customers cannot compensate for the losses caused by nearby customers. To this end, we constructed a game-theoretical queueing model in Wang et al. (2023) to study the effectiveness of the policy by carefully examining the resultant customer behavior, system throughput, and welfare.

In the model, customers live at different distances from a service location and need to decide whether to seek service. They make their decisions based on the service value, service fee, travel cost and expected wait time to obtain the service once they arrive at the service location. The most relevant prior work to the model is the work by Rajan et al. (2019) which considers travel cost and waiting cost to obtain service for patients who need to see a medical specialist. Similar to our model, customers (patients) in theirs have heterogeneous travel costs because their distances from the service (specialist) location are different, and they decide whether to seek service based on comparing costs to service value. The researchers focus on whether the specialist should offer telemedicine service in addition to in-person service, in order to accommodate patients who live far away and are not attracted to in-person service. To achieve the same goal, we explore the effectiveness of the distance-based service priority policy which gives customers who have to travel farther to the service location higher service priority. Although both the approach in Rajan et al. (2019) and our approach can improve system throughput, the advantage of our approach is that it may still be effective for services that cannot be provided remotely, e.g., dining services from restaurants or vaccination services from healthcare providers.

2 Model Preliminaries and FIFO Benchmark

We consider a service provider offering a physical service to customers living in a specific area. The service requires traveling and waiting and is modeled as an unobservable queueing system. More specifically, the travel cost of a customer is determined by the distance between the customer's residence location and the service location, and the expected wait time to obtain service is determined by the service discipline chosen by the service provider. As a benchmark, we first consider the scenario where the service provider uses the ordinary FIFO service discipline. It specifies that anyone who arrives at the service location earlier will be served before others who arrive later. Customers' service needs arise according to a Poisson process with rate Λ, that is, Λ indicates the arrival rate of potential customers to the system. A single server serves the queue, and the service time is exponentially distributed with rate μ and independent among customers. We use $\rho \equiv \Lambda/\mu$ to denote the system's potential workload.

When a service need arises, customers decide whether to seek service based on the service value, service fee, travel cost and expected wait time to obtain service

2 Model Preliminaries and FIFO Benchmark

once they arrive at the service location, and they do not renege if they decide to join the service system. We denote the service reward by V and service fee by B. We assume the distances between customers' locations and the service location form a uniform distribution with support $[0, \bar{x}]$ where $\bar{x}$ is the farthest distance where service demand arises. In other words, customers who have the service need live at heterogeneous distances from the service location. We denote customers' unit travel cost as d. Finally, we denote the expected wait time to obtain service once customers arrive at the service location (which includes the delay in the queue and service time) as W and customers' unit waiting cost as c. Based on these notations, the expected utility of seeking service for a customer with "distance" x, denoted by $U(x)$, can be expressed as

$$U(x) = V - B - d \cdot x - c \cdot W \text{ for } x \in [0, \bar{x}], \tag{6.1}$$

and we normalize the utility of customers who decide not to seek service to 0. Because whether or not customers decide to seek service determines the expected wait time to obtain service (W), which in turn determines the utility of customers who seek service ($U(x)$), an equilibrium analysis is necessary.

To simplify the notation for subsequent analysis, we use $S \equiv \mu(V-B)/c = (V-B)/(c/\mu)$ to denote the net service value (not considering travel and waiting costs), $V - B$, normalized by the expected service cost, c/μ. We will refer to S as the normalized service value in the rest of the paper. We assume $S \geq 1$ because otherwise no customers will choose to join the system even if no other person is in the system (i.e., even when $W = 1/\mu$). We also use $T \equiv \mu d\bar{x}/c = (d\bar{x})/(c/\mu)$ to denote the maximum travel cost, $d\bar{x}$, normalized by the expected service cost, c/μ. We will refer to T as the normalized travel cost in the rest of the chapter. In particular, when customers' unit travel cost increases (i.e., $d \uparrow$) or when they are distributed over longer distances (i.e., $\bar{x} \uparrow$), the normalized travel cost T will also increase.

Because customers are heterogeneous in terms of their distance to the service location, we consider an asymmetric equilibrium strategy parameterized by their distance $x \in [0, \bar{x}]$. In particular, we consider a general, mixed strategy $q(x) \in [0, 1]$ which specifies that a potential customer with distance $x \in [0, \bar{x}]$ will choose to seek service with probability $q(x)$ and not to seek service with probability $1 - q(x)$. A pure strategy of either joining or not joining (i.e., $q(x) \in \{0, 1\}$) is naturally a special case. An equilibrium, denoted by subscript e, is such that no customer can improve his or her expected utility by a unilateral change of strategy, that is, any customer cannot benefit from changing his or her probability of seeking service while all other customers stick to the equilibrium strategy.

Given an equilibrium strategy $q_e(x)$ for $x \in [0, \bar{x}]$, (i) the service provider's system throughput (or the effective arrival rate of customers to the system) is

$$\lambda_e = \Lambda \int_0^{\bar{x}} q_e(x)/\bar{x}\, dx, \tag{6.2}$$

(ii) customer welfare, denoted by CW, is the total utility of all customers given by

$$CW = \Lambda \int_0^{\bar{x}} q_e(x) U(x) / \bar{x} \, dx, \qquad (6.3)$$

and (iii) social welfare, denoted by SW, is the summation of customer welfare and service revenue, given by

$$SW = CW + B\lambda_e = \Lambda \int_0^{\bar{x}} q_e(x) [U(x) + B] / \bar{x} \, dx. \qquad (6.4)$$

2.1 FIFO Service Discipline

As a benchmark, we first consider the ordinary FIFO service discipline when all customers who choose to obtain the service will be served according to the order of arrival to the system. We use the superscript F to denote the FIFO case. The expected wait time to obtain service (W^F) is the same for all customers under FIFO, however, travel cost increases in the distance customers must travel to get to the service location. This implies that

$$U^F(x) = V - B - d \cdot x - c \cdot W^F \text{ for } x \in [0, \bar{x}], \qquad (6.5)$$

where the waiting time expression is standard (for an $M/M/1$ system). Because $U^F(x)$ is strictly decreasing in x, there exists some threshold $x^F \in [0, \bar{x}]$ such that in equilibrium potential customers will choose to join the system if and only if their distance satisfies $x < x^F$ where x^F can be uniquely determined by

$$x^F = \max\{x \mid U^F(x) \geq 0, x \in [0, \bar{x}]\}. \qquad (6.6)$$

This implies the (unique) equilibrium strategy is a pure strategy, which can be characterized as

$$q_e^F(x) = \begin{cases} 1 \text{ if } x \in [0, x^F]; \\ 0 \text{ if } x \in (x^F, \bar{x}]. \end{cases}$$

We can derive the system throughput, customer welfare and social welfare under the FIFO service discipline based on (6.2)–(6.4) accordingly.

3 Distance-Based Service Priority Policy

We now study customer behavior under the distance-based service priority policy which will be simply referred to as the "priority policy" when there is no ambiguity and denoted by the superscript P for the remainder of the chapter. Under such a policy, a customer who arrives at the system with distance x will receive (preemptive) service priority over any customers in the system with a distance $x' < x$.[1] That is, the priority of customers increases with the distance they must travel to get to the service location. It is worth noting that there is a continuum of priority levels because the distances between the customers' locations and the service provider's location are continuously distributed. We assume that the service provider can verify customers' distance information. This can be done at the facility check-in where customers present their IDs.

We define the distance of the farthest potential customer who decides to seek service under an equilibrium strategy as $\tilde{x}$. Based on (6.1), we must have $\tilde{x} = \max\{x | V - B - d \cdot x - c/\mu \geq 0, x \in [0, \bar{x}]\}$ because this customer will receive service priority over any other customers who have decided to seek service and his or her expected waiting time to obtain service is simply the expected service time $1/\mu$. It can be derived that

$$\tilde{x} = \min\{\bar{x}(S-1)/T, \bar{x}\} \tag{6.7}$$

and any customers with distance $x > \tilde{x}$ will not join the service system under the equilibrium.

When a strategy $q(x)$ is adopted by all customers with distance $x < \tilde{x}$, the expected utility for a customer with a particular distance x ($x \leq \tilde{x}$) is given by

$$U^P(x) = V - B - d \cdot x - c \cdot W^P(x) \tag{6.8}$$

where $W^P(x)$ is the expected wait time to obtain service upon arrival and can be derived as

$$W^P(x) = \mu^{-1}\left[1 - \rho\left(\int_x^{\tilde{x}} q(t)dt\right)/\bar{x}\right]^{-2}, \tag{6.9}$$

where the customer with distance x will not be affected by customers with a distance smaller than x because of service priority, and the fraction of customers who own priority over this customer is $\left(\int_x^{\tilde{x}} q(t)dt\right)/\bar{x}$, see, e.g., Eqn (9) in Haviv and Oz (2018). We derive customers' equilibrium strategy for the distance-based service priority policy in the following propositions.

---

[1] All of our main insights continue to hold under the non-preemptive priority rule.

Proposition 1 *When $T \leq S - 1$, we have $\tilde{x} = \bar{x}$ and customers' equilibrium strategy under the priority policy is characterized by $q_e^P(x) = \frac{T}{2\rho}(S - Tx/\bar{x})^{-\frac{3}{2}}$ for $x \in [0, \max\{\hat{x}, 0\})$ and by $q_e^P(x) = 1$ for $x \in [\max\{\hat{x}, 0\}, \bar{x}]$, where $\hat{x} \in [\bar{x} - \bar{x}/\rho, \bar{x}]$ uniquely solves $S = T\hat{x}/\bar{x} + [1 - \rho + \rho\hat{x}/\bar{x}]^{-2}$.*

Proposition 2 *When $T > S - 1$, we have $\tilde{x} = (S - 1)\bar{x}/T < \bar{x}$ and customers' equilibrium strategy under the priority policy is given as follows.*

(1) *If $T \in (0, 2\rho]$, we have $q_e^P(x) = \frac{T}{2\rho}(S - Tx/\bar{x})^{-\frac{3}{2}}$ for $x \in [0, \tilde{x}]$ and $q_e^P(x) = 0$ for $x \in (\tilde{x}, \bar{x}]$.*
(2) *If $T \in (2\rho, (\sqrt{S} + S)\rho]$, we have $q_e^P(x) = \frac{T}{2\rho}(S - Tx/\bar{x})^{-\frac{3}{2}}$ for $x \in [0, \check{x}]$, $q_e^P(x) = 1$ for $x \in [\check{x}, \tilde{x}]$ and $q_e^P(x) = 0$ for $x \in (\tilde{x}, \bar{x}]$, where $\check{x} = [2(S - T/\rho) - 1 + \sqrt{4T/\rho + 1}]\bar{x}/(2T)$.*
(3) *If $T \in (\rho(\sqrt{S} + S), \infty)$, we have $q_e^P(x) = 1$ for $x \in [0, \tilde{x}]$ and $q_e^P(x) = 0$ for $x \in (\tilde{x}, \bar{x}]$.*

Propositions 1–2 fully characterize customers' equilibrium strategies under the priority policy for the entire parameter space. Note that for given system parameters $(\Lambda, \mu, V, B, c, d, \bar{x})$, customers' equilibrium strategy is unique. We illustrate the four cases described in Proposition 1 and Proposition 2/(1),(2),(3) in Fig. 6.1a–d, respectively. In particular, the solid lines in Fig. 6.1 represent customers' equilibrium strategies under the priority policy while the dash lines correspond to customers' equilibrium strategies under the FIFO service discipline as a benchmark.

Some interesting observations emerge from Fig. 6.1. First, while under the FIFO service discipline customers' equilibrium strategy in terms of the probability of seeking service is always monotone decreasing in their distance to the service location, it is no longer the case under the priority policy. Under the priority policy, customers' equilibrium strategy in terms of the probability of seeking service can be monotone increasing (Fig. 6.1a), monotone decreasing (Fig. 6.1d) or even non-monotonic (Fig. 6.1b–c). This is because customers' hassle cost to obtain service is no longer monotone increasing with distance like in the FIFO case. In particular, customers' hassle cost consists of travel cost to get to the service location and expected wait time/cost to obtain service once they arrive. Under the priority policy, although the travel cost continues to increase in customers' distance from the service location, the expected wait time/cost to obtain service is decreasing. As a result, customers who live at a medium distance from the service location may end up with the highest motivation to seek service as they can avoid paying high waiting costs incurred by the short-distance customers and avoid paying high travel costs incurred by the long-distance customers (see, e.g., Fig. 6.1c). This leads to the non-monotonic equilibrium strategy among customers under the priority policy where the probability of seeking service first increases and then decreases in customers' distance from the service location. The cases of monotone increase and monotone decrease can be regarded as special cases of the general first-increase-then-decrease structure and will be discussed in greater detail below.

3 Distance-Based Service Priority Policy

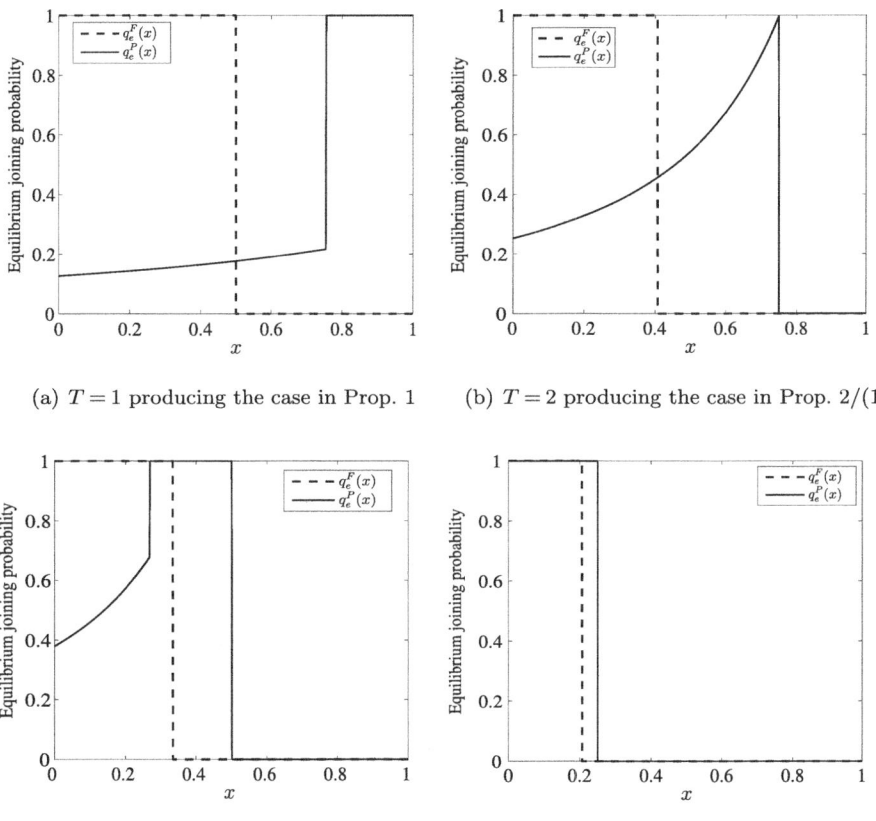

Fig. 6.1 Illustration of equilibrium strategies under the FIFO and distance-based service priority policies. (Note that $S = 2.5$ and $\rho = \mu = c = \bar{x} = 1$ for all panels while the value of T varies)

We observe from Fig. 6.1 (by comparing the solid lines on the four subfigures) that as T increases progressively from 1 to 2, then to 3, and then to 6, fewer and fewer long-distance customers choose to seek service in equilibrium under the priority policy. In other words, a greater value of the normalized travel cost discourages long-distance customers from seeking service compared to a smaller value under the priority policy. Recall that an increase in the normalized travel cost can be the result of an increased unit travel cost (d) or a longer distance over which the customers are distributed ($\bar{x}$). Nevertheless, either change will reduce the priority policy's effectiveness in attracting long-distance customers to join the service system because an increased travel cost ($d \uparrow$ and/or $\bar{x} \uparrow$) makes the waiting-cost savings for long-distance customers due to distance-based service priorities less significant relative to travel costs.

4 Comparison between Priority and FIFO Policies

To compare the (distance-based service) priority policy to the FIFO benchmark, we assume that system parameters (i.e., Λ, μ, V, B, c, d, $\bar{x}$) are the same under the two. We first compare the equilibrium system throughput in the following result.

Proposition 3 *Comparing λ_e^P and λ_e^F, we have the following.*

(1) *If $T \leq S - \sqrt{S}$, then $\lambda_e^P = \lambda_e^F = \Lambda$ for $\rho \leq \bar{\rho}_P$ and $\lambda_e^P < \lambda_e^F$ for $\rho > \bar{\rho}_P$.*
(2) *If $S - \sqrt{S} < T \leq S - 1$, then $\lambda_e^P = \lambda_e^F = \Lambda$ for $\rho \leq \bar{\rho}_F$, $\lambda_e^P > \lambda_e^F$ for $\bar{\rho}_F < \rho < T/S$, and $\lambda_e^P < \lambda_e^F$ for $\rho > T/S$.*
(3) *If $T > S - 1$, then $\lambda_e^P > \lambda_e^F$ for $\rho < T/S$, and $\lambda_e^P < \lambda_e^F$ for $\rho > T/S$.*

Proposition 3 provides a full comparison between λ_e^P and λ_e^F. On the one hand, when the system load is sufficiently low and the normalized travel cost is small, both the FIFO and the priority policies achieve full market coverage (i.e., $\lambda_e^P = \lambda_e^F = \Lambda$), see Proposition 3/(1). This is because the travel and service waiting costs are both low for all customers who will enjoy joining the service under either policy. On the other hand, when the system load is sufficiently high, the FIFO policy induces a strictly higher system throughput than the priority policy, see Proposition 3/(2)–(3)—recall we commented earlier that customers are more reluctant to join the service under the priority policy with an increase in the system workload. Therefore, the priority mechanism is efficient in improving the system throughput compared to the FIFO policy only when the system load is intermediate and the travel cost is large. We show in the following result that for a given system load, the priority policy results in higher system throughput than the FIFO policy as long as the travel cost is sufficiently large.

Corollary 1 *For any given ρ, we have that $\lambda_e^P \geq \lambda_e^F$ if $T > \max\{\rho S, S - \sqrt{S}\}$.*

Corollary 1 reveals that the priority policy can improve the system throughput compared to the FIFO scheme, especially when the (normalized) travel cost is sufficiently large. Recall from the discussion after Propositions 1–2 that when the normalized travel cost is small, the priority policy gives long-distance customers significant incentives to join the system. However, this is at the cost of losing medium- and short-distance customers (see, e.g., Fig. 6.1a) because these customers would be overtaken by long-distance customers while waiting to obtain service and thereby have reduced incentives to seek service under the priority policy. Overall, the extra throughput brought by long-distance customers under the priority policy cannot compensate for the loss of throughput caused by medium and short-distance customers, making the total throughput less than that of the FIFO benchmark.

In contrast, when the normalized travel cost is sufficiently large, the priority policy (or the FIFO policy) does not offer long-distance customers enough incentives to join the system. However, customers who live at a medium distance from the service location and who would not join the system under the FIFO scheme will now have incentives to join under the priority policy because they are given service priorities (over the short-distance customers) which reduces their expected wait time to obtain service. This may discourage a portion of the short-distance customers who would join the system under the FIFO scheme from seeking service under the priority policy. However, the rest of the short-distance customers, if not all of them, can be retained under the priority policy because their travel costs are low enough to tolerate the increase in the service waiting time. Overall, the extra throughput brought by medium-distance customers under the priority policy exceeds the loss of throughput caused by short-distance customers, making the total throughput exceed that of the FIFO scheme (see, e.g., Fig. 6.1c–d).

As mentioned earlier, increasing system throughput is critical for service providers. As such, we quantify the potential of the priority policy to increase the system throughput in the next result. We define the throughput improvement (of the priority policy over the FIFO policy) as $TI(T, S) = (\lambda_e^P - \lambda_e^F)/\lambda_e^F$.

Proposition 4 *The service throughput/coverage can be increased by up to 50% by the priority policy.*

Proposition 4 suggests that by simply adapting to the priority policy, service providers can increase system throughput by as much as half, which makes the priority policy very enticing. We supplement the result in Proposition 4 using a contour plot (Fig. 6.2) to show how the throughput improvement varies for different normalized travel cost T and service value S (note that $S > 1$ due to our model assumption in Sect. 2). In Fig. 6.2, each curve in the contour plot joins points of equal value of the throughput improvement $TI(T, S)$.

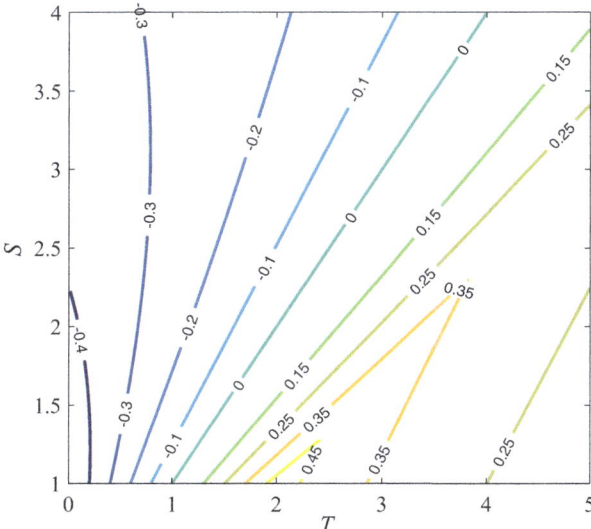

Fig. 6.2 Contour plot of throughput improvement, $TI(T, S)$. Note. $\Lambda = \mu = c = B = \bar{x} = 1$ while T and S vary ($S > 1$ by model assumption in Sect. 2)

We observe from Fig. 6.2 that first, the priority policy increases system throughput compared to the FIFO benchmark if and only if the normalized travel cost T is large (as predicted by Corollary 1). Second, the priority policy is most effective in increasing system throughput when the normalized service value S is small and the normalized travel cost T is about twice as large (e.g., when S is close to 1 and T is close to 2). This is because when the service value is relatively low, the service would not attract any customers who live more than a mere short distance away under the FIFO service discipline, making the priority policy more effective in increasing throughput because of its ability to attract medium- and long-distance customers. Given a value of S, an intermediate T value achieves the largest percentage of throughput improvement under the priority policy over the FIFO policy which corresponds to the right incentive level that attracts the most medium- and short-distance customers to join the system. In contrast, when the value of T is too small, only long-distance customers join the system and throughput cannot be improved by the priority policy compared to the FIFO policy, as explained after Corollary 1. When the value of T is too large, no long-distance and too few medium-distance customers are attracted to the service, again diminishing the effectiveness of the priority policy in terms of improving throughput (also see the graphical illustrations in Fig. 6.1c–d).

The direct consequence of an increase in system throughput when customers' travel costs are sufficiently large, is higher server utilization and longer average wait time to obtain service. In particular, the wait time for short-distance customers will notably increase because they are de-prioritized for service requests under the (distance-based service) priority policy. To this end, we next compare welfare of the priority policy to that of the FIFO policy when T is sufficiently large.

Proposition 5 *For any given S, there exists $\hat{T}$ such that $SW^P > SW^F$ and $CW^P < CW^F$ if $T > \hat{T}$.*

Proposition 5 shows that when the normalized travel cost is sufficiently large (i.e., when $T > \hat{T}$), the priority policy not only increases the throughput of the system (Corollary 1) but also achieves higher overall social welfare which is the sum of customer welfare and service revenue. However, the increase in social welfare is driven by the higher service revenue (i.e., $B\lambda_e^P > B\lambda_e^F$) because customer welfare is reduced (i.e., $CW^P < CW^F$). It can be shown that $\hat{T} \to \infty$ when $B \downarrow 0$. Therefore, when the underlying service provided is free for the customers (i.e., $B = 0$), social welfare which is the same as customer welfare will be reduced under the priority policy compared to the FIFO policy (i.e., $SW^P = CW^P < CW^F = SW^F$ when $B = 0$).

Moreover, Proposition 5, together with Corollary 1, shows that when the normalized travel cost is sufficiently large (i.e., when $T > \hat{T}$), the average customer utility of those who join the system is smaller under the priority policy compared to the FIFO policy (i.e., $CW^P/\lambda_e^P < CW^F/\lambda_e^F$ because $CW^P < CW^F$ by Proposition 5 and $\lambda_e^P > \lambda_e^F$ by Corollary 1). In Fig. 6.3, we illustrate equilibrium customer utility under the FIFO and priority policies when $T > \hat{T}$. It is clear from the figure that the

4 Comparison between Priority and FIFO Policies

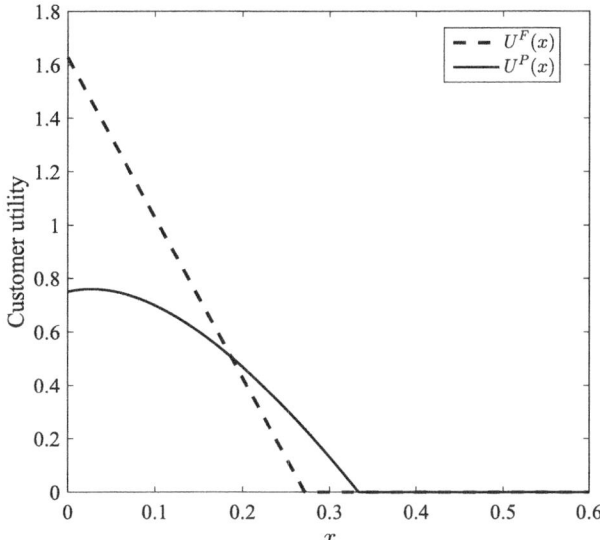

Fig. 6.3 Illustration of customer utility under the FIFO and priority policies when $T > \hat{T}$

Note. $\Lambda = \mu = B = c = \bar{x} = 1$, $T = 6$, $S = 3$ and $\hat{T} = 5.53$.

priority policy is making the utility of short-distance customers lower while that of some customers with a longer distance higher. Thus, short-distance customers are asked to subsidize others under the priority policy by giving up their FIFO service rights. Essentially, hassle cost for customers who seek service includes travel cost and service waiting cost, and the priority policy tries to balance it among customers who will join the system—the nearby (resp., distant) customers incur less (resp., more) travel cost and the priority policy assigns them more (resp., less) service wait. As a result, the priority policy makes total utility more evenly distributed among customers, compared to the FIFO policy, generating more beneficiaries and resulting in higher system throughput. However, the per-capita utility among all customers who end up joining the system is reduced.

The discussion above demonstrates that while the service provider can improve system throughput and service revenue and the society can increase social welfare by adapting to the priority policy when customers' travel costs are sufficiently large, customers overall or on average can suffer. In other words, the social welfare is improved at the expense of customer welfare. In what follows, we propose a possible remedy to coordinate service revenue and customer welfare under the priority policy when the normalized travel cost is sufficiently large (i.e., when $T > \hat{T}$). The idea is to have the service provider give back some revenue to the customers under the priority policy so that both the service revenue and customer welfare can be improved compared to the FIFO benchmark. When the service is free of charge (i.e., $B = 0$), the service provider does not collect any revenue. Therefore, we focus on the case when $B > 0$ and propose a distance-based service rebate $R(x)$ for customers who decide to join the system. That is, a customer with distance x will pay an effective service price of $B - R(x)$ if he or she decides to obtain the service. We denote the corresponding equilibrium system throughput, service revenue, social welfare and customer welfare with the rebate scheme (still under the priority policy) as $\hat{\lambda}_e^P, \hat{\Pi}^P, \hat{SW}^P$ and $\hat{CW}^P$, respectively, where $\hat{SW}^P = \hat{\Pi}^P + \hat{CW}^P$.

Proposition 6 *Consider $B > 0$. Let $R(x) = \alpha[V - B - xd - \frac{c}{\mu[1-\rho(\tilde{x}-x)/\tilde{x}]^2}]$ for $x \in [0, \tilde{x}]$ where*

$$\alpha \in \left(\frac{T(T/\rho - S + 1)\left(T/\rho + S - \sqrt{(T/\rho - S)^2 + 4T/\rho}\right)}{(S-1)(T - (S+1)\rho)\left(\sqrt{(T/\rho - S)^2 + 4T/\rho} + T/\rho + S\right)} - 1, \right.$$

$$\left. \frac{\mu B(T/\rho - S + 1)\left(\sqrt{(T/\rho - S)^2 + 4T/\rho} + S - T/\rho - 2\right)}{c(S-1)^2(T/\rho - S - 1)} \right).$$

Then in equilibrium $\hat{\lambda}_e^P > \lambda_e^P$, $\hat{\Pi}^P > \Pi^F$, $\hat{SW}^P > SW^F$ and $\hat{CW}^P > CW^F$ for $T > \hat{T}$.

Proposition 6 shows that the proposed rebate scheme in the proposition can enable the priority policy to achieve a win-win-win situation between the service provider, society and customers when when the normalized travel cost is sufficiently large (i.e., when $T > \hat{T}$). We now detail the results by providing more information. First, by performing extensive numerical experiments we can confirm that the rebate $R(x)$ is always smaller than the service fee B, although this remains analytically challenging to prove. Second, for any given α, it can be shown that $R(x)$ decreases in x, that is, the rebate is less for customers with longer distance who are already compensated by higher service priority under the priority policy.

Furthermore, the $R(x)$ in Proposition 6 is structured such that it does not change any customers' decision as to whether to seek service under the priority policy when $T > \hat{T}$. Consequently, the equilibrium with or without the proposed rebate scheme stays the same. Social welfare under the priority policy with or without the proposed rebate scheme also stays the same (i.e., $SW^P = \hat{SW}^P$) because the rebate can be simply regarded as a transfer price between the service provider and customers, which has no impact on the total social welfare. It is worth noting that there can be (possibly many) other distance-based price-adjustment mechanisms that will also enable the priority policy to achieve a win-win-win situation between the service provider, society and customers when $T > \hat{T}$. However, the one outlined in Proposition 6 retains the same equilibrium and social welfare compared to the original no-adjustment case.

Because social welfare (or total customer welfare and service revenue) under the priority policy is higher than that under the FIFO policy when $T > \hat{T}$ (Proposition 5), we can use $R(x)$ to allocate welfare between the service provider and customers (by redistributing the service provider's revenue to the customers) so that the resultant customer welfare and service revenue under the priority policy are both higher than those under the FIFO policy. This is essentially guaranteed by the specified range of α given in Proposition 6: When α is at the lower limit of the

4 Comparison between Priority and FIFO Policies

specified range, the service provider will give the smallest rebate to the customers so that the customer welfare under the priority policy (with the rebate) is equivalent to that under the FIFO policy. In contrast, when α is at the higher limit of the specified range, the service provider will give back the largest rebate to the customers so that the service revenue under the priority policy (with the rebate) is equivalent to that under the FIFO policy. Finally, when α falls in the middle of the specified range, both customer welfare and service revenue will end up being strictly higher under the priority policy (with the rebate) than their counterparts under the FIFO policy. Increasing α would redistribute more of the service provider's payoffs to the customers, leading to lower service revenue but higher customer welfare.

Finally, in Fig. 6.4, we illustrate customer utility before and after the rebate, and compare it to the FIFO benchmark. It is clear that the rebate increases customers' utility. For the parameters used in the example in Fig. 6.4, it can be computed that the total social welfare under the priority policy and the FIFO policy satisfy $SW^P = S\hat{W}^P = 0.5 > 0.492 = SW^F$ (an increase of 1.63%). Moreover, it can be computed that $\Pi^P = 0.333 > \Pi^F = 0.271$ but $CW^P = 0.167 < CW^F = 0.221$, so the priority policy without the rebate would increase system throughput (or service revenue) and social welfare at the expense of customer welfare, compared to the FIFO policy. However, $\hat{\Pi}^P = 0.274 > \Pi^F = 0.271$ (an increase of 1.11%) and $C\hat{W}^P = 0.226 > CW^F = 0.221$ (an increase of 2.26%) with the rebate, implying that the rebate scheme can properly coordinate service revenue and customer welfare to make the priority policy desirable for all stakeholders including the service provider, customers, and society as a whole.

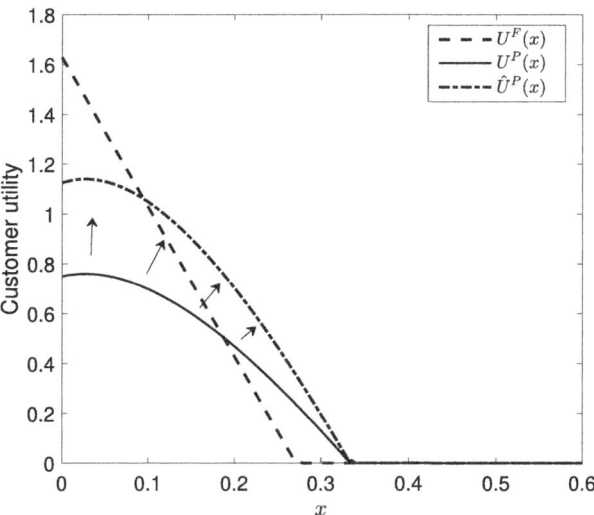

Note. $\Lambda = \mu = B = c = \bar{x} = 1$, $T = 6$, $S = 3$ and $\hat{T} = 5.53$.

Fig. 6.4 The effect of rebate on customer utility when $\alpha = 0.35$

5 Two-Dimensional Service Area

In the model above, we assumed that distances between potential customers and the service location were distributed uniformly on the support of $[0, \bar{x}]$, i.e., the probability density function for a potential service request to come from a customer with distance $x \in [0, \bar{x}]$ is $1/\bar{x}$. Implicitly, we were assuming in the main model that customers live uniformly in a linear city with the service provider located at one end of the city.

We now extend the earlier model by considering a two-dimensional circular service area where potential customers are distributed uniformly. We assume the farthest potential customers live at a distance $\bar{x}$ away from the service provider. Because all points in a plane that are equidistant from the service location form a circle, the probability density function for a potential service request to come from a customer with distance $x \in [0, \bar{x}]$ is $2\pi x/\pi \bar{x}^2 = 2x/\bar{x}^2$ (circumference of the circle with radius x divided by the area of the circle with radius $\bar{x}$). It is clear that the distances between potential customers and the service location are no longer uniformly distributed over $[0, \bar{x}]$. Rather, more customers are located at a larger distance from the service provider than at any smaller distance because there are more customers located on an outer circle than on an inner circle.

We assume all other model assumptions remain the same as before. Then, under the FIFO policy, there continues to exist a threshold distance $x_2^F \in [0, \bar{x}]$ such that in equilibrium potential customers will choose to join the system if and only if their distance satisfies $x < x^F$. This implies that the utility for a customer with distance x to seek service is

$$U_2^F(x) = V - B - d \cdot x - c \cdot W_2^F \text{ for } x \in [0, \bar{x}] \text{ where } W_2^F = [\mu - (x_2^F)^2 \Lambda/\bar{x}^2]^{-1} \quad (6.10)$$

because the proportion of customers who decide to join is $\pi(x_2^F)^2/[\pi \bar{x}^2] = (x_2^F)^2/\bar{x}^2$, and thus the effective arrival rate is $(x_2^F)^2 \Lambda/\bar{x}^2$. It follows that x_2^F can be uniquely determined by

$$x_2^F = \max\{x | U_2^F(x) \geq 0, x \in [0, 1]\}. \quad (6.11)$$

Based on (6.10) and (6.11), we can derive that $x_2^F = \min\{\tilde{x}_2^F, \bar{x}\}$, where $\tilde{x}_2^F$ uniquely solves $U_2^F(\tilde{x}_2^F) = 0$.

For the priority policy, we continue to use $\tilde{x}$ to denote the distance of the farthest potential customer who decides to seek service under an equilibrium strategy. We have $\tilde{x} = \max\{x | V - B - d \cdot x - c/\mu \geq 0, x \in [0, \bar{x}]\}$ as in the main model, and it follows that $\tilde{x} = \min\{\bar{x}(S-1)/T, \bar{x}\}$. When a mixed strategy $q(x)$ is adopted by all customers with distance $x < \tilde{x}$, the proportion of customers who own priority over a tagged customer with distance x is $\pi \left(\int_x^{\tilde{x}} q(t) dt^2\right)/[\pi \bar{x}^2] = \left(\int_x^{\tilde{x}} q(t) dt^2\right)/\bar{x}^2$. It follows that the expected utility for a customer with a particular distance x ($x \leq \tilde{x}$)

6 Optimal Service Fee B

to seek service can be derived as

$$U_2^P(x) = V - B - d \cdot x - c \cdot W_2^P(x) \text{ where } W^P(x)$$

$$= \mu^{-1}\left[1 - \rho\left(\int_x^{\tilde{x}} q(t)dt^2\right)/\bar{x}^2\right]^{-2} \quad (6.12)$$

based on (6.9). With the utility function shown in (6.12), it is analytically intractable to fully characterize customers' equilibrium strategy under the priority policy for the entire parameter space. However, we can analytically compare the FIFO and priority policies when the normalized travel cost T is sufficiently large, in the following Proposition 7.

Proposition 7 *Assuming customers are distributed uniformly over a two-dimensional circular service area, there exists $\bar{T}$ such that $\lambda_e^P > \lambda_e^F$, $\Pi^P > \Pi^F$, $CW^P > CW^F$ and $SW^P > SW^F$ if $T > \bar{T}$.*

Proposition 7 shows that when the service area is two-dimensional rather than one-dimensional which was assumed in the main model, the priority policy continues to improve system throughput, service revenue, and social welfare compared to the FIFO policy when the normalized travel cost is sufficiently large. However, unlike the main model, where customer welfare was lower under the priority policy than under the FIFO policy, even customer welfare is improved under the priority policy. This is because the priority policy reduces the utility of customers with shorter distances and improves that of customers with longer distances. With the two-dimensional service area under consideration, there are now significantly more customers who are farther away from the service provider, and the priority policy can improve the utility of these customers at the cost of reducing the utility of a smaller number of customers, thereby increasing overall customer welfare. This result further demonstrates the potential of the priority policy, which can lead to a win-win-win solution on its own between the service provider, customers, and society as a whole, especially when customers' travel costs are significant.

6 Optimal Service Fee B

Thus far, when we compare the FIFO and priority policies, we assume that the service fee B is exogenously given. However, service providers can charge different service fees under the FIFO and priority policies. This may be especially true for for-profit service providers whose goal is to maximize revenue. In this section, we consider the situation by assuming that the service provider will charge optimal service fees, denoted by B^F and B^P, under the FIFO and priority policies, respectively, such that $B^F = \arg\max_{B \geq 0} B\lambda_e^F(B)$ and $B^P = \arg\max_{B \geq 0} B\lambda_e^P(B)$. We assume $\rho \geq 1$ to focus on the nontrivial case where not all potential customers can be served, namely, an overloaded system. All other model assumptions remain the same as the main model in Sects. 2–4. The following two lemmas characterize B^F and B^P, and show that they are unique for any given system parameters $(\Lambda, \mu, V, c, d, \bar{x})$.

Lemma 1 *The optimal fee of the service provider under the FIFO policy, B^F, is the unique solution of B that solves*

$$T/\rho + S - B\left(1 + \frac{T/\rho - S}{\sqrt{4T/\rho + (T/\rho - S)^2}}\right)\mu/c - \sqrt{4T/\rho + (T/\rho - S)^2} = 0.$$

where $S = \mu(V - B)/c$ as before.

Lemma 2 *The optimal fee of the service provider under the priority policy, B^P, is given by*

$$B^P = \begin{cases} \hat{B}, & \text{if } T < T_1; \\ \frac{c\sqrt{1+4T/\rho}+2V\mu-c-2cT/\rho}{2\mu}, & \text{if } T_1 \leq T < T_2, \\ \frac{V\mu-c}{2\mu}, & \text{if } T \geq T_2, \end{cases}$$

where $\hat{B} \in (0, V)$ is the unique solution of B that solves $2S\left(\sqrt{S} - 1\right) - B\mu/c = 0$, T_1 is the unique solution of T which solves $\frac{c\sqrt{1+4T/\rho}+2V\mu-c-2cT/\rho}{2\mu} = \hat{B}$, and $T_2 = \frac{\rho[1+V\mu/c-\sqrt{2(1+V\mu/c)}]}{2}$.

What is clear from the above results is that while B^F is continuous in the normalized travel cost T, B^P is a piecewise function of it. This is because the system throughput is continuous in T under the FIFO policy but piecewise in T under the priority policy. Based on these results, we can derive the following comparison results on system throughput, service revenue, and social welfare in equilibrium between the FIFO and priority policies.

Proposition 8 *When service fees are set optimally by the service provider, there exists $\bar{\bar{T}}$ such that $\lambda_e^P > \lambda_e^F$, $B^P \lambda_e^P(B^P) > B^F \lambda_e^F(B^F)$ and $SW^P > SW^F$ if $T > \bar{\bar{T}}$.*

Proposition 8 indicates that when the normalized travel cost is sufficiently large, the priority policy improves system throughput, service revenue and social welfare compared to the FIFO policy. In addition, we have verified through extensive numerical experiments that when T is sufficiently large, customer welfare is lower under the priority policy than under the FIFO policy. In other words, the results shown in Propositions 1 and 5 from the main model are robust even when the service provider sets optimal service fees instead of having fixed service fees.

7 Comparison to Price Discrimination Strategy

The priority policy we propose here awards residents who live farther away from the service provider with a higher service priority, but all customers are charged the same service price. In this section, we compare the priority policy to the traditional price discrimination strategy (PDS) from the revenue management literature where for our context customers traveling different distances are charged different service prices but no one receives service priority over others.

We assume the service price decreases with the distance that customers must travel, in order to provide customers who live farther away with more incentive to seek service. In particular, we assume the service price $P(x) \geq 0$ is given by $\bar{P} - \delta \cdot x$ where $\bar{P}$ is the intercept and δ is the slope. In the rest of this section, we use the superscript D to denote the price discrimination strategy. The expected utility of a customer with distance x is therefore given by

$$U^D(x) = V - P(x) - d \cdot x - c \cdot W^F \text{ for } x \in [0, \bar{x}] \text{ with } W^F = (\mu - x^F \Lambda/\bar{x})^{-1},$$

where the waiting time expression is standard for a FIFO $M/M/1$ system. We focus on the case $\delta \leq d$ to ensure that $U^D(x)$ decreases in x (otherwise the customers will join if and only if their distance is sufficiently large). It follows that there exists a threshold distance $x^D \in [0, \bar{x}]$ such that in equilibrium potential customers will choose to join the system if and only if their distance satisfies $x < x^D$ where x^D can be uniquely determined by

$$x^D = \max\{x | U^D(x) \geq 0, x \in [0, \bar{x}]\}.$$

It can be derived that $x^D = \left[T_D/\rho + S_D - \sqrt{4T_D/\rho + (T_D/\rho - S_D)^2}\right]\bar{x}/(2T_D)$, where $S_D = \mu(V - \bar{P})/c$ and $T_D = \mu(d - \delta)\bar{x}/c$. Furthermore, we derive the system throughput, service revenue, customer welfare and social welfare under the price discrimination strategy. In what follows, we first compare the price discrimination policy to the (non-price-discrimination) FIFO benchmark, and then to our proposed priority policy in this chapter.

7.1 Comparing PDS to the FIFO Benchmark

Consider the (non-price-discrimination) FIFO policy with service price B as a benchmark (see Sect. 2.1). It is clear that the price discrimination policy has the potential to achieve higher system throughput, or higher service revenue, or higher social welfare, or higher customer welfare one at a time with the right choices of $\bar{P}$ and δ because the benchmark is simply a special case with $\bar{P} = B$ and $\delta = 0$. However, our next result demonstrates that with carefully selected parameters, the price discrimination policy can actually achieve higher system throughput, higher service revenue, higher social welfare and higher customer welfare all at the same time, compared with the FIFO policy.

Proposition 9 *For fixed δ, the price discrimination policy achieves higher system throughput, higher service revenue, higher social welfare and higher customer welfare at the same time if and only if $P_1(\delta) < \bar{P} < \min\{P_2(\delta), P_3(\delta)\}$, where $P_1(\delta)$ and $P_2(\delta)$ are the smaller and larger roots of the equation $x^D[\bar{P} - \delta x^D/2] - Bx^F = 0$ with respect to $\bar{P}$, and $P_3(\delta) = V - c\left(T_D\sqrt{d/(d-\delta)}x^F - \frac{\bar{x}^2}{\rho\sqrt{d/(d-\delta)}x^F - \bar{x}}\right)/\mu\bar{x}$.*

7.2 Comparing PDS to the Priority Policy

According to Propositions 6 and 9, the distance-based service priority policy and the price discrimination strategy can both be superior in all aspects compared to the FIFO policy. Nevertheless, how do they compare to each other? The next result reveals that they each have their own advantages. Denote by $\bar{\lambda}_e^X$, $\overline{\Pi}^X$ the maximal system throughput and service revenue that can be achieved, for $X = P, D$.

Proposition 10 $\overline{\Pi}^D > \overline{\Pi}^P$ and $\bar{\lambda}_e^D < \bar{\lambda}_e^P$.

Proposition 10 shows that while the price discrimination strategy has the potential to achieve higher service revenue, the distance-based service priority policy has the potential to achieve higher system throughput. It is well known that price discrimination allows a producer to extract most, if not all, of customer surplus, therefore it is not surprising that the price discrimination strategy works especially well to capture revenue. In contrast, the distance-based service priority policy is more efficient in improving the system throughput compared to the price discrimination policy.

8 Concluding Remarks

In this chapter, we introduced an innovative distance-based service priority policy (shortened as "priority policy" below). The idea is to assign higher service priority to customers who must travel farther for a physical service that requires waiting. As a result, customers who are located far away from the service location can save waiting time to obtain service, which provides them with a new incentive to consider seeking service—these customers would not have been interested in seeking the service under the first-come-first-served policy due to their high travel costs *and* the high waiting costs to obtain service.

We demonstrated that the priority policy can significantly increase system throughput by attracting more customers to seek service, and the increase can be up to 50% compared to the ordinary first-come-first-served service discipline. We then showed that the priority policy can increase social welfare while benefiting the service provider. This, however, may come at the cost of customer welfare. We proposed a possible remedy to coordinate service revenue and customer welfare when the situation happens, making the priority policy beneficial to all stakeholders.

We now discuss some practical and fairness issues related to implementing the priority policy to conclude this chapter. For the policy to work, it is important that the service provider be transparent about the policy and disclose its procedure to all potential customers so that they can make informed decisions. The service provider also needs to be able to verify the residence information of any customers who choose to seek service and maintain a proper service sequence based on their distance-based service priorities. Verification of the residence information can be done at the facility check-in or by installing self-service check-in kiosks with ID and address authentication capability. Such technology is widely available at airports, casinos and government agencies. Customers can then sit in an open waiting area and they will be called by name (or by their ticket number if tickets are issued from the check-in kiosks) when it is their turn for service. The service provider can then ask customers to go up for service in the order of their service priority, effectively achieving a continuum of priority levels. In practice, it may also be more feasible to implement a few discrete distance-based service priority classes. This would be similar to airlines' boarding lines for numbered groups (e.g., Groups 1–5). Group 1 can include customers who live farthest from the service location, and they will be given the highest service priority. Group 2 is the second farthest with the next highest service priority, followed by Group 3, and so on. There should be clear signs to guide arriving customers to their designated line.

Finally, we argue that the associated fairness concerns for the distance-based service priority policy may be less protruding compared to the traditional price discrimination strategy. This is because many people consider price discrimination unfair, and price discrimination can even be unlawful under certain circumstances (e.g., gender-based insurance premium prices). The priority policy, however, is more about helping disadvantaged people—that is, providing kindness and convenience to those who live in remote areas and have to travel long distances to reach the service provider. In general, people experience happiness and a sense of fulfillment when helping those in need, and recent research in service operations further suggests that customers are willing to sacrifice their own utility to help others waiting in line (Ülkü et al. 2023). This means that the priority policy is unlikely to receive pushbacks among de-prioritized customers who live near the service provider.

References

Haviv M, Oz B (2018) Self-regulation of an unobservable queue. Manag Sci 64(5):2380–2389
Rajan B, Tezcan T, Seidmann A (2019) Service systems with heterogeneous customers: investigating the effect of telemedicine on chronic care. Manag Sci 65(3):1236–1267

Ülkü S, Hydock C, Cui S (2023) Social queues (cues): impact of others' waiting in line on one's service time. Manag Sci 68(11):7958–7976

Wang Z, Cui S, Fang L (2023) Distance-based service priority: an innovative mechanism to increase system throughput and social welfare. Manuf Serv Oper Manag 25(1):353–369

Open Access This chapter is licensed under the terms of the Creative Commons Attribution 4.0 International License (http://creativecommons.org/licenses/by/4.0/), which permits use, sharing, adaptation, distribution and reproduction in any medium or format, as long as you give appropriate credit to the original author(s) and the source, provide a link to the Creative Commons license and indicate if changes were made.

The images or other third party material in this chapter are included in the chapter's Creative Commons license, unless indicated otherwise in a credit line to the material. If material is not included in the chapter's Creative Commons license and your intended use is not permitted by statutory regulation or exceeds the permitted use, you will need to obtain permission directly from the copyright holder.

Chapter 7
In-Queue Priority Purchase

1 Introduction

This chapter is based on Wang et al. (2021) and builds a queueing-game-theoretic model that explicitly captures self-interested customers' dynamic *in-queue* priority-purchasing behavior. In-queue decisions give customers more flexibility and make the pay-for-priority option always available—even after customers join the system. Modeling the behavior of dynamic in-queue priority-purchasing is no easy task. When deciding whether to purchase priority, customers must make a delicate trade-off between the priority premium they pay and the waiting time they expect to save, which, in turn, depends on how many other customers are seeking service and competing for priority. Additionally, self-interested customers must take into account all possible future events of the queue and decide not only *whether* to purchase priority (as in the upon-arrival case in the literature) but also *when* to do so (assumed away by the upon-arrival case). These actions, in turn, shape the underlying queueing dynamics. Capturing this feedback loop necessitates (challenging) equilibrium analysis.

In this chapter, we formulate the problem of in-queue priority purchases as a dynamic game played by homogeneous customers in a queueing system. We first consider a simultaneous upgrade rule whereby customers who have not yet upgraded to priority simultaneously decide whether to upgrade at any time while they are waiting in the queue. We show that any threshold strategy cannot be sustained in equilibrium under some intuitive criteria. Furthermore, we introduce a tractable small buffer system that can hold at most two customers (including the customer in service). We analytically confirm, without assuming intuitive criteria, that such a small buffer system indeed cannot support a pure-strategy equilibrium in which some customers purchase priority.

Next, we consider an alternative sequential upgrade rule whereby each time there is a new customer arrival, the service provider sequentially asks non-priority customers one by one whether to purchase priority, with the first customer in line being called upon first, then the second one, and so on. Today's mobile Internet makes it exceedingly easy to manage such a system efficiently. We first introduce the cases of sufficiently light traffic and sufficiently heavy traffic. Under sufficiently low traffic, customers can effectively act myopically by ignoring future arrivals. We establish the existence of a pure-strategy equilibrium of the following structure: each time the arrival of a new customer causes the low-priority queue length to tentatively reach a given threshold (given in closed form), the second last customer (and no one else) upgrades; the newcomer will be the next customer to upgrade if the low-priority queue length temporarily reaches the threshold again (due to an arrival) before the newcomer is served. This equilibrium structure implies that the low-priority queue length can never exceed the above threshold (and can only temporarily stay at the threshold). This property is preserved under any traffic intensity in equilibrium even though the maximum low-priority queue length would likely decrease with traffic. In particular, under sufficiently heavy traffic, we show that when the priority price is not too high, the equilibrium is such that as soon as the ordinary queue amasses two customers, the first ordinary customer upgrades to the priority queue. We then again turn to a small buffer system that can hold at most two customers and analytically characterize the pure-strategy equilibrium for any traffic intensity.

Finally, we numerically solve for the pure-strategy equilibrium of sequential in-queue priority purchases in a system that can hold at most three customers under various traffic intensities and priority prices. We find instances in which as soon as the number of ordinary customers reaches three, it triggers the upgrade of the very first customer but not the second or third customer, defying the equilibrium structure previously identified. Nevertheless, we numerically observe that in such a system (sequential), in-queue priority purchases still generate less revenue than upon-arrival priority purchases, corroborating the analytical insight gleaned from the small buffer system.

While we study customers' in-queue priority-purchasing behavior, a few other recent papers consider customers' in-queue reneging decisions, e.g., see Assaf and Haviv (1990), Afèche and Sarhangian (2015), Maglaras et al. (2017), Ata and Peng (2018), and Cui et al. (2022) for various theoretical models of reneging. Specifically, Afèche and Sarhangian (2015) study the reneging behavior in priority queues, who assume two exogenously fixed streams of customers (ordinary and priority) arriving to a priority queue without any priority premium involved, and study how being bumped by the priority customers triggers in-queue reneging behavior of the ordinary customers (the priority customers may balk upon arrival but do not have any incentive to renege after joining).

2 Model Description

Consider an M/M/1 service system. Customers arrive at the system according to a Poisson process with rate λ. The service times are independent and exponentially distributed with rate μ. Customers do not balk or renege. Hence, we focus on the case $\lambda < \mu$ to ensure system stability. Customers are delay-sensitive and their waiting cost per unit time is C. Consistent with the literature, the values of λ, μ, and C are common knowledge.

By default, each customer upon arrival is an *ordinary customer*, i.e., a non-priority customer, and decides whether and when to purchase priority throughout her stay in the system (from the arrival epoch to the departure epoch). The priority price is $P(>0)$ and is nonrefundable. Hence, the decision to upgrade to priority is irrevocable. Once an ordinary customer purchases priority, she becomes a *priority customer* and obtains *preemptive* priority for service over all other ordinary customers. The queue disciplines within the ordinary and priority lines are both FIFO. The state of the system is described by $\{N_o, N_p\}$, where $N_o \in \mathbb{N}_0 := \{0\} \cup \mathbb{N}$ and $N_p \in \mathbb{N}_0$ correspond to the number of ordinary customers and the number of priority customers in the system (including the one in service, if any), respectively. Throughout her time in the system, each customer observes the system state and her position in the queue.

Customers are fully rational in our model in that (i) they act to maximize their own expected utility (or equivalently, minimize the expected cost) at any given time upon and after arriving to the system, and (ii) they take into consideration the actions of other customers, including the current customers in the system as well as any future arrivals. To that end, customers are able to calculate the probabilities for all different sample paths according to which the system evolves. Given that the priority premium is nonrefundable, once any customer has purchased priority, they have no more actions to take. We consider two different rules that can be imposed on the specific timing of priority upgrades: the simultaneous upgrade rule and the sequential-upgrade rule .

3 Simultaneous Upgrade Rule

In this section, we consider a simultaneous upgrade rule specified as follows. Each ordinary customer in the system *continuously* evaluates the options of purchasing and not purchasing priority—until she either upgrades to priority or completes service. The evaluation and priority upgrade are instantaneous. Thus, *at any time point*, all (ordinary) customers *simultaneously* decide whether to upgrade to priority.

When multiple ordinary customers decide to upgrade, it is imperative to specify the order in which these customers join the priority line, i.e., their service order (because the order affects the calculation of customers' expected utilities and hence the equilibrium analysis). We adopt the *first-come-first-upgrade rule*, i.e., customers who upgrade at the same time will join the priority line according to their order of arrival to the system, which is also their order in the ordinary line. First-come-first-upgrade is arguably the fairest and most natural rule for customers.

3.1 Equilibrium Definition

We set up the in-queue priority-purchasing problem under the simultaneous rule as a dynamic game. We focus on Markovian priority-purchasing strategies that depend on the system state $\{N_o, N_p\}$ (i.e., the numbers of ordinary and priority customers in the system), and the position of a given customer within the ordinary line (due to the first-come-first-upgrade rule). The information set an ordinary customer acts on can thus be described by a three-dimensional position vector (i, j, k), where $i \in \mathbb{N}$ indicates the position of the customer in the ordinary line including any ordinary customer at the server, $j \in \mathbb{N}_0$ the number of ordinary customers behind her in the ordinary line, and $k \in \mathbb{N}_0$ the number of customers already in the priority queue. For example, if the only customer in the system is an ordinary customer at the server, then her position vector is $(i, j, k) = (1, 0, 0)$. By definition, at any system state $\{N_o, N_p\}$ with $N_o \geq 1$, any ordinary customer's position vector (i, j, k) must satisfy $i + j = N_o$ and $k = N_p$.

Given the position vector (i, j, k), each ordinary customer chooses between "Yes" (for purchasing priority) and "No" (for not purchasing priority). A (Markovian) *strategy* $\sigma : \mathbb{N} \times \mathbb{N}_0 \times \mathbb{N}_0 \to \{Y, N\}$ is a mapping from the position vector (i, j, k) to a <u>Y</u>es or <u>N</u>o priority-purchasing action. We use Σ to denote the strategy space. Because customers are homogeneous, we consider symmetric (pure) strategies. When all customers follow strategy σ, we call system state $\{N_o, N_p\}$ a *stable state under* σ if and only if (i) $N_o = 0$, or (ii) $N_o > 0$ and $\sigma(i, N_o - i, N_p) = N$ for all $i \in \{1, 2, \ldots, N_o\}$. That is, at a stable state (under σ), the strategy σ specifies that all of the ordinary customers, if any, do not purchase priority (i.e., to stay "stable"). A system state that is not stable under σ will be referred to as a *transient state under* σ. See Fig. 7.1 for an illustration of the system dynamics when customers follow a specific strategy.

Define the value function $V(i, j, k) : \mathbb{N} \times \mathbb{N}_0 \times \mathbb{N}_0 \to \mathbb{R}$ as the expected utility (or the continuation value) of an ordinary customer at position (i, j, k). We use $\mathcal{V}$ to denote the value-function space. Note that $V(i, j, k)$ is time-homogeneous because the underlying queueing system evolves according to a time-homogeneous Markov chain.

Definition 1 A symmetric pure-strategy equilibrium under the simultaneous upgrade rule is characterized by any strategy and value-function pair $(\sigma, V) \in \Sigma \times \mathcal{V}$ that satisfies Conditions (7.1), (7.3a)–(7.3b), (7.4), and (7.5):

$$V(i, j, k) = \begin{cases} -P - \left[k + \sum_{s=1}^{i-1} \mathbb{1}_{\{\sigma(s, i+j-s, k)=Y\}} + 1 \right] \frac{C}{\mu}, & \text{if } \sigma(i, j, k) = Y, \\ V(i', j', k'), & \text{otherwise,} \end{cases} \quad \forall (i, j, k) \in \mathbb{N} \times \mathbb{N}_0 \times \mathbb{N}_0,$$

(7.1)

3 Simultaneous Upgrade Rule	123

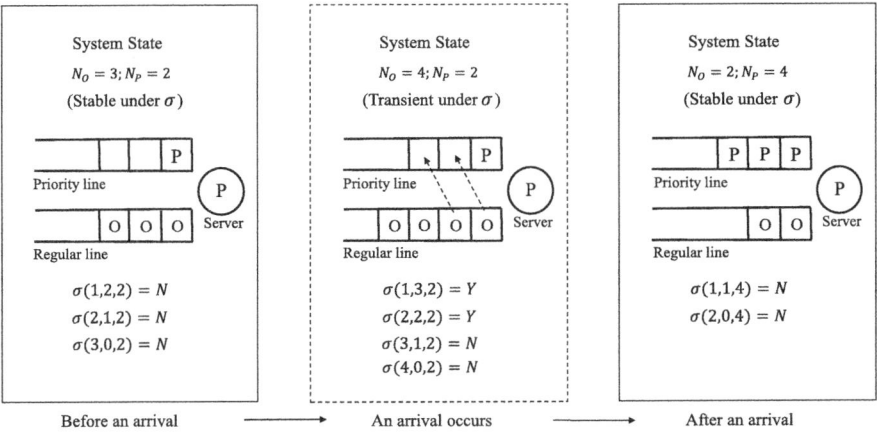

Note. O's and P's in the figure represent ordinary and priority customers, respectively. As a new arrival occurs (middle panel), the four ordinary customers (including the arrival) act simultaneously according to strategy σ and the first-come-first-upgrade rule. If σ were an equilibrium strategy, no ordinary customer has an incentive to unilaterally deviate from $\sigma(i,j,k)$ given her position (i,j,k) at any stable or transient state under σ.

Fig. 7.1 System dynamics as an arrival occurs, assuming customers follow strategy σ specified in each box

where (i', j', k') is as specified by

$$i' := i - \sum_{s=1}^{i-1} \mathbb{1}_{\{\sigma(s,i+j-s,k)=Y\}},$$

$$j' := j - \sum_{s=i+1}^{i+j} \mathbb{1}_{\{\sigma(s,i+j-s,k)=Y\}}, \tag{7.2}$$

$$k' := k + \sum_{s=1}^{i-1} \mathbb{1}_{\{\sigma(s,i+j-s,k)=Y\}} + \sum_{s=i+1}^{i+j} \mathbb{1}_{\{\sigma(s,i+j-s,k)=Y\}}.$$

In particular, $\forall (i, j, k) \in \mathbb{N} \times \mathbb{N}_0 \times \mathbb{N}_0$, if $\sigma(s, i+j-s, k) = N$ for all $s = 1, \ldots, i+j$, then:

$$V(i, j, k) = -\frac{C}{\lambda + \mu} + \frac{\mu}{\lambda + \mu} V(i, j, k-1)$$
$$+ \frac{\lambda}{\lambda + \mu} V(i, j+1, k), \quad \forall (i, j, k) \in \mathbb{N} \times \mathbb{N}_0 \times \mathbb{N}, \tag{7.3a}$$

$$V(i, j, 0) = -\frac{C}{\lambda + \mu} + \frac{\mu}{\lambda + \mu} V(i-1, j, 0)$$

$$+ \frac{\lambda}{\lambda + \mu} V(i, j+1, 0), \quad \forall (i,j) \in \mathbb{N} \times \mathbb{N}_0, \tag{7.3b}$$

$$V(0, j, 0) \equiv 0, \quad \forall j \in \mathbb{N}_0, \tag{7.4}$$

$$V(i, j, k) = \max \left\{ -P - \left[k + \sum_{s=1}^{i-1} \mathbb{1}_{\{\sigma(s, i+j-s, k) = Y\}} + 1 \right] \frac{C}{\mu}, \right.$$

$$\left. V(i', j', k') \right\}, \quad \forall (i, j, k) \in \mathbb{N} \times \mathbb{N}_0 \times \mathbb{N}_0, \tag{7.5}$$

where (i', j', k') is as specified by (7.2). □

In Definition 1, Conditions (7.1), (7.3a)–(7.3b), and (7.4) pin down the value function V (through a system of linear equations) for a given strategy σ. Specifically, Condition (7.1) gives recursive formulas of the value function when state transitions occur due to priority upgrades without changing the total number of customers in the system. If σ requires that an ordinary customer with position (i, j, k) purchase priority at the cost of premium P, then she will join the priority line with the $\left[k + \sum_{s=1}^{i-1} \mathbb{1}_{\{\sigma(s, i+j-s, k) = Y\}} + 1 \right]^{th}$ position in the priority line according to the first-come-first-upgrade rule, which means she must wait behind the original k priority customers and all upgraders who are originally ahead of her. Her expected waiting cost until service completion is thus $\left[k + \sum_{s=1}^{i-1} \mathbb{1}_{\{\sigma(s, i+j-s, k) = Y\}} + 1 \right] C/\mu$. If instead she chooses not to purchase priority, her position vector changes from (i, j, k) to (i', j', k') as specified by (7.2), which indicates that her updated position i' in the ordinary line is her original position i less than the number of upgraders who are originally ahead of her; the updated number of customers waiting behind her j' is the original number j less than the number of upgraders who are originally behind her; and the updated number of priority customers k' is the original number k plus the total number of upgraders.

Note that Condition (7.1) is applicable to both transient and stable states, although for a stable state, it would simply give a trivial identity equation, i.e., $V(i, j, k) = V(i, j, k)$. Hence, Conditions (7.3a)–(7.3b) add to Condition (7.1) by specifying the recursive formulas of the value function for stable states (in which everyone in the ordinary line chooses "N" according to σ). A stable state evolves if and only if an arrival or departure event occurs, which (unlike transitions in Condition (7.1)) changes the total number of customers in the system. Specifically, the mean time till the next (arrival or departure) event is $1/(\lambda + \mu)$, during which each ordinary customer incurs a waiting cost of C per unit of time. If an event occurs, it is an arrival with probability $\lambda/(\lambda + \mu)$, in which case, the number of customers waiting behind any ordinary customer is incremented by one. On the other hand, with probability $\mu/(\lambda+\mu)$, a departure occurs as the next event, in which case, either the number of priority customers is decremented by one if originally there is at least one priority customer (see Condition (7.3a)) or the position of any ordinary customer moves up by one otherwise (see Condition (7.3b)). On the other hand, Condition (7.4) specifies boundary conditions for absorbing states of service completion.

Note that while the value function V is determined by Conditions (7.1), (7.3a)–(7.3b), and (7.4) for a given strategy σ, there is no guarantee that σ is an equilibrium. Hence, Condition (7.5) acts as a consistency check that ensures the continuation value $V(i, j, k)$ is indeed the maximum expected utility any customer with position (i, j, k) can obtain (even if they could choose differently than $\sigma(i, j, k)$), provided that all other customers follow σ. That is, when all customers adopt σ, no one can strictly improve their expected utility at any position (i, j, k) by unilaterally deviating from the action specified by $\sigma(i, j, k)$, which implies that the best response to σ coincides with σ itself. Taken together, Conditions (7.1), (7.3a)–(7.3b), (7.4), and (7.5) close the feedback loop to qualify σ as an *equilibrium strategy*.

3.2 Analysis

The strategy space and the value-function space of the game are massive. To facilitate equilibrium analysis, we first propose three intuitive criteria on value functions. This enables us to focus on a reasonable subspace of $\Sigma \times \mathcal{V}$ that complies with these criteria.

Intuitive Criteria

We propose three intuitive criteria on value functions as follows:

Criterion 1 $V(i+1, j, k) \leq V(i, j, k)$.

Criterion 2 $V(i, j+1, k) \leq V(i, j, k)$.

Criterion 3 $V(i-1, j, k+1) \leq V(i, j, k)$.

Criterion 1 states that all else being equal, an ordinary customer does not receive a higher expected utility when there are more customers ahead of her in the ordinary line. Criterion 2 specifies that all else being equal, an ordinary customer does not receive a higher expected utility when there are more customers behind her in the ordinary line. Criteria 1 and 2 are consistent with the intuition that a non-priority customer cannot be better off with a more congested system (corresponding to more potential competitors for priority). On the other hand, Criterion 3 states that for an ordinary customer, when the number of ordinary customers ahead of her in the ordinary line and the number of priority customers in the priority line add up to a constant, the customer (weakly) prefers the scenario with fewer priority customers. The intuition here is that any customer already in the priority line will be served before the tagged ordinary customer with certainty regardless of whether she upgrades, whereas a customer ahead of her in the ordinary line may not be served before her if she upgrades in a timely manner and the other person does not.

Roadmap

The rest of this section is devoted to proving that pure equilibrium strategies do not exist under the intuitive criteria. In particular, we proceed with the following two-step approach which is also illustrated by the corresponding Venn diagrams in Fig. 7.2.

Step 1. We establish that any pure-strategy equilibrium subject to intuitive criteria must be of a state-dependent threshold type. In particular, combining the equilibrium conditions from Definition 1 (which characterize a subset of $\Sigma \times \mathcal{V}$, denoted by $\mathcal{E}$) with the three intuitive criteria (corresponding to set $\mathcal{I}$), we show that if a pure-strategy equilibrium exists, it must be of a state-dependent threshold

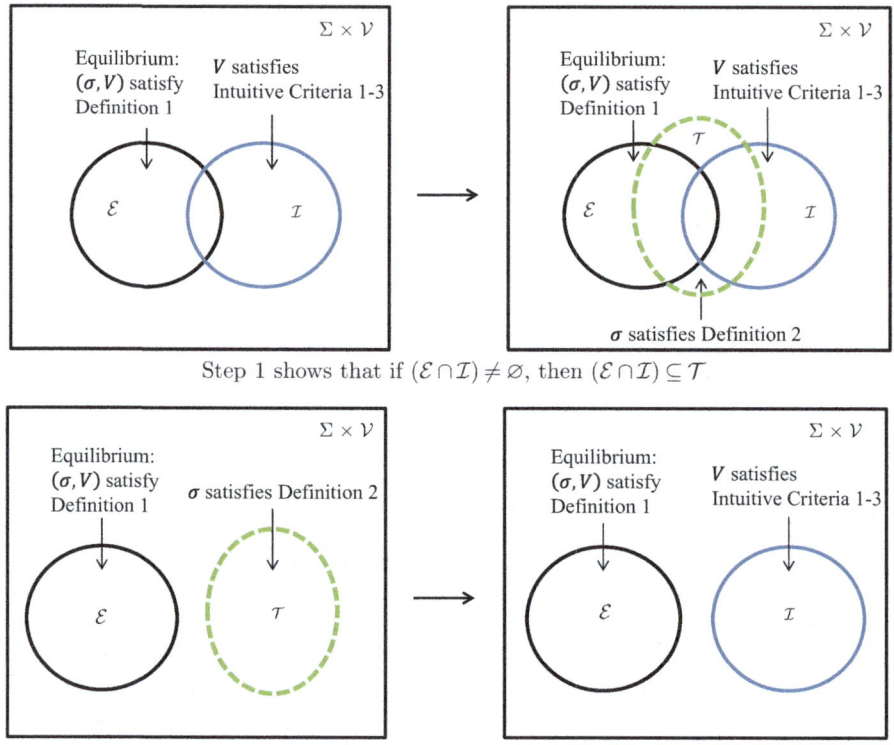

Fig. 7.2 Illustration of the analytical roadmap

type (the set of such threshold strategies is denoted by $\mathcal{T}$). That is, Step 1 shows that if $(\mathcal{E} \cap \mathcal{I}) \neq \varnothing$, then $(\mathcal{E} \cap \mathcal{I}) \subseteq \mathcal{T}$.

Step 2. We show that any state-dependent threshold strategy cannot be an equilibrium, i.e., $(\mathcal{E} \cap \mathcal{T}) = \varnothing$. The result implies $(\mathcal{E} \cap \mathcal{I}) \nsubseteq \mathcal{T}$, and by the contrapositive argument of Step 1, we can conclude that $(\mathcal{E} \cap \mathcal{I}) = \varnothing$. That is, there does not exist any pure-strategy equilibrium of our game that would satisfy the intuitive criteria. In other words, a pure-strategy equilibrium, even if it ever existed, would be peculiar and thus might be of little practical interest.

3.2.1 Step 1: Equilibrium Structure

In this subsection, we search for the equilibrium structure subject to Definition 1 and Criteria 1–3. Hence in this step, we treat the three intuitive criteria as underlying *assumptions* for all the derivations. For brevity, we do not repeatedly state in each of the formal results in Step 1 their reliance on the three intuitive criteria. We develop some supporting lemmata first.

Lemma 1 *In equilibrium, under Criteria 1–3, for any system state* $\{N_o, N_p\} = \{i + j, k\}$, *if* $\sigma(i, j, k) = N$, *we must have* $\sigma(i+s, j-s, k) = N$ *for all* $s \in \{1, 2, \ldots, j\}$.

Lemma 1 implies that under any equilibrium strategy, an ordinary customer does not purchase priority unless all other customers ahead of her in the ordinary line do. This is consistent with the first-come-first-upgrade rule whereby an ordinary customer with a more advanced (resp., backward) position in the ordinary line also receives a more advanced (resp., backward) position in the priority line, when the two of them decide to upgrade to priority at the same time.

Lemma 2 *In equilibrium,* $V(i, j, k) - V(i, j, k+1) \geq C/\mu$.

Lemma 2 gives a lower bound for the difference between $V(i, j, k)$ and $V(i, j, k+1)$. Intuitively, when there is one more priority customer in the line (all else being equal), an ordinary customer's expected utility is reduced by at least the waiting cost of a service period, but could be more because waiting longer in the ordinary line (if she does not upgrade) further increases the likelihood of being overtaken (by more other customers).

Lemma 3 *In equilibrium,*

(i) *if* $\sigma(1, j, k) = N$, *then* $\sigma(1, j', k') = N$ *for all* $j' \in \{0, 1, \ldots, j\}$ *and* $k' \in \{0, 1, \ldots, k\}$;
(ii) *if* $\sigma(1, j, k) = Y$, *then* $\sigma(1, j', k') = Y$ *for all* $j' \in \{j, j+1, \ldots\}$ *and* $k' \in \{k, k+1, \ldots\}$.

Lemma 3 suggests that the first customer in the ordinary line is more inclined to purchase priority when the lines are longer (either due to more customers waiting behind in the ordinary line or due to more customers waiting ahead in the priority line). Intuitively, more other customers standing in the ordinary line provide the first customer with a greater incentive to upgrade since their presence spells more competition for priority. More customers being in the priority line also motivate priority-purchasing because a longer waiting time caused by these priority customers implies that the first customer is likely to encounter more future arrivals who pose a threat as prospective competitors for priority.

Based on Definition 1 and Criteria 1–3 and using Lemmas 1–3 as stepping stones, we now establish the structure of pure-strategy equilibrium in the following Theorem 1. Note that it is a necessary condition for any equilibrium strategy under the three intuitive criteria.

Theorem 1 *A pure-strategy equilibrium under the three intuitive criteria must be of a state-dependent threshold type as specified by Definition 2.*

Definition 2 For a weakly decreasing sequence of nonnegative integers $\{n_s\}_{s \in \mathbb{N}_0}$ such that

$$n_0 = \infty \geq n_1 \geq n_2 \geq \ldots \geq n_{(\underline{m}-1)} > n_{\underline{m}} = 0 = n_{(\underline{m}+1)} = n_{(\underline{m}+2)}, \ldots \quad (7.6)$$

with $\underline{m} \leq \left\lceil \frac{\mu P + C}{C} \right\rceil$, we define the following strategy σ: For any $N_o \in \mathbb{N}$ and $N_p \in \mathbb{N}_0$,

$$\sigma(i, N_o - i, N_p) = \begin{cases} Y & \text{if } i \in \{1, 2, \ldots, \bar{n}_{\{N_o, N_p\}}\}, \\ N & \text{if } i \in \{\bar{n}_{\{N_o, N_p\}} + 1, \bar{n}_{\{N_o, N_p\}} + 2, \ldots, N_o\}, \end{cases} \quad (7.7)$$

where

$$\bar{n}_{\{N_o, N_p\}} = \min\{s | N_p + s \leq n_{(N_o - s)} - 1, s \in \mathbb{N}_0\}. \quad (7.8)$$

Let us unpack Theorem 1. First, it states that given any state $\{N_o, N_p\}$, an equilibrium strategy is a state-dependent threshold strategy that specifies that the first and only the first $\bar{n}_{\{N_o, N_p\}}$ ordinary customers should purchase priority; see Eq. (7.7). Therefore, $\bar{n}_{\{N_o, N_p\}}$ also corresponds to the number of ordinary customers who purchase priority at state $\{N_o, N_p\}$ under an equilibrium strategy. Note that $\bar{n}_{\{N_o, N_p\}}$ is well-defined by Eq. (7.8) and $\bar{n}_{\{N_o, N_p\}} \leq N_o$ because N_o is an element that belongs to the set $\{s | N_p + s \leq n_{(N_o - s)} - 1, s \in \mathbb{N}_0\}$. Because only customers at the front of the ordinary line purchase priority, the FIFO service order is preserved. Second, Theorem 1 indicates that $\bar{n}_{\{N_o, N_p\}}$ should be derived for any given $\{N_o, N_p\}$ from a weakly decreasing integer sequence $\{n_s\}_{s \in \mathbb{N}_0}$ *that only depends on the system parameters but not the system state*; see Eq. (7.8). It is easier to interpret the relationship between an equilibrium strategy and $\{n_s\}_{s \in \mathbb{N}_0}$ through the lens of an equivalent condition presented in the following Corollary 1.

Corollary 1 *In equilibrium, for any given system state $\{N_o, N_p\}$, we have $\sigma(i, N_o - i, N_p) = Y$ if and only if $N_p + s \geq n_{(N_o - s)}$ for $s \in \{0, 1, 2, \ldots, i - 1\}$.*

The second implication of Theorem 1 is the following Corollary 2.

Corollary 2 *In equilibrium, the occurrence of a departure event in a stable state will not trigger any customer to purchase priority.*

Corollary 2 follows directly from the condition in Corollary 1 because by plugging $s = 0$, we know that a system state is stable if and only if $N_p < n_{N_o}$. When a departure event occurs to a stable state, i.e., N_p is reduced by 1 if $N_p \geq 1$ or N_o is reduced by 1 if $N_p = 0$, the condition $N_p < n_{N_o}$ is preserved because n_{N_o} is weakly decreasing in N_o (Theorem 1).

3.2.2 Step 2: Nonexistence of Pure-Strategy Equilibria

Thus far, Theorem 1, together with Corollaries 1 and 2, has presented a clear view of the equilibrium structure—if equilibrium strategies exist. To characterize the equilibrium strategies under Criteria 1–3, it is sufficient to focus on the state-dependent threshold strategies in Definition 2. In this step, we now prove that any pure strategy given by Definition 2 cannot be sustained in equilibrium.

Theorem 2 *Any pure strategy defined by Definition 2 cannot be sustained in equilibrium. That is, $(\mathcal{E} \cap \mathcal{T}) = \emptyset$. Furthermore, under the simultaneous upgrade rule, pure-strategy equilibria do not exist if the intuitive criteria hold. That is, $(\mathcal{E} \cap \mathcal{I}) = \emptyset$.*

We will provide some intuition for why pure-strategy equilibria do not exist through the lens of a tractable small buffer system that has a buffer size $K = 2$, i.e., a system that can hold at most two customers (including the customer in service if any). A firm understanding of this simplified setting will shed light on our main model that does not have a buffer limit (i.e., $K = \infty$).

3.3 A Small Buffer System

In this subsection, we analyze a small buffer system with $K = 2$ to sharpen intuition. For notational convenience, we define traffic intensity $\rho \triangleq \lambda/\mu$ and normalized price $v_P \triangleq \mu P/c$. Since a small buffer system is always stable, we relax the assumption $\lambda < \mu$, i.e., traffic intensity ρ can be less than or greater than 1.

Theorem 3 *Consider a small buffer system with $K = 2$ subject to the simultaneous upgrade rule. If $v_P > 1$, then no customer purchasing priority is an equilibrium. Otherwise, i.e., if $v_P \leq 1$, there exist no pure-strategy equilibria.*

Theorem 3 shows that in a small buffer system, no customer purchasing priority is an equilibrium strategy for customers when the priority price is high ($v_P > 1$). This is intuitive because customers would never purchase priority if the priority price is higher than the maximum expected reduction in delay cost.

More importantly, when the priority price is not too high ($v_P \leq 1$), a pure-strategy equilibrium does not exist (note that this result does not rely on the intuitive criteria as an assumption). In this case, customers have conflicting interests: a customer that is ahead in the queue only has an incentive to upgrade if the customer behind her upgrades, whereas the customer that is behind in the queue only gains from upgrading if the customer ahead does not upgrade.

When buffer size K increases, "no customers purchasing priority" will be sustained in equilibrium for any $v_P > K - 1$. On the other hand, if $v_P \leq K - 1$, we conjecture that no pure-strategy equilibria exist. Note that as K increases, the condition $v_P > K - 1$ becomes more difficult to satisfy. When $K \uparrow \infty$, we conjecture that there will not be any pure-strategy equilibrium for any $P > 0$ (we have proved this under the caveat of three intuitive criteria in Theorem 3).

The nonexistence of pure-strategy equilibria implies that the simultaneous upgrade rule may be troublesome to implement. Similar phenomenon can be found in ticket queues, where Kerner et al. (2017) prove that any threshold strategies cannot be an equilibrium. In addition, the simultaneous rule requires real-time updates of system states without delay (as all the customers move at the same time), which may also pose implementation challenges.

4 Sequential Upgrade Rule

In this section, we consider an alternative, sequential upgrade rule specified as follows. Each time a new customer arrives, the service provider sequentially asks each ordinary customer one at a time whether they wish to purchase priority, with the first customer in line being called upon first, then the second one, and so on, until all the ordinary customers are asked. Unlike the simultaneous upgrade rule, customers in this case cannot purchase priority until it is their turn. They have a single opportunity to upgrade each time a new customer arrives, and if they choose not to upgrade this time, they must wait until the next customer arrival for a new upgrade opportunity. The sequential upgrade rule can be implemented with the aid of today's mobile Internet, which may efficiently automate the inquiry and upgrade process.

4.1 Equilibrium Definition

We set up the in-queue priority-purchasing problem under the sequential rule as a dynamic game. Consider an ordinary customer whose position vector is (i, j, k), where i is the number of ordinary customers ahead of and including her; j, the number of ordinary customers behind her; and k, the number of priority customers. When it is her turn to upgrading, we define her (Markovian) strategy to be $\sigma(i, j, k) \in \{Y, N\}$, where "$Y$" indicates "upgrade" (or purchase priority) and "N"

4 Sequential Upgrade Rule

indicates "no." Note that in most sequential games, it is necessary to specify a player's strategy as a function of the possible strategies of all the other players who move before she does (which would be cumbersome). However, in our case, this information is subsumed by a customer's position vector when she is about to decide on upgrading. In other words, what matters to a customer is not how she reaches her position vector, but what the position vector is at the moment of decision-making. Therefore, for our purpose, it suffices to condition customer strategies only on the position vectors, instead of tracking the history of previous customers' moves.

Next, we define the value function. Let $V_x(i, j, k)$ denote the expected utility of a customer with position vector (i, j, k) when the x-th ordinary customer is about to decide on upgrading, for $x = 1, \ldots, i + j + 1$. Specifically, $V_i(i, j, k)$ is the expected utility of customer (i, j, k) when it is her turn to upgrade (right before she acts); $V_{i+j+1}(i, j, k)$ is the expected utility of customer (i, j, k) when the upgrade process is complete (i.e., after all the ordinary customers have been asked).

Definition 3 A symmetric pure-strategy equilibrium under the sequential upgrade rule is characterized by any strategy and value-function pair (σ, V) that satisfies Conditions (7.9)–(7.13):

$$V_x(i, j, k) = \begin{cases} V_x(i-1, j, k+1), & \text{if } \sigma(x, i+j-x, k) = Y, \\ V_{x+1}(i, j, k), & \text{otherwise,} \end{cases}$$
$$\forall x = 1, \ldots, i-1, i \geq 2, (j, k) \in \mathbb{N}_0 \times \mathbb{N}_0, \qquad (7.9)$$

$$V_i(i, j, k) = \begin{cases} -\frac{c(k+1)}{\mu} - P, & \text{if } \sigma(i, j, k) = Y, \\ V_{i+1}(i, j, k), & \text{otherwise,} \end{cases} \quad \forall (i, j, k) \in \mathbb{N} \times \mathbb{N}_0 \times \mathbb{N}_0, \qquad (7.10)$$

$$V_x(i, j, k) = \begin{cases} V_x(i, j-1, k+1), & \text{if } \sigma(x, i+j-x, k) = Y, \\ V_{x+1}(i, j, k), & \text{otherwise,} \end{cases}$$
$$\forall x = i+1 \ldots, i+j, (i, j, k) \in \mathbb{N} \times \mathbb{N} \times \mathbb{N}_0, \qquad (7.11)$$

$$V_{i+j+1}(i, j, k) = -\frac{C}{\lambda + \mu} + \frac{\mu}{\lambda + \mu} V_{i+j+1}(i, j, k-1)$$
$$+ \frac{\lambda}{\lambda + \mu} V_1(i, j+1, k), \quad \forall (i, j, k) \in \mathbb{N} \times \mathbb{N}_0 \times \mathbb{N}, \qquad (7.12a)$$

$$V_{i+j+1}(i, j, 0) = -\frac{C}{\lambda + \mu} + \frac{\mu}{\lambda + \mu} V_{i+j}(i-1, j, 0)$$
$$+ \frac{\lambda}{\lambda + \mu} V_1(i, j+1, 0), \quad \forall (i, j) \in \mathbb{N} \times \mathbb{N}_0, \quad (7.12\text{b})$$
$$V_{j+1}(0, j, 0) \equiv 0, \quad \forall j \in \mathbb{N}_0, \quad (7.12\text{c})$$

$$V_i(i, j, k) = \max\left\{-\frac{c(k+1)}{\mu} - P, V_{i+1}(i, j, k)\right\}, \quad \forall (i, j, k) \in \mathbb{N} \times \mathbb{N}_0 \times \mathbb{N}_0. \quad \square$$
$$(7.13)$$

In Definition 3, Conditions (7.9) specify the state transition due to the action of the x-th ordinary customer who moves before customer (i, j, k) does. If the x-th ordinary customer upgrades, then customer (i, j, k)'s position vector becomes $(i-1, j, k+1)$ (because now there is one fewer ordinary customers ahead of her but one more customer in the priority line). Note that the next customer who gets to choose whether to upgrade is still the x-th customer in the ordinary line as the original x-th customer joins the priority line. If the x-th ordinary customer does not upgrade, then customer (i, j, k)'s position vector is unchanged before the next customer upgrades, and now the next customer will be the $(x+1)$-th customer in the ordinary line. Conditions (7.10) specify the state transition due to customer (i, j, k)'s action. Conditions (7.11) specify the state transition due to the action of a customer who moves after customer (i, j, k) does. Conditions (7.12a) through (7.12c) specify the state transition due to arrivals and departures. Note that a new arrival triggers a new round of priority upgrades starting from the first customer in the ordinary line, and therefore the subscript of the value function is reset to 1. Conditions (7.13) ensure that customers indeed maximize their expected utility by choosing strategy σ provided that other customers choose σ. While Definition 3 applies to a system without a buffer limit, we can easily modify Conditions (7.12a) through (7.12c) by imposing boundary conditions that accommodate any finite buffer K.

Given the complexity of the problem, it is challenging to solve for the equilibrium in general, but we can nevertheless analytically characterize the equilibrium both under sufficiently light traffic and sufficiently heavy traffic, which will shed some light on the equilibrium structure in general.

4.2 Sufficiently Light or Heavy Traffic

We first examine a case of sufficiently light traffic in which arrival rate λ is much smaller than service rate μ (i.e., $\lambda \ll \mu$) such that customers do not need to concern themselves with future arrivals that are not yet present in the system (because $\lambda \ll \mu$ implies that any existing customers in the system will be served long before any

4 Sequential Upgrade Rule

future customers arrive). We first define a threshold-type "X-strategy" below in Definition 4.

Definition 4 (X-**Strategy**) Whenever the number of ordinary customers reaches $X + 1$, the X-th customer (or equivalently the second last customer) and only that customer upgrades.

Theorem 4 shows the X-strategy will arise in equilibrium under sufficiently low traffic.

Theorem 4 *When* $\lambda \ll \mu$, *the X-strategy as defined in Definition* 4 *with* $X = \lceil v_P \rceil$ *is a pure-strategy equilibrium, where* $v_P = \mu P / C$.

Under sufficiently light traffic ($\lambda \ll \mu$), customers compete only with existing customers and can act myopically without loss of optimality. In essence, the underlying game reduces to a one-shot sequential game. To understand the equilibrium in Theorem 4, consider the example of $v_P = 1.5$. In this case, $\lceil v_P \rceil = 2$, which implies that the maximum stable ordinary-queue length is 2. As soon as a new customer arrives, the number of customers in the ordinary queue temporarily reaches 3, which triggers the upgrade of the second customer (while the first and third customers stay put), and the newcomer becomes the one to occupy the second position. In this simple case, it is easy to verify the equilibrium. Customer 1 loses C/μ by being overtaken, which is better than paying $P = 1.5C/\mu$ to secure her position. Given that Customer 1 does not upgrade, Customer 2 loses $0.5C/\mu$ by upgrading (paying $1.5C/\mu$ and overtaking one customer), which is better than losing C/μ by being overtaken by Customer 3 (Customer 3 would upgrade if neither Customers 1 nor 2 were to upgrade). Given that Customer 1 stays put and Customer 2 upgrades, Customer 3 is better off not upgrading as she would incur a net cost of $0.5C/\mu$ if he were to upgrade (overtaking Customer 1 and paying $1.5C/\mu$).

Theorem 5 *If and only if* $\rho \geq \sqrt{v_P} - 1$, *the X-strategy as defined in Definition* 4 *with* $X = 1$ *is a pure-strategy equilibrium, i.e., in this equilibrium, the first and only the first customer upgrades whenever the number of ordinary customers reaches* 2.

Theorem 5 shows that under sufficiently heavy traffic, an equilibrium arises in which as soon as two ordinary customers are present, the first customer upgrades. Note that if the normalized priority price is low, i.e, $v_P \leq 1$, the condition $\rho \geq \sqrt{v_P} - 1$ will in fact be satisfied by any traffic intensity ρ, i.e., the aforementioned equilibrium strategy holds for any traffic intensity. In this case, since $\lceil v_P \rceil = 1$, the equilibrium strategy is the same as the one identified in Theorem 4. Nevertheless, for $v_P \in (1, 4)$, combining Theorems 4 and 5 indicates that the equilibrium strategy under sufficiently heavy traffic (when forward-looking customers must take into account future arrivals) disagrees with the equilibrium strategy under sufficiently light traffic (when customers can act myopically). Although the exact equilibrium strategy differs, the equilibrium structure is still the same, both belonging to the families of X-strategies.

4.3 Small Buffer Systems

In this subsection, we introduce customers' equilibrium strategies in small buffer systems to sharpen intuition. Specifically, we first analytically introduce a queueing system that can hold at most two customers (i.e, $K = 2$). We will then numerically introduce a queueing system that can hold at most three customers (i.e., $K = 3$).

4.3.1 $K = 2$

If a single ordinary customer is present in the queue, it is straightforward that the customer will not upgrade. Thus, since $K = 2$, specifying customer strategies when there are two ordinary customers will pin down the equilibrium. Theorem 6 characterizes the pure-strategy equilibrium through a tuple in which the first (resp., second) element indicates the first (resp., second) ordinary customer's strategy.

Theorem 6 *Consider a small buffer system with $K = 2$ subject to the sequential upgrade rule. The unique pure-strategy equilibrium is (Y, N) if $v_P \leq 1$ and (N, N) otherwise.*

When the priority price is high ($v_P > 1$), it is intuitive that no customers purchase priority. However, unlike the simultaneous case (as shown in Theorem 3), when the priority price is not too high ($v_P \leq 1$), a pure-strategy equilibrium exists, and in equilibrium, the first customer upgrades while the second customer does not. Under the sequential upgrade rule, the first customer gets to decide first. Should she upgrade, she would lose P; should she not upgrade, the second customer would upgrade, causing the first customer to lose C/μ. Since $P \leq C/\mu$ (or equivalently $v_P \leq 1$), the first customer is better off not upgrading, which, in turn, removes the incentive for the second customer to upgrade. Based on the equilibrium strategy given in Theorem 6, we further derive the priority revenue in Corollary 3 below.

Corollary 3 *Consider a small buffer system with $K = 2$ subject to the sequential upgrade rule. The priority revenue per unit time as a function of v_P is given by*

$$\Pi^{SQ}_{K=2}(v_P) = \begin{cases} \frac{C\rho^2 v_P}{1+\rho+\rho^2}, & \text{if } v_P \leq 1; \\ 0, & \text{if } v_P > 1. \end{cases}$$

Next, we compare the priority revenue generated from in-queue priority purchases subject to the sequential upgrade rule with that from the classical upon-arrival priority purchase under $K = 2$. To be clear, in the upon-arrival priority purchase scheme, customers are presented with the option to purchase priority only upon arrival, and if they choose not to purchase the moment they arrive, they cannot do so later. The literature has shown that customers in this case follow a threshold strategy in equilibrium: they purchase if and only if the queue length they see upon arrival reaches a certain threshold. We select the *Pareto-dominant* equilibrium in which all

4 Sequential Upgrade Rule

customers have higher expected utility than they would in other equilibria. Note that the Pareto-dominant equilibrium effectively corresponds to the one with the highest threshold. Proposition 1 characterizes the equilibrium and the corresponding priority revenue when customers can purchase priority only upon arrival.

Proposition 1 *Consider a small buffer system with $K = 2$ where customers can purchase priority only upon arrival. The unique Pareto-dominant pure-strategy equilibrium strategy is given below.*

- *If $v_P \leq \min\{\rho, 1\}$, then all customers purchase priority.*
- *If $\rho < v_P < 1$, then a customer purchases priority if and only if she sees one (ordinary) customer in the system upon arrival.*
- *If $v_P \geq 1$, then no customers purchase priority.*

The priority revenue per unit time as a function of v_P is given by

$$\Pi_{K=2}^{ARR}(v_P) = \begin{cases} \frac{C\rho(1+\rho)v_P}{1+\rho+\rho^2}, & \text{if } v_P \leq \min\{\rho, 1\}; \\ \frac{C\rho^2 v_P}{1+\rho+\rho^2}, & \text{if } \rho < v_P < 1; \\ 0, & \text{if } v_P \geq 1. \end{cases}$$

Next, we compare the maximum revenue (by optimizing over the priority price) of upon-arrival priority purchase, $\Pi_{K=2}^{ARR}$, and that of in-queue priority purchase subject to the sequential rule, $\Pi_{K=2}^{SQ}$, where

$$\Pi_{K=2}^{ARR} = \max_{v_P} \Pi_{K=2}^{ARR}(v_P), \quad \Pi_{K=2}^{SQ} = \max_{v_P} \Pi_{K=2}^{SQ}(v_P).$$

Theorem 7 *Consider a small buffer system with $K = 2$. The optimal revenue of upon-arrival priority purchases is higher than that of in-queue priority purchases subject to the sequential rule, i.e., $\Pi_{K=2}^{ARR} > \Pi_{K=2}^{SQ}$.*

Theorem 7 shows that in a small buffer system with $K = 2$, the upon-arrival priority purchase scheme yields higher revenue than in-queue priority purchase, although the latter presents customers with more upgrade opportunities. Recall that in-queue priority purchases lessen customers' fear of being overtaken if they do not purchase priority upon arrival by allowing them to defer their purchase decision. As a result, customers have less of an incentive to purchase than they would in the upon-arrival case, causing the in-queue purchase scheme to fall short of the upon-arrival purchase scheme in terms of priority revenue.

While in-queue priority purchases create more selling opportunities for the service provider, Theorem 7 tells a cautionary tale against this practice. This implies that the service provider may instead benefit from giving customers a *buy-it-or-lose-it* ultimatum when they arrive.

4.3.2 K = 3

As a proof of concept, we numerically solve for the pure-strategy equilibrium of sequential in-queue priority purchases in a system that can hold at most three customers (i.e., $K = 3$). In each numerical instance, we enumerate all the possible strategies σ; for each given σ, we solve a modified version of Conditions (7.9) through (7.12c) that accommodates the finite-buffer system of $K = 3$ (a system of linear equations) for the corresponding value function V; we then check if V satisfies (7.13); if so, the (σ, V) pair is an equilibrium. In all the numerical instances tested, we have consistently found a unique equilibrium.

By Table 7.1, we observe four types of possible equilibria:

(1) Whenever the ordinary queue length reaches 2, the first customer upgrades.
(2) Whenever the ordinary queue length reaches 3, the first customer upgrades.
(3) Whenever the ordinary queue length reaches 3, the second customer upgrades.

First, as the arrival rate (and thus traffic intensity) increases, customers are more prone to upgrade (in the sense that we see more Y's and fewer N's). This contrasts the case of $K = 2$, in which the equilibrium strategy does not vary with traffic (see Theorem 6), but makes intuitive sense because a higher traffic intensity implies that future arrivals pose a greater threat, which warrants more preemptive upgrades. Second, when $\lambda = 0.5$ (a case of light traffic), the equilibrium behavior is of type (3) and indeed agrees with the one identified in Theorem 4 for sufficiently light traffic. Third, when the traffic intensity is higher ($\lambda = 0.6, 0.7, 0.8, 0.9$), the equilibrium behavior departs from what occurs under light traffic. In particular, when $\lambda = 0.6, 0.7, 0.8$, the equilibrium is of type (2), and it is not the second (to the last) customer but the first customer who upgrades. When $\lambda = 0.9$, the equilibrium is of type (1) and the queue length only needs to reach 2, instead of 3, to trigger an upgrade. Fourth, the number of priority customers (0 or 1) does not affect the equilibrium strategy, i.e., $\sigma(1, 1, 0) = \sigma(1, 1, 1)$ and $\sigma(2, 0, 0) = \sigma(2, 0, 1)$. In fact, we can analytically prove this result, as shown in Theorem 8.

Table 7.1 The equilibrium strategies of sequential in-queue priority purchase under various arrival rates for $K = 3$

Arrival rate	$\lambda = 0.5$	$\lambda = 0.6$	$\lambda = 0.7$	$\lambda = 0.8$	$\lambda = 0.9$
$\sigma(1, 1, 0)$	N	N	N	N	Y
$\sigma(2, 0, 0)$	N	N	N	N	Y
$\sigma(1, 2, 0)$	N	Y	Y	Y	Y
$\sigma(2, 1, 0)$	Y	Y	Y	Y	Y
$\sigma(3, 0, 0)$	Y	Y	Y	Y	Y
$\sigma(1, 1, 1)$	N	N	N	N	Y
$\sigma(2, 0, 1)$	N	N	N	N	Y
Type	(3)	(2)	(2)	(2)	(1)

$\mu = 1, C = 1, P = 1.5$

4 Sequential Upgrade Rule

Theorem 8 *Consider a small buffer system with $K = 3$ subject to the sequential upgrade rule. In a pure-strategy equilibrium, $\sigma(1, 1, 0) = \sigma(1, 1, 1)$ and $\sigma(2, 0, 0) = \sigma(2, 0, 1)$.*

We caution that the result of Theorem 8 (the equilibrium strategy being independent of the number of priority customers) is likely driven by the assumption $K = 3$ and is not meant to be interpreted as a general result that applies to systems with any buffer size. What is special about $K = 3$ is that if there is one priority customer and two ordinary customers in the system, then the system is already full. As a result, the two ordinary customers would not be very concerned about future arrivals (because they know the next event can only be a departure). Hence, their strategy in equilibrium is no different than if the priority customer did not exist. However, this reasoning would not generalize to a system with a larger buffer, and it is reasonable to conjecture that ordinary customers would act differently should the number of priority customers in the system differ.

We also numerically compare the priority revenue generated in sequential in-queue priority purchases with that in the upon-arrival purchasing model. The results are reported in Fig. 7.3. We observe that in the system of $K = 3$, sequential in-queue priority purchases still generate less revenue than upon-arrival priority purchases (for a given priority price and under the optimal priority price), which parallels the analytical insight gleaned from the small buffer system with $K = 2$ (see Theorem 7).

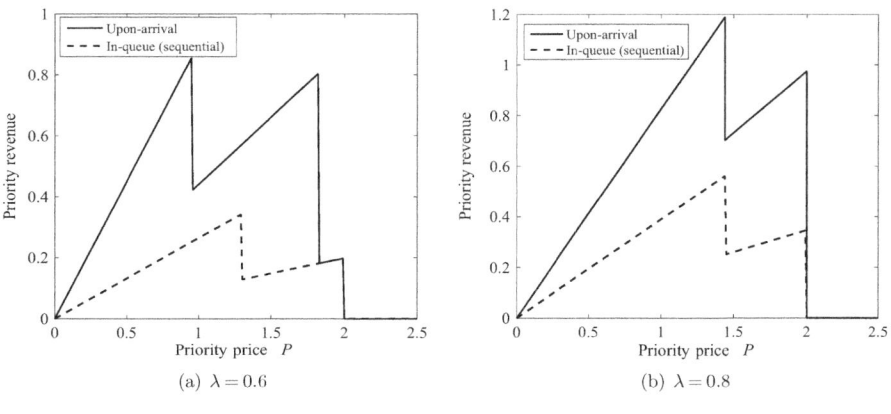

Note. $\mu = 1, C = 1$.

Fig. 7.3 Comparison of priority revenues for $K = 3$

5 Concluding Remarks

The extant priority-purchasing literature has restricted attention to the case where customers who would like to purchase priority must do so upon arrival to the service system. This chapter seeks to fill this gap by formulating a dynamic game that models customers' in-queue priority-purchasing behavior. When the simultaneous upgrade rule is imposed, we find that pure-strategy equilibria do not exist under certain intuitive criteria, contrasting the extant literature which instead shows the existence and sometimes multiplicity of pure-strategy equilibria when customers can only purchase priority upon arrival.

However, when the sequential upgrade rule is implemented, pure-strategy equilibria may exist. The upgrading behavior can be complex. Under sufficiently light traffic, if the number of ordinary customers accumulates to a certain threshold, then it is always the second last customer who upgrades, but in general, it could be a customer from another position and the queue-length threshold that triggers an upgrade can also vary with the traffic intensity. Under sufficiently heavy traffic and a not-too-high priority price, as soon as two ordinary customers gather, the first customer will upgrade. Our analytical and numerical results on systems with relatively small buffers consistently show that in-queue priority purchases do not yield as much revenue as upon-arrival priority purchases.

References

Afèche P, Sarhangian V (2015) Rational abandonment from priority queues: equilibrium strategy and pricing implications. In: Working paper, University of Toronto

Assaf D, Haviv M (1990) Reneging from processor sharing systems and random queues. Math Oper Res 15(1):129–138

Ata B, Peng X (2018) An equilibrium analysis of a multiclass queue with endogenous abandonments in heavy traffic. Oper Res 66(1):163–183

Cui S, Veeraraghavan SK, Wang J, Zhang Y (2022) Observational reneging. Available at SSRN 3290868

Kerner Y, Sherzer E, Yanco MA (2017) On non-equilibria threshold strategies in ticket queues. Queueing Syst 86(3–4):419–431

Maglaras C, Yao J, Zeevi A (2017) Observational learning and abandonment in a congested queue. In: Working paper, Columbia University

Wang Z, Yang L, Cui S, Wang J (2021) In-queue priority purchase: a dynamic game approach. Queueing Syst 97(3):343–381

Open Access This chapter is licensed under the terms of the Creative Commons Attribution 4.0 International License (http://creativecommons.org/licenses/by/4.0/), which permits use, sharing, adaptation, distribution and reproduction in any medium or format, as long as you give appropriate credit to the original author(s) and the source, provide a link to the Creative Commons license and indicate if changes were made.

The images or other third party material in this chapter are included in the chapter's Creative Commons license, unless indicated otherwise in a credit line to the material. If material is not included in the chapter's Creative Commons license and your intended use is not permitted by statutory regulation or exceeds the permitted use, you will need to obtain permission directly from the copyright holder.

The manufacturer's authorised representative in the EU is Springer Nature Customer Service Centre GmbH, Europaplatz 3, 69115 Heidelberg, Germany. If you have any concerns regarding our products, please contact ProductSafety@springernature.com

Printed and bound by CPI Group (UK) Ltd, Croydon, CR0 4YY

25/03/2026

02078170-0015